Moral Responsibility and the Problem of Many Hands

"Ibo van de Poel, Lambèr Royakkers, and Sjoerd D. Zwart have assembled the most comprehensive treatment yet of the problem of many hands, which has confounded assessments of individual responsibility in contexts of joint action and diffuse causality. Not only do they cogently capture the nature of this problem, both descriptively and formally, but they offer three compelling solutions to it, which should be of political as well as philosophical interest."

—*Steven Vanderheiden, Associate Professor of Political Science at the University of Colorado at Boulder, USA*

When many people are involved in an activity, it is often difficult, if not impossible, to pinpoint who is morally responsible for what, a phenomenon known as the 'problem of many hands'. This term is increasingly used to describe problems with attributing individual responsibility in collective settings in such diverse areas as public administration, corporate management, law and regulation, technological development and innovation, healthcare, and finance. This volume provides an in-depth philosophical analysis of this problem, examining the notion of moral responsibility and distinguishing between different normative meanings of responsibility, both backward-looking (accountability, blameworthiness, and liability) and forward-looking (obligation, virtue). Drawing on the relevant philosophical literature, the authors develop a coherent conceptualisation of the problem of many hands, taking into account the relationship, and possible tension, between individual and collective responsibility. This systematic inquiry into the problem of many hands pertains to discussions about moral responsibility in a variety of applied settings.

Ibo van de Poel is Anthoni van Leeuwenhoek Professor in Ethics and Technology at Delft University of Technology, The Netherlands.

Lambèr Royakkers is Associate Professor of Ethics and Technology in the School of Innovation Sciences at Eindhoven University of Technology, The Netherlands.

Sjoerd D. Zwart is Assistant Professor of Philosophy and Technology at Delft and Eindhoven Universities of Technology, The Netherlands.

Routledge Studies in Ethics and Moral Theory

1 **The Contradictions of Modern Moral Philosophy**
Ethics after Wittgenstein
Paul Johnston

2 **Kant, Duty and Moral Worth**
Philip Stratton-Lake

3 **Justifying Emotions**
Pride and Jealousy
Kristján Kristjánsson

4 **Classical Utilitarianism from Hume to Mill**
Frederick Rosen

5 **The Self, the Soul and the Psychology of Good and Evil**
Ilham Dilman

6 **Moral Responsibility**
The Ways of Scepticism
Carlos J. Moya

7 **The Ethics of Confucius and Aristotle**
Mirrors of Virtue
Jiyuan Yu

8 **Caste Wars**
A Philosophy of Discrimination
David Edmonds

9 **Deprivation and Freedom**
A Philosophical Enquiry
Richard J. Hull

10 **Needs and Moral Necessity**
Soran Reader

11 **Reasons, Patterns, and Cooperation**
Christopher Woodard

12 **Challenging Moral Particularism**
Edited by Mark Norris Lance, Matjaž Potrč, and Vojko Strahovnik

13 **Rationality and Moral Theory**
How Intimacy Generates Reasons
Diane Jeske

14 **The Ethics of Forgiveness**
A Collection of Essays
Christel Fricke

15 **Moral Exemplars in the *Analects***
The Good Person is *That*
Amy Olberding

16 **The Phenomenology of Moral Normativity**
William H. Smith

17 **The Second-Person Perspective in Aquinas's Ethics**
Virtues and Gifts
Andrew Pinsent

18 **Social Humanism**
A New Metaphysics
Brian Ellis

19 **Ethics Without Morals**
In Defence of Amorality
Joel Marks

20 **Evil and Moral Psychology**
Peter Brian Barry

21 **Aristotelian Ethics in Contemporary Perspective**
Edited by Julia Peters

22 **Modern Honor**
A Philosophical Defense
Anthony Cunningham

23 **Art and Ethics in a Material World**
Kant's Pragmatist Legacy
Jennifer A. McMahon

24 **Defending Associative Duties**
Jonathan Seglow

25 **Consequentialism and Environmental Ethics**
Edited by Avram Hiller, Ramona Ilea, and Leonard Kahn

26 **The Ethics of Vulnerability**
A Feminist Analysis of Social Life and Practice
Erinn C. Gilson

27 **Eudaimonic Ethics**
The Philosophy and Psychology of Living Well
Lorraine Besser-Jones

28 **The Philosophy and Psychology of Character and Happiness**
Edited by Nancy E. Snow and Franco V. Trivigno

29 **Moral Responsibility and the Problem of Many Hands**
Ibo van de Poel, Lambèr Royakkers, and Sjoerd D. Zwart

Moral Responsibility and the Problem of Many Hands

Ibo van de Poel, Lambèr Royakkers, and Sjoerd D. Zwart

With contributions by Tiago de Lima, Neelke Doorn, and Jessica Nihlén Fahlquist

LONDON AND NEW YORK

First published 2015
by Routledge

2 Park Square, Milton Park, Abingdon, Oxfordshire OX14 4RN
711 Third Avenue, New York, NY 10017

Routledge is an imprint of the Taylor & Francis Group, an informa business

First issued in paperback 2018

Copyright © 2015 Taylor & Francis

The right of Ibo van de Poel, Lambèr Royakkers, and Sjoerd D. Zwart to be identified as authors of this work has been asserted by them in accordance with sections 77 and 78 of the Copyright, Designs and Patents Act 1988.

All rights reserved. No part of this book may be reprinted or reproduced or utilised in any form or by any electronic, mechanical, or other means, now known or hereafter invented, including photocopying and recording, or in any information storage or retrieval system, without permission in writing from the publishers.

Notice:
Product or corporate names may be trademarks or registered trademarks, and are used only for identification and explanation without intent to infringe.

Library of Congress Cataloging-in-Publication Data
Poel, Ibo van de, 1966–
   Moral responsibility and the problem of many hands / Ibo van de Poel, Lambèr Royakkers, and Sjoerd D. Zwart ; with contributions by Tiago de Lima, Neelke Doorn, and Jessica Nihlen Fahlquist. — 1 [edition].
      pages cm. — (Routledge studies in ethics and moral theory ; 29)
   Includes bibliographical references and index.
   1. Responsibility.   2. Decision making—Moral and ethical aspects.
3. Common good.   I. Title.
   BJ1451.P64 2015
   170—dc23
   2014041915

ISBN: 978-1-138-83855-0 (hbk)
ISBN: 978-1-138-34671-0 (pbk)

Typeset in Sabon
by Apex CoVantage, LLC

Contents

List of Figures and Tables	ix
Acknowledgements	xi
Introduction	1
IBO VAN DE POEL AND LAMBÈR ROYAKKERS	
1 **Moral Responsibility**	12
IBO VAN DE POEL	
2 **The Problem of Many Hands**	50
IBO VAN DE POEL	
3 **A Formalisation of Moral Responsibility and the Problem of Many Hands**	93
TIAGO DE LIMA AND LAMBÈR ROYAKKERS	
4 **Responsibility and the Problem of Many Hands in Networks**	131
SJOERD D. ZWART	
5 **A Procedural Approach to Distributing Responsibility**	167
NEELKE DOORN	
6 **Responsibility as a Virtue and the Problem of Many Hands**	187
JESSICA NIHLÉN FAHLQUIST	
Conclusions: From Understanding to Avoiding the Problem of Many Hands	209
IBO VAN DE POEL AND SJOERD D. ZWART	
About the Authors	219
Index	223

Figures and Tables

FIGURES

3.1	A graphic representation of a CEDL model.	96
3.2	A CEDL model for the Light Bulb and Light Switch scenario.	100
3.3	A CEDL model for the Light Bulb and Light Switch scenario where w_0 and w_2 are violation states.	111
3.4	The CEDL model $M = \langle \mathcal{O}, W, \mathcal{K}, \mathcal{T}, \mathcal{V} \rangle$ for the example in Section 3.4.5.	122

TABLES

1.1	Taxonomy of responsibility meanings	14
1.2	Aims of attributing responsibility	20
1.3	Conditions for accountability and blameworthiness	25
1.4	Routes for acquiring responsibility-as-obligation	35
1.5	Routes to accountability for φ	39
1.6	Conditions for proper attribution of responsibility	41
1.7	Implications of the attribution of responsibility and the related aims of attributing responsibility	42
2.1	Aims of attributing responsibility	54
2.2	Three types of collectives	57
2.3	Conditions for three main kinds of responsibility	61
2.4	Employee Safety	67
3.1	The axiomatisation of CEDL	103
3.2	The joint actions and valuation function $\mathcal{V}$ for the model M in Figure 3.4	123
5.1	Moral issues related to social acceptance	178
5.2	Summary of empirical findings of the workshop	179

Acknowledgements

This book is the product of many hands. Ibo van de Poel, Lambèr Royakkers, and Sjoerd D. Zwart are the authors of the Introduction, Chapters 1, 2, and 4, and the Conclusion. As they also edited the other chapters, they are accountable for the content of the entire book. The three contributors (Tiago de Lima, Neelke Doorn, and Jessica Nihlén Fahlquist) are only accountable for their own chapter. Still, they also added to the discussions and ideas to be found in the other chapters.[1] The research team formed by the authors and contributors worked together on the project *Moral Responsibility in R&D Networks,* which was funded by the Netherlands Organization for Scientific Research (NWO). The project formally ended in 2012, but the present volume bears witness to its informal continuation long after that date.

The Introduction is written by Ibo van de Poel and Lambèr Royakkers.

Chapter 1 is written by Ibo van de Poel with a contribution of Neelke Doorn to section 1.2.3, and of Jessica Nihlén Fahlquist to section 1.3.1. It contains (brief) excerpts from:

- Van de Poel, I. 2011. "The relation between forward-looking and backward-looking responsibility." In *Moral responsibility. Beyond free will and determinism*, edited by N. Vincent, I. van de Poel and J. van den Hoven, 37–52. Dordrecht: Springer. (Several paragraphs in the sections 1.2.1, 1.2.2, 1.3.2, 1.4.1, 1.5, and 1.5.1).
- Doorn, N. 2012. "Responsibility ascriptions in technology development and engineering: Three perspectives." *Science and Engineering Ethics* 18 (1):69–90. (Several paragraphs in section 1.2.3)
- van de Poel, I., J. Nihlen Fahlquist, N., Doorn, S. Zwart, and L. Royakkers. 2012. "The problem of many hands: Climate change as an example." *Science and Engineering Ethics*, 18(1), 49–68. (Several paragraphs in section 1.3.1)

Chapter 2 is written by Ibo van de Poel. It contains (brief) excerpts from:

- van de Poel, I., J. Nihlen Fahlquist, N., Doorn, S. Zwart, and L. Royakkers. 2012. "The problem of many hands: Climate change as an example."

xii *Acknowledgements*

Science and Engineering Ethics, 18(1), 49–68. (Several paragraphs in section 2.1, 2.2, and 2.6)
- Van de Poel, I., and L. Royakkers 2011. *Ethics, technology and engineering*. Oxford: Wiley-Blackwell. (Several paragraphs in section 2.5)
- Van de Poel, I., and J. Nihlen Fahlquist, 2012. "Risk and responsibility." In *Handbook of risk theory* edited by S. Roeser, R. Hillerbrand, M. Peterson, and P. Sandin , 877–907. Dordrecht: Springer. (One paragraph in section 2.4)

Chapter 3 is written by Tiago de Lima and Lambèr Royakkers. The authors are grateful to Frank Dignum, whose helpful suggestions and comments have led to substantial improvements of this chapter.

Chapter 4 is written by Sjoerd D. Zwart. Its case description in sections 4.3.1 and 4.3.2 contains (brief) excerpts from sections 3 and 4 of: Doorn, N., L. Royakkers, and R. Raven. 2011. "Distribution of responsibility in socio-technical networks: The Promest case." *Technology Analysis & Strategic Management* 23(4), 453–471.

Chapter 5 is written by Neelke Doorn with contributions by Ibo van de Poel and Sjoerd D. Zwart. It contains excerpts from:

- Van de Poel, I., and S. Zwart 2010. "Reflective Equilibrium in R&D Networks." *Science, Technology, & Human Values* 35(2), 174–199. (Several paragraphs in section 5.2.1, 5.2.2 and 5.3.3)
- Doorn, N. (2010). "A procedural approach to distributing responsibilities in R&D networks". *Poiesis & Praxis. International Journal of Technology Assessment and Ethics of Science* 7(3), 169–188. (Several paragraphs in section 5.2, 5.3.1 and 5.4)

Chapter 6 is written by Jessica Nihlen Fahlquist with a contribution of Ibo van de Poel to section 6.6.

The Conclusion is written by Ibo van de Poel and Sjoerd D. Zwart.

The editing of the entire manuscript was done by Ibo van de Poel, Lambèr Royakkers, and Sjoerd D. Zwart.

This book is the result of the research program "Moral Responsibility in R&D Networks", which was supported by the Netherlands Organization for Scientific Research (NWO) under grant number 360–20–160.

NOTE

1. Fortunately (or unfortunately), it is likely that none of the errors contained can be traced back to one author.

Introduction

Ibo van de Poel and Lambèr Royakkers

0.1 PROBLEMATIC RESPONSIBILITY: THE *DEEPWATER HORIZON* DISASTER[1]

On 20 April 2010 the crew of the *Deepwater Horizon* drilling rig, stationed in the Gulf of Mexico for exploratory drilling on the Macondo Well, was carrying out test procedures. During these tests, control of the well was lost which resulted in a large flow of well fluids up the riser. The fluids were diverted to a mud/gas separator which vents above the main deck. This in turn led to a large release of hydrocarbons onto the main deck which quickly engulfed the rig in a hydrocarbon gas cloud. At approximately 9:49 pm ignition of the gas cloud occurred, resulting in several explosions, and a fire ensued on the rig which eventually led to the deaths of eleven workers and at least a dozen serious injuries. It is estimated that nearly five million barrels of hydrocarbons were released into the gulf over a period of nearly three months after the blowout. The disaster is considered the largest accidental marine oil spill in the history of the petroleum industry.

Deepwater Horizon was a mobile, temporary rig designed to drill the well that was intended to find out whether there was a viable reservoir of hydrocarbon and if so, to make it safe and ready for a more permanent production rig. This involved drilling a deep bore hole in stages and filling the casing with cement. The main companies involved in the *Deepwater Horizon* operations were British Petrol (the well owner also responsible for the design of the well and for leasing the rig), Transocean (the owner and operator of the rig that also providing the rig crew), and Halliburton (responsible for the cement operations).

On 9 April the final section of the well was drilled to a total depth of 18,360 feet (5,300 m), and the next day the cement job was started to seal the well bore from the reservoir sands. The sealing with casing and cement was finished on 17 April. On 20 April pressure tests were conducted to demonstrate well integrity. Among the tests carried out was a negative pressure test, which placed the well in a controlled underbalanced state to test the integrity of the mechanical barriers. An underbalanced state is a state in which there is more pressure on the reservoir side, so that the hydrocarbons

2 Ibo van de Poel and Lambèr Royakkers

will flow out of the well. The negative pressure test showed that hydrocarbons were leaking into the well, but BP's well site leaders misinterpreted the result. It appears that they did so in part because they accepted a rather implausible theory suggested by certain experienced members of the Transocean rig crew. Transocean rig personnel then missed a number of further signals indicating that hydrocarbons had entered the well and were rising to the surface during the final hour before the blowout actually occurred. By the time they recognised a blowout was occurring, they tried to activate the rig's blowout preventer to prevent an explosion, but the blowout preventer emergency function failed to seal the well. Hydrocarbons flowed past the blowout preventer and were rushing upward through the riser pipe to the rig floor. Given the large quantity of hydrocarbon released ignition was most likely: explosions followed.

The root technical cause of the blowout was the fact that the cement that BP and Halliburton had pumped to the bottom of the well on 17 April did not seal off hydrocarbons in the formation. The cement slurry was poorly designed, which was known because Halliburton's own internal tests showed that the design was unstable.

According to the Chief Counsels Report "all of the technical failures at Macondo can be traced back to management errors by the companies involved in the incident" (National Commission on the BP Deepwater Horizon Oil Spill and Offshore Drilling 2011a: x). The presented list contains many errors, such as

- BP did not adequately supervise the work of its contractors, who in turn did not deliver to BP all the benefits of their expertise;
- BP personnel on the rig were not properly trained and supported, and all three companies [BP, Halliburton, and Transocean] failed to communicate key information to people who could have made a difference;
- BP did not adequately identify or address risks created by last-minute changes to well design and procedures;
- Halliburton appears to have done little to supervise the work of its key cementing personnel and does not appear to have meaningfully reviewed data that should have prompted it to redesign the Macondo cement slurry;
- Transocean did not adequately train its employees in emergency procedures and kick detection, and did not inform them of crucial lessons learned from a similar and recent near-miss drilling incident.

The National Commission on the BP Deepwater Horizon Oil Spill and Offshore Drilling established by President Obama to recommend ways of preventing and mitigating the impact of any future spills that result from offshore drilling released a final report on 5 January 2011. In this report the Commission did not place the blame for the accident on anyone, but stated that "[t]hough it is tempting to single out one crucial misstep or point the finger at one bad actor as the cause of the *Deepwater Horizon* explosion, any such explanation provides a dangerously incomplete picture of what happened—encouraging the very kind of complacency that led to the accident in the first place" (National Commission on the BP Deepwater Horizon Oil Spill and Offshore Drilling 2011b: viii). Rather, the Commission concluded that "the accident of April 20 was avoidable. It resulted from clear mistakes made in the first instance by BP, Halliburton, and Transocean, and by government officials who, relying too much on industry's assertions of the safety of their operations, failed to create and apply a program of regulatory oversight that would have properly minimized the risk of deepwater drilling" (National Commission on the BP Deepwater Horizon Oil Spill and Offshore Drilling 2011b: 127). In their accident investigation report, published on 8 September 2010, BP also concluded that no single action caused the incident, "[r]ather a complex and interlinked series of mechanical failures, human judgements, engineering design, operational implementation and team interfaces came together to allow the initiation and escalation of the accident. Multiple companies, work teams and circumstances were involved over time" (BP 2010: 11). This shows how difficult it is to pinpoint responsibility and blame in cases in which many actors are involved. Furthermore, all three companies, BP, Halliburton, and Transocean, blamed each other for various events that caused the blowout.[2] As a consequence, it is not amazing that the legal proceedings have still not entirely settled which of the several companies and individuals involved are legally responsible for the spill and its effects.[3]

0.2 THE PROBLEM OF MANY HANDS

Technical failures or disasters like the one of the *Deepwater Horizon* explosion often present the question about who is responsible. Disasters are, however, typically the result of the interaction between the actions of many different agents, including engineers, users, governments, companies, managers, and the like. One might assume that if all of the agents were to behave individually responsibly, the overall result would be beneficial for society. This assumption does not always hold water: the fragmentation of decision-making leads to different parts of the organisation focusing purely on their areas of responsibility, and thus not feeling responsible for safety as a whole. For example, BP did not adequately supervise the work of its contractors, and Halliburton appears to have done little to supervise the work of its key cementing personnel. So, different organisations were responsible for supervision, but no one had overall authority. Thompson (2014) concludes from this that the responsibility design was diffuse, which probably contributed to the disaster. In addition, the principal agency for regulating the drilling, the federal Minerals Management Service (MMS), granted exceptions, such as exempting a 'special exception' in 2009 from the obligation for *Deepwater Horizon* to comply with the National Environment Policy Act, and had never achieved the reform of its regulatory oversight of drilling safety consonant with practices that most countries had embraced decades earlier (National Commission on the BP Deepwater Horizon Oil Spill and Offshore Drilling 2011b: 71). Furthermore, MMS conducted since 2005 at least 16 fewer inspections aboard the *Deepwater Horizon* than it should have under the policy (Huffington Post 2010).

The *Deepwater Horizon* blowout then is an example of what we call in this book the problem of many hands (PMH), a term that was originally coined by Dennis Thompson (1980). The PMH typically describes the problem where a lot of people are involved in an activity, like a complex drilling project, therefore making it difficult to identify where the responsibility for a particular outcome lies. In part this is a practical problem. It is often difficult in complex organisations or projects to identify and prove who was responsible for what (Bovens 1998). Especially for outsiders it is usually very difficult, if not impossible, to know who contributed to, or could have prevented a certain action, who knew or could have known what, et cetera. This is especially problematic if one wants responsibility to have juridical implications, because the law requires evidence of irresponsible behaviour and this evidence has to meet a certain standard of proof.

The PMH is also a moral problem because it may turn out that nobody can reasonably be held morally responsible for a disaster. This is morally problematic for at least two independent reasons. The first is that many people, including victims, members of the public and also the engineering community, may find it morally unsatisfactory that if a disaster occurs, nobody can be held responsible. Of course, the search for somebody to blame may be misunderstood, but at least in some situations it seems reasonable to say that someone should bear responsibility. In fact, some philosophers have introduced the notion of collective responsibility to deal with the intuition that there is more to responsibility in complex cases than just the sum of the responsibilities of the individuals considered in isolation (see Chapter 2). Intuitively, we may say that a collective is responsible in cases where, had it been an action performed by one person, he or she would have been held responsible. This addresses the intuition that for outsiders it should not make a difference whether a complex project was undertaken by one person or by a large number of persons in a division of labour. The second reason for attributing responsibility is the desire to learn from mistakes, and to do better in the future. If nobody is held morally responsible for a disaster, this may not happen.

The PMH then typically refers to undesirable outcomes in collective setting for which it is hard or even impossible to hold an individual or organisation (like a company or the government) responsible. In an earlier publication, we have defined the PMH as follows:

> A problem of many hands occurs if there is a gap in a responsibility distribution in a collective setting that is morally problematic.
>
> (van de Poel et al. 2012: 63)

Introduction 5

In this book, we will develop a conceptualisation of the PMH that is line with this general characterisation but which is, we believe, more precise and better traceable. We will understand the PMH as the occurrence of the situation in which the collective can reasonably be held morally responsible for an outcome, whereas none of the individuals can reasonably be held morally responsible for that outcome.

0.3 MEANINGS OF RESPONSIBILITY

It could be argued that in cases like the *Deepwater Horizon* blowout, there is actually not one problem of many hands, but at least two. One is the PMH with respect to backward-looking responsibility, i.e., the impossibility to hold an individual (or organisation) responsible after the disaster has occurred. However, there is also the PMH referring to forward-looking responsibility, i.e., the problem that the responsibility to prevent such blow-outs is not well organised, so that no individual (or organisation) is responsible for preventing the disaster. These two PMHs are of course not completely unrelated, but it is important to distinguish them because, the one does not necessarily imply the other. Solutions to the PMH for backward-looking responsibility do not necessarily also contribute to solve the PMH for forward-looking responsibility, and might even have detrimental effects.

To untangle the various problems of many hands that might occur, we will in this book distinguish five *moral* meanings of responsibility, three of which are backward-looking (accountability, blameworthiness, and liability) and two of which are primarily forward-looking (obligation, virtue). We will argue that these different moral meanings can be associated with different aims (or purposes) for why we attribute responsibility, for example blameworthiness is associated with the aim of moral retribution. For each meaning of responsibility, we will also distinguish a number of conditions under which it is properly applied. Despite its huge extent, we did not find such a comparative approach in the philosophical literature on responsibility where most contributions tend to focus on one meaning of responsibility (i.e., blameworthiness) and one specific condition (i.e., free will). In many real-world contexts, free will is typically one of the least problematic conditions for responsibility, and other meanings of responsibility—apart from blameworthy—are relevant as well.

We are aware that our distinction between the different meanings of responsibility and the discussion of conditions for the applicability of each meaning might strike the reader as somewhat artificial. Arguably, responsibility is a notion with different shades of meanings rather than there being entirely different concepts of responsibility. The conditions we discuss are also often not strict conditions (in the sense of necessary and sufficient conditions), but rather reasons or considerations for holding someone

6   *Ibo van de Poel and Lambèr Royakkers*

appropriately responsible that function in an argument or plea for why someone is responsible or not for something.

0.4   THE DISCREPANCY BETWEEN INDIVIDUAL AND COLLECTIVE RESPONSIBILITY

In the *Deepwater Horizon* case, a cause of the PMH was the distribution of information over the various actors. According to the Chief's Counsels Report BP, Halliburton, and Transocean "failed to communicate key information to people who could have made a difference" (National Commission on the BP Deepwater Horizon Oil Spill and Offshore Drilling 2011a: x). For example, due to the way information was distributed, BP could not reasonably have known that the cement was poorly designed. The crucial point is that applying the knowledge of each individual in isolation might yield a different result than applying it to the entire group of actors at once. This is why we might sometime judge that none of the individuals could reasonably foresee a certain harm, whereas at the collective level that same harm is foreseeable, which means that the collective satisfies the knowledge condition for responsibility, even if none if the individuals satisfies the condition.

The discrepancy between applying the responsibility conditions to the individuals and to the collective can also occur regarding other conditions, like wrong-doing. An example is the responsibility of individual car drivers to the greenhouse effect. Individual car drivers by using their car emit concentrations of greenhouse gases that are—considered in isolation—completely harmless (assuming that there is a level below which greenhouse gas emissions have no effect); all car drivers together, however, introduce a considerable risk for future generations. What is essential about this example is that whereas none of the individuals is doing something wrong or is at fault, at the collective level there is obviously harm done, so it would be natural to assume that there is also wrong-doing at the collective level.

The PMH can also arise due to a combination of conditions for responsibility. For example, an employee of a company who knows of a defect in a product may—due to the hierarchical nature of the organisation and the specific procedures within the organisation—lack the freedom to repair the defect or to warn customers about it. His superior may have the freedom to act but maybe could not have known the defect.

The idea that there can be a discrepancy between individual and collective moral responsibility is not new. In fact, in the philosophical literature various accounts can be found that allow for the possibility of non-distributive collective responsibility, i.e., collective responsibility that is not distributed over (individual) members of a collective but only applies to the collective in its entirety (e.g. Feinberg 1968; French 1984; May 1992; Copp 2007; Pettit 2007; Isaacs 2011). What is new in our account is that we interpret this

Introduction 7

discrepancy in terms of the problem of many hands; in doing so we build on a suggestion made, but not further elaborated, by Bovens (1998).

The account of collective responsibility that we offer in this book does not assume that collective have intentions; we rather speak of collective (or shared) aims. Because in our account collectives have no intentions, some of the aims we have in attributing responsibility, like moral retribution, cannot be achieved by solely attributing responsibility to the collective. The reason is that moral retribution presupposes an intentional action, and if collectives have no intentions we cannot *morally* blame them, and we therefore cannot achieve the aim of *moral* retribution (even if we can punish collectives in other, non-moral ways).

If, as we hold, some of the aims of attributing responsibility cannot be achieved by solely attributing responsibility to the collective, the discrepancy between collective and individual responsibility becomes a problem, and it is for that reason that we speak of a *problem* of many hands if a collective is responsible for some harm without any of its individual members being responsible for that harm.

The account that we develop in this way makes it not only possible to offer a much more precise characterisation of the PMH than early authors have done, it also offers a framework with which we can envision and discuss possible solutions to the PMH.

0.5 OVERVIEW OF THE BOOK

The aim of the book is to develop a conceptual framework for moral responsibility and the PMH that makes it possible to devise possible solutions to the PMH. The first three chapters of the book develop this conceptual framework. Chapters 4–6 discuss possible solutions to the PMH.

Chapter 1 presents a conceptual analysis of moral responsibility. We start with introducing a taxonomy of the various meanings of responsibility and distinguish five main normative meanings of responsibility, three of which are backward-looking (accountability, blameworthiness, and liability), and two of which are forward-looking (obligation, virtue). After discussing the relational nature of responsibility and the various reasons we have for attributing responsibility, we analyse each of the five normative notions in depth. For each, we discuss the conditions under which the meaning of responsibility applies and we discuss the (normative) implications of the meaning of responsibility. For example, responsibility as blameworthiness applies under five conditions (capacity, causality, wrong-doing, freedom, knowledge) and implies that it is appropriate to blame the responsible agent for some action or outcome. We end Chapter 1 with discussing the relationship between the different meanings of responsibility that follows from our conceptualisation.

Chapter 2 elaborates a conceptualisation of the PMH and provides examples of the PMH in three different kinds of collective settings. We start

8 *Ibo van de Poel and Lambèr Royakkers*

by taking up the suggestion by Mark Bovens that the PMH has to do with the potential discrepancy between individual and collective responsibility. We propose to understand the PMH as the situation in which a collective can be appropriately held responsible for something whereas no individual within the collective can be appropriately held responsible for that same thing. Because responsibility can have different meanings, as we have seen in Chapter 1, we can distinguish different versions of the PMH. Next we discuss the notion of collective responsibility, which has been the subject of philosophical debate. We propose a notion of collective responsibility that does not presuppose collective intentions or a collective mind, but that nevertheless may be more than the sum of individual responsibilities. Building on the relevant philosophical literature, we propose to distinguish among three types of collectives: (1) organised groups, (2) collectives involved in a joint action, and (3) occasional collections of individuals that can reasonably be expected to organise themselves into a collective. For each, we discuss, through an example, how the PMH might occur.

Chapter 3 develops a formalisation of the main ideas in Chapters 1 and 2. Using the basic concepts through which the meanings of responsibility are defined, we construct a logic which enables to express sentences like 'individual i is accountable for φ', 'individual i is blameworthy for φ' and 'individual i has the obligation to see to it that φ'. This formalisation clarifies the definitions of responsibility given in Chapter 1 and highlights their differences and similarities. It also helps to assess the consistency of the formalisation of responsibility, not only by showing that definitions are not inconsistent, but also by providing a formal demonstration of the relation between three main meanings of responsibility (accountability, blameworthiness, and obligation) argued for in Chapter 1. Moreover, the formal account can be used to derive new properties of the concepts. Chapter 3 also develops a formal tool that can help to detect the occurrence of the PMH. To do so, we define a logical framework for reasoning about collective and individual responsibility. This logic extends the Coalition Epistemic Dynamic Logic (CEDL). We add a notion of group knowledge, generalize the definitions of individual responsibility to groups of agents, and give a formal definition for the PMH.

Chapter 4 describes how the PMH might occur in networks. The term network is often used to describe social settings that are less formally and hierarchically organised than organised groups but in which nevertheless significant social ties exists between the various agents involved. Networks are probably more prone to the PMH than organised groups due to the absence of formal and hierarchical relations. In Chapter 4, we analyse the PMH in networks by discussing in detail the example of the collapse of a manure processing factory, which to a considerable extent had to solve the agricultural manure problem in the Netherlands. We discuss the PMH with respect to different meanings of responsibility (obligation, accountability and blameworthiness) in this case and explore to what extent these versions of the PMH are mutually related. We also discuss how the PMH in networks may be avoided or at least alleviated through institutional design, i.e., the deliberate design of social institutions. We do so by looking at three organisational dimensions of networks: (1) power: an agent has power over another agent if the first agent can impose actions on the second agent that are in the interest of the first agent, (2) coordination: the flow of information and knowledge between agents and, (3) control: we speak of control if an agent monitors the behaviour of another actor and provides for fall-back options. In this chapter, we will investigate how these three types of relations influence the occurrence of the PMH.

The lessons we draw in Chapter 4 may be seen as tentative heuristics for the institutional design of organisations and networks that help to prevent the occurrence of PMHs. In Chapters 5 and 6, we will consider other ways of preventing, or dealing with, the PMH. In Chapter 5 we develop a procedural approach to distributing responsibility that might help to avoid the PMH. It is inspired by procedural approaches in political philosophy, in particular John Rawls' approach of the wide reflective equilibrium and overlapping consensus. The chapter focuses on responsibility-as-obligation and starts with noticing that people might have different, and potentially conflicting, rationales for distributing responsibility-as-obligation, which may lead to disagreement about the distribution of responsibility in collective settings and, hence, to the occurrence of the PMH. This pluralism of responsibility rationales is, we suggest, sometimes irreducible as each of them might be able to survive the test of scrutiny by public reason. The solution we suggest is therefore to be found in a fair procedure. We present an approach that might help to trace disagreements about the distribution of responsibility and might help to overcome this disagreement by constructively developing an overlapping consensus on the distribution of responsibility. We show how the approach might be applied in network settings by an example in which we examined the approach in practice.

In Chapter 6, we discuss responsibility-as-virtue as a way to deal with the PMH. The occurrence, and the potential avoidance, of the PMH depend on social institutions and procedures but also on individuals and their character traits. Responsibility-as-virtue is a much more open-ended than the other normative meanings distinguished in Chapter 1. It therefore offers additional possibilities for dealing with the PMH. Chapter 6 develops a more detailed account of responsibility-as-virtue and argues that it consists in care, moral imagination, and practical wisdom. It is shown how these three dimensions might help in avoiding or alleviating the occurrence of the PMH. We argue that these dimensions do not only depend on individuals but may also be nurtured by organisational and institutional settings, which have implications for how such settings are to be designed. This is illustrated by a discussion of the responsibility for dealing with the risks of new technology.

In the conclusion we return to our characterisation of the PMH in Chapter 2. We argue that, and why, our characterisation captures the main

10 Ibo van de Poel and Lambèr Royakkers

characteristics of the PMH that we have seen throughout the book. We also discuss possible ways to avoid the PMH by formulating five hypotheses on the basis of Chapter 3–6 about under which condition the PMH is less likely to occur.

NOTES

1. *Sources*: Office of the Maritime Administrator (2011), National Academy of Engineering and National Research Council (2011), and National Commission on the BP Deepwater Horizon Oil Spill and Offshore Drilling (2011a; 2011b).
2. Steven Mufson, "BP, Transocean, Halliburton Blamed by Presidential Gulf Oil Spill Commission," *Washington Post*, 6 January 2011. http://www.washingtonpost.com/wp-dyn/content/article/2011/01/05/AR2011010504631.html. Accessed 2 August 2014.
3. "Deepwater Horizon Litigation," *Wikipedia,* http://en.wikipedia.org/wiki/Deepwater_Horizon_litigation. Accessed 2 August 2014.

REFERENCES

Bovens, M. 1998. *The quest for responsibility. Accountability and citizenship in complex organisations*. Cambridge: Cambridge University Press.
BP. 2010. *Deepwater Horizon. Accident investigation report*, 8 September 2010. (http://noaa.ntis.gov/view.php?pid=NOAA:ocn662664692)
Copp, D. 2007. "The collective moral autonomy thesis." *Journal of Social Philosophy* 38(3): 369–388.
Feinberg, J. 1968. "Collective responsibility." *Journal of Philosophy* 65(21): 674–688.
French, P.A. 1984. *Collective and corporate responsibility*. New York: Columbia University Press.
Huffington Post. 2010. Deepwater Horizon inspections: MMS skipped monthly inspections on doomed rig, 16 May 2010. (http://www.huffingtonpost.com/2010/05/16/deepwater-horizon-inspect_n_578079.html)
Isaacs, T.L. 2011. *Moral responsibility in collective contexts*. Oxford: Oxford University Press.
May, L. 1992. *Sharing responsibility*. Chicago: University of Chicago Press.
National Academy of Engineering and National Research Council. 2011. *Macondo Well-Deepwater Horizon blowout*. Washington, D.S.: Publisher National Academies Press.
National Commission on the BP Deepwater Horizon Oil Spill and Offshore Drilling. 2011a. *Macondo : the Gulf oil disaster* (Chief Counsel's report). Washington, D.C.: National Commission on the BP Deepwater Horizon Oil Spill and Offshore Drilling. (http://www.eoearth.org/files/164401_164500/164423/full.pdf)
National Commission on the BP Deepwater Horizon Oil Spill and Offshore Drilling. 2011b. *Deepwater. The Gulf oil disaster and future of offshore drilling*. Washington, D.C.: National Commission on the BP Deepwater Horizon Oil Spill and Offshore Drilling. (http://www.gpo.gov/fdsys/pkg/GPO-OILCOMMISSION/content-detail.html)
Office of the Maritime Administrator. 2011. *Deepwater Horizon marine casualty investigation report* (nr. 2213). Reston: Republic of the Marshall Islands Maritime Administrator. (https://www.register-iri.com/miReports/)

Pettit, Ph. 2007. "Responsibility incorporated." *Ethics* 117(2): 171–201.

Thompson, D.F. 1980. "Moral responsibility and public officials: The problem of many hands." *American Political Science Review* 74(4): 905–916.

Thompson, D.F. (2014). "Responsibility for failures of government: The PMH." *American Journal of Public Administration* 44(3): 259–273.

van de Poel, I., J. Nihlén Fahlquist, N. Doorn, S. Zwart, and L. Royakkers. 2012. "The Problem of Many Hands: Climate Change as an Example." *Science and Engineering Ethics* 18(1): 49–68.

1 Moral Responsibility

Ibo van de Poel

1.1 INTRODUCTION

What do we mean when we say that someone is responsible for something? This question is remarkably hard to answer. Or better, it does not have one correct answer. Sometimes, by saying that some agent i is responsible for some state-of-affairs φ, we mean to express that it would be appropriate to blame or praise agent i for φ being the case (depending on whether φ is desirable or not); sometimes we, however, mean to say that i should bring about φ, or at least do everything in i's power to bring about φ. We also might also intend to say that i is to account for φ being the case (or not being the case), or—if the occurrence of φ has caused damage to another agent j, is to pay damages to j.

Responsibility, then, has a multiplicity of meanings. These meanings are, however, not unrelated. An agent i may be responsible-as-blameworthy for φ because that same agent i did not properly fulfil her responsibility to avoid φ from occurring. A shipping company may be responsible (as-blameworthy) for a shipping disaster because it did not fulfil its responsibility to take measures to avoid a disaster, such as having qualified personnel, good equipment, inspection schemes, et cetera. Although the various meanings of responsibility are related to each other, these relationships are not straightforward or simple, as we will see in this chapter.

Therefore, it is useful to investigate the meanings of responsibility and the relation between these different meanings. This chapter develops a conceptualization of moral responsibility. By doing so, it lays the ground for the other chapters in this book, especially the next chapter, in which we try to understand and conceptualise the so-called problem of many hands with respect to moral responsibility. The focus in this chapter will be on notions of *moral* responsibility, i.e., responsibility that is grounded in moral considerations, rather than legal or organisational considerations and rules.

The approach in this chapter is conceptual in nature, i.e., it will proceed by distinguishing and clarifying different meanings of responsibility and their relations. In doing so, we will build on accounts of responsibility that have been offered by other thinkers and that can be found in daily language.

Moral Responsibility 13

At some points, we will make choices with respect to how we understand the relevant terms and their relations that are substantial or even normative. Such choices seem inevitable if one wants to sketch a coherent picture. Nevertheless, we have tried to provide an account that is general and abstract enough to apply to different, more substantive notions of responsibility.

This chapter is structured as follows. We start with an overview of different meanings of responsibility, suggesting five major normative meanings of responsibility, three of which are primarily backward-looking (accountability, blameworthiness, and liability), and two which are primarily forward-looking (virtue and obligation). In section 1.2 we provide an account of responsibility as a relational concept and we discuss different reasons one might have for attributing responsibility. Sections 1.3 and 1.4 propose conceptualisations of respectively backward-looking and forward-looking responsibility. Section 1.5 discusses the relation between forward-looking and backward-looking responsibility. The final section concludes with some conceptual relations between the different meanings of responsibility that follow from the chapter.

1.2 THE CONCEPT OF RESPONSIBILITY

In section 1.2.1, we introduce a taxonomy of meanings of responsibility that list four descriptive and five normative meanings of responsibility. In the remainder of this chapter, and the book, we will focus on the normative meanings of responsibility. (We give more precise definitions of all these meanings of responsibility in sections 1.3 and 1.4.) In section 1.2.2., we discuss responsibility as a relational concept, and in section 1.2.3, we pay attention to the reasons we may have for attributing the various normative meanings of responsibility.

1.2.1 Meanings of Responsibility

The term 'responsibility' has different meanings. It is therefore useful to distinguish some of the main meanings of the concept.[1] Table 1.1 lists, to this end, various meanings of responsibility. The first four meanings are more or less descriptive: responsibility-as-cause, role,[2] authority,[3] and capacity describe something that is the case or not. The other five are normative. They imply a normative evaluation, as in responsibility-as-virtue and responsibility-as-blameworthiness, or a prescription, as in responsibility-as-obligation and in responsibility-as-liability (to pay damages, offer excuses, put the situation right, et cetera). Responsibility-as-accountability seems to imply both an evaluation as well as a prescription; the agent is supposed to account for something because an action or outcome can be laid at her feet.[4] Our focus here will be on the normative meanings of responsibility.

The first two normative meanings are primarily forward-looking (prospective) in nature. This is most obvious for responsibility-as-obligation; it

14 *Ibo van de Poel*

Table 1.1 Taxonomy of responsibility meanings

---

1. Descriptive

Responsibility-as-cause	Being the cause. As in: The earth quake is responsible for the death of 100 people.
Responsibility-as-task	Having the task. As in: The train driver is responsible for driving the train.
Responsibility-as-authority	Having the authority or being in charge. As in: He is responsible for the project, meaning he is in charge of the project.
Responsibility-as-capacity	The ability to act in a responsible way. This includes, for example, the ability to reflect on the consequences of one's actions, to form intentions, and to deliberately choose an action and act upon it.

2. Normative

2a Normative and Forward-looking

Responsibility-as-virtue	The disposition (character trait) to act responsibly. As in: He is a responsible person.
Responsibility-as-obligation	The obligation to see to it that something is the case. As in: He is responsible for the safety of the passengers, meaning he is responsible to see to it that the passengers are transported safely.

2a Normative and Backward-looking

Responsibility-as-accountability	The obligation to account for one's actions and their outcomes.
Responsibility-as-blameworthiness	The appropriateness of blame. As in: He is responsible for the car accident, meaning he can be blamed for the car accident happening.
Responsibility-as-liability	The obligation to remedy a situation or to compensate for it. As in: He is liable to pay damages.

---

relates to something that is—usually—not yet the case. Responsibility-as-virtue is often primarily understood as being forward-looking (e.g Ladd 1991, Bovens 1998); it relates to responsibilities an agent actively assumes and to a certain attitude, rather than to blame (or praise). Nevertheless, one could well argue that a responsible person is one who is willing to account for his actions and who accepts blame and liability where that is due (Williams 2008).

Responsibility-as-accountability, blameworthiness, and liability are backward-looking in the sense that they usually apply to something that has occurred. Nevertheless, accountability and liability have a forward-looking (prescriptive) element in the sense that the agent is supposed to do something (in the future): to account for his actions, to pay damages, and the like.

Most of the philosophical literature on responsibility tends to focus on backward-looking responsibility and often understands backward-looking responsibility in terms of reactive attitudes (e.g. Wallace 1994, Strawson 1962). That is to say, if it is reasonable to hold someone responsible for something, it is considered reasonable to have certain reactive attitudes to that person in respect of the thing for which the person is held responsible. Although such reactive attitudes may take different forms, the most common denominator seems to be blame. We will, therefore, call this meaning of responsibility 'responsibility-as-blameworthiness'.

It should be noted that responsibility-as-blameworthiness is not the only meaning of backward-looking moral responsibility. Two other main meanings are responsibility-as-accountability and responsibility-as-liability (Van de Poel 2011, Davis 2012). We will understand accountability basically in the sense of being obliged to account for one's actions and their outcomes. Moral liability is related to obligations to victims of one's action, like being obliged to pay damages or to remedy an injustice caused.

Some of the normative meanings of responsibility are related to, or rely on, the descriptive meanings of responsibility. Responsibility-as-virtue is closely related to responsibility-as-capacity. But whereas the latter only refers to the ability to act responsibly, responsibility-as-virtue refers to the actual disposition, also surfacing in actions, to be a responsible person. Similarly, responsibility-as-obligation is closely related to responsibility-as-task.[5] Tasks are typically formulated in terms of seeing to it that something is the case. The difference is that not every task or role defines a moral obligation. So, whereas it might be said that Eichmann had the task (responsibility) that the Jews were effectively transported to the concentration camps, it does not follow that he had a (moral) obligation to see to it that they were effectively transported. In fact, because the transport was part of an immoral plan, aiming at the extinction of the Jews, he might even have had a moral obligation to see to it that they were not effectively transported.

Although responsibility-as-accountability, responsibility-as-blameworthiness, and responsibility-as-liability are in meaning not directly related to one of the descriptive notions, it is often assumed that responsibility-as-cause and responsibility-as-capacity are preconditions for holding someone accountable, liable, or for blaming someone. Blameworthiness, in turn, is sometimes seen as a condition for moral liability. It is also often believed that responsibility-as-task or responsibility-as-authority may lead to responsibility-as-accountability, especially if the former responsibilities are not properly discharged.

16 *Ibo van de Poel*

1.2.2 Responsibility as a Relational Concept

In most of its meanings, responsibility refers to a relation between at least two entities. The most basic form this relation takes is:

(1) *i is responsible for φ*

In which i is some agent and φ can refer to actions, state of affairs (outcomes), tasks, or realms of authority. Two meanings of responsibility, however, seem to resist this conceptualisation, namely responsibility-as-capacity and responsibility-as-virtue.[6] Capacity and virtue are better understood as a 'property', or characteristic of the agent i, rather than as a relation between an agent i and some φ. This is not to say that it never makes sense to particularise responsibility-as-capacity or responsibility-as-virtue to a particular φ. We might, for example, say that someone is a responsible parent but an irresponsible engineer (both in the virtue sense).[7] However, for both responsibility-as-capacity and responsibility-as-virtue, it makes sense to say that i is responsible full stop, whereas that appears impossible for all other meanings.

Responsibility can also be understood as a triadic relational concept. Duff (2007: 23–30) argues that normative notions of responsibility are best understood according to the following scheme:[8]

(2) *i is responsible for φ to j*

In which j is some agent, usually different from i. In cases of forward-looking responsibility, (2) reflects the fact that we may have specific responsibilities to different people. Professionals like engineers, for example, have different responsibilities to their employer, to their colleagues, to their clients, and to the public. What they owe to their clients is different from what they owe to their employer or to the public; their responsibilities to these different groups of agents may even conflict.[9]

More generally, (2) may be seen as a reflection of the fact that forward-looking responsibilities may arise from the specific relations we have with specific people (cf. Scheffler 1997). This is not to deny that we may also have responsibilities to ourselves, or general responsibilities. These may be seen as special cases in which j is i, or in which j is humanity (or morality, or God, if one wishes). In the case of forward-looking responsibility (2) might then be understood as follows:

(3) *i is forward-looking responsible for φ to j means that i owes it to j to see to it that φ*

How is (2) to be understood for backward-looking notions of responsibility like accountability and blameworthiness? Duff (2007: 23) suggests that j is

Moral Responsibility 17

"a person or body who has the standing to call me to answer for X [φ]". More generally, j may be any agent who can fittingly, i.e., fairly or reasonably, hold i responsible for φ. This may be expressed as follows:

(4) *i is backward-looking responsible for φ to j means that it is appropriate for j to hold i responsible for φ*

Holding responsible here includes holding accountable or blaming. Duff suggests that the ones to which I owe something (the agent j in (3)) is the same as the one for whom it would be appropriate to hold me backward-looking responsible (the agent j in (4)). This suggestion, however, seems false. I may have a forward-looking responsibility to future generations to limit my emissions of greenhouse gases with an eye to global warming, but it does not follow that they are the only ones who can hold me accountable (or blameworthy) for not limiting my emissions of greenhouse gases. In fact, they may never be able to hold me accountable because future generations do not exist yet, and when they (hopefully) exist in the future I may not live anymore. There may nevertheless be others, including myself, who can properly hold me accountable for my emissions of greenhouse gases.

It has indeed been suggested that in cases of moral, backward-looking responsibility, in contrast to legal, organisational, or social responsibility, it is in principle appropriate for anyone to hold me accountable (or blameworthy) under certain conditions. The reference to j, in other words, is superfluous for moral responsibility. In fact, Strawson's conceptualisation of backward-looking responsibility as the fittingness of certain reactive attitudes can be understood along the following lines (Zimmerman 2009):

(5) *i is backward-looking responsible for φ means it is fitting to adopt some reactive attitude toward i in respect of φ*

Or, in a formulation that closely resembles a proposal by Wallace (1994: 92):

(6) *i is backward-looking responsible for φ if and only if it is fitting to hold i responsible for φ*

Formulations (5) and (6) suggest that the fittingness of reactive attitudes is independent from the specific agent j, so that the reference to j becomes superfluous. An interesting criticism of formulations like (5) and (6) is offered by Kutz (2000: 17–65). He admits that in cases of moral responsibility, it might be appropriate for anyone to hold me accountable or to express certain reactive attitudes. However, which reactive attitudes are appropriate or under which conditions it is fitting to hold some agent i responsible may well depend on the specific relation between i and j, so that the reference to j is not superfluous.

A specific case is the situation when j is i. Consider the following example.[10] During a departmental meeting I make a statement or an argument that turns out to be insulting for one of the other participants in the meeting. Let's suppose that my statement cannot in general be considered insulting or inappropriate, nor could I have known that my words would be insulting. Because of this excusable ignorance, it seems inappropriate for other participants in the meeting to hold me responsible (blameworthy) for what turned out to be an insult. For the same reason I am morally allowed not to blame myself, nor should I feel guilty. Nevertheless, it would not be inappropriate if I felt guilty and offered her excuses. In fact, doing so might, depending on the exact circumstances, be laudable or virtuous. This example suggests two things. First, I can appropriately take responsibility for some φ even if it would be inappropriate for others to hold me responsible for that φ. Second, I have a degree of choice in taking responsibility. Of course, I cannot reasonably take responsibility for anything, nor can I reasonably escape responsibility for some things. However, within the bounds of reason and morality, I have some freedom for taking responsibility for certain things or not.

The possibility of taking responsibility seems to undermine formulations (5) and (6). In fact, it is also not fully captured by (4) because, as the example suggests, there may be situations in which it would be both appropriate, i.e., rationally and morally allowable, not to take responsibility and to take responsibility. Whether an agent is, or rather becomes, responsible in such situations depends on the volitional choice of that agent.

1.2.3 Why Do We Attribute Responsibility?

In the philosophical literature on moral responsibility, it is often assumed that the aim for ascribing responsibility is retribution. In the traditional view, being morally responsible means that the person is an appropriate candidate for reactive attitudes, such as blame or praise (Fischer and Ravizza 1998, Miller 2004, Strawson 1962). Because moral responsibility in this view is related to reactive attitudes, which may have consequences for the well-being of an agent, the ascription of moral responsibility is only warranted if these reactive attitudes and their consequences are merited or deserved (Eshleman 2014, Magill 2000, Wallace 1994, Watson 1996, Zimmerman 1988). This perspective on moral responsibility might therefore be called merit-based. In addition to this traditional perspective, we might also distinguish a consequentialist perspective and a rights-based perspective.

In the consequentialist perspective, the most important question when ascribing responsibility is not whether the reactive response triggered by the responsibility ascription is warranted but whether the reactive response would likely lead to a desired outcome, such as improved behaviour by the agent (Eshleman 2014). According to a strict consequentialist view, the responsibility ascription that yields the best consequences is the morally optimal responsibility ascription. Responsibilities, in this view, do not take specific actions of persons as their object, but they rather have the character of obligations to see to it that a certain state of affairs is brought about (or prevented). As such, responsibilities are outcome and result oriented (Van den Hoven 1998: 107).

A third approach for ascribing responsibilities is based on the no harm principle. This implies that "actions are right if and only if: either there are no (possible) consequences for others; or those who will experience the (possible) consequences have consented to the actions after having been fully informed of the possible consequences" (Zandvoort 2005a: 46). The aim of this approach is remedial: it refers to the duty or obligation to put a situation right (Miller 2004). One way to effectuate the rights-based approach is the (legal) requirement of strict liability, which holds that actors are unconditionally required to repair or fully compensate for any damage to others that may result from their actions, regardless of culpability or fault (Honoré 1999, Vedder 2001, Zandvoort 2005b). Hence, the question of responsibility is reduced to the question 'Who caused the particular outcome?' (causal responsibility). As such, blame is not the guiding concept in ascribing responsibility.[11]

The three approaches each depart from a particular moral background theory in that they each try to answer a different moral question.[12] The merit-based approach fits into a deontological framework, which is primarily a theory of 'right actions'. The rights-based approach fits into an ethics of rights and freedoms (see e.g. Mackie 1977, Nozick 1974). This theory shares with deontological ethics that it takes 'action' as the primary object of evaluation. Where deontological ethics departs from duties, a right-based discourse departs from people's individual rights and freedom and uses these to determine which actions are permissible and which are not. In both cases, the content of the responsibility ascription is an action that ought to be abstained from (merit-based) or that ought to be done (rights-based): to breach a duty is to perform a blameworthy action (merit-based) or to be liable for compensation (rights-based). The consequentialist approach has a different focus. Rather than on particular actions, the consequentialist approach is focused on states of affairs. It does not prescribe what action ought to be done, but rather what should be achieved.

Different approaches thus emphasise different aims for attributing responsibility. The function of a responsibility distribution does, however, not just depend on one's ethical theory or perspective, but also on the sense of responsibility on which one is focused. Responsibility-as-blameworthiness is, for example, typically connected to retribution. Forward-looking responsibility-as-obligation will often be connected to efficacy. Liability often aims at remediation and doing justice to victims. Accountability may be connected to restoring or maintaining the moral community (cf. Kutz 2000).[13] Finally, responsibility-as-virtue might be interpreted as expressing due care, as we

20   *Ibo van de Poel*

Table 1.2   Aims of attributing responsibility

Meaning of responsibility	Aim of attributing responsibility
Backward-looking	
Responsibility-as-blameworthiness	Retribution
Responsibility-as-accountability	Maintaining moral community
Responsibility-as-liability	Remediation, Justice to victims
Forward-looking	
Responsibility-as-obligation	Efficacy
Responsibility-as-virtue	Due care to others

will further elaborate in Chapter 6. Table 1.2 summarises these aims of attributing responsibility.

This also means that the different perspectives on responsibility focus on different meanings of responsibility. The merit-based perspective mainly focuses on blameworthiness; the rights-based perspective on accountability; and the consequentialist perspective on responsibility-as-obligation to see to it that φ. This does, however, not mean that the perspectives have nothing to say on the other senses of responsibility. For example, in the consequentialist perspective, responsibility-as-blameworthiness may be attributed to the basis of its motivational force in relation to responsibility-as-obligation.

1.3   BACKWARD-LOOKING RESPONSIBILITY

Below we will discuss three different meanings of backward-looking responsibility (blameworthiness, accountability, and liability) and their application. In doing so we will make a distinction between the conditions under which a certain concept applies (e.g., i is responsible-as-blameworthy) and the (normative) implications of that application (e.g., it is appropriate to blame i for φ).

This distinction we make between conditions and implications is similar to the distinction that Ransdell (1971) makes between the *connotation* and the *import* of a term. The connotation describes the conditions under which a term is properly applied to an item; the import describes the (normative) implications of that application. He gives the following example of the distinction:

> being a physician connotes, on the hand, that the person has satisfactory completed a certain amount of education and training in connection with an accredited institution, but the import of the term is given by the codes of ethics applicable to such a person.
>
> (Ransdell 1971: 393)

Rather than speaking of connotation, we will speak of the *conditions* under which a term applies. For example, we will argue that an agent is responsible-as-blameworthy if the following five conditions are met: capacity, causality, knowledge, freedom, and wrong-doing. We will speak of the *implication* rather than the import of this application: e.g., if an agent is responsible-as-blameworthy, an implication is that it is appropriate to blame that agent.

1.3.1 Responsibility-as-Blameworthiness

Ascribing responsibility-as-blameworthiness to an agent i for φ has the following implication:

> (*Implication 1*) *i is responsible-as-blameworthy for φ implies that it is appropriate to adopt a blaming reactive attitude toward i in respect of φ,*

where i is some agent, and φ an action or state-of-affairs.

Following the literature on responsibility, we will assume that an agent can reasonably be held responsible-as-blameworthy if, and only if, certain conditions are met. The conditions of responsibility-as-blameworthiness have been discussed throughout the history of philosophy and there are countless different views on the relevance and priority of them. Still, we think a common framework can be defined that contains the main types of conditions mentioned in the literature. We will not take a stance as to whether all conditions are equally important, or as to the exact content of the conditions. The point of this discussion is merely to provide a framework that helps to discuss when it is reasonable to hold someone responsible.

Below, we will argue that the following conditions together capture the general notion of when it is reasonable to hold an agent morally responsible-as-blameworthy:

1. Capacity
2. Causality
3. Knowledge
4. Freedom
5. Wrong-doing

Capacity

The first condition, 'capacity', is closely related to the question of moral agency. Philosophers and non-philosophers alike commonly exempt some groups of human beings from responsibility, for example, children and people with mental disorders, because they lack the capacity to act responsibly (Wallace 1994, cf. Austin 1956–57). In the literature, there has been discussion whether animals or even machines should be awarded moral agency and hence should be eligible for normative assessment, although

22   *Ibo van de Poel*

few actually defend such positions (Shapiro 2006, Johnson 2006). The discussion of whether it is appropriate to ascribe responsibility to collective entities also focuses on this condition (see section 2.3.1). It is essentially a question of whether collectives are eligible for normative assessment.

Causality

The second condition is that the agent in question actually caused that for which she is being held responsible-as-blameworthy. We call this the condition of causality. Some theorists treat causality as *the* condition for moral responsibility: if an agent causes harm to another she is responsible for that even if she could not have foreseen it or was not acting voluntarily. This is so because either there is an individual as well as a societal interest to hold everyone who caused harm responsible or because people feel justified regret when they cause harm regardless of why or how they caused harm (Honoré 1999, Williams 1999, Zandvoort 2000, Vedder 2001).

Most people do not ascribe responsibility to an agent unless she appears to have contributed causally to that for which she is held responsible. The question is what sense of causation one should adopt, and how strong the causal link should be in order for someone to reasonably be held responsible. Similarly, causation is not the only condition to which most people refer when holding others responsible.

Knowledge

Aristotle argued that an agent is not responsible-as-blameworthy if the action was performed involuntarily. To be voluntary, an action should not have been performed under coercion or ignorance. We call the latter the knowledge condition. Like the causality condition, the knowledge condition is much more complicated in the technological age than it was at the time of Aristotle's analysis. One could argue that, for example, engineers are only responsible for what they actually know or are aware of. However, this neglects the reasonable notion that engineers also have a duty to know or find out some things. This duty is entailed by their role as engineers, as professionals who have knowledge and experience that goes beyond the knowledge and experience of laypeople. The knowledge condition then has a normative aspect; it relates to what people should know, or can reasonably be expected to know. People are only excused by nonculpable ignorance.

Freedom

The second excusing condition has been called the freedom condition, or the control condition. If the agent was acting under coercion, she is not responsible (Aristotle 2000). If an agent i is coerced to do φ, it is not reasonable to hold her responsible for φ or for the consequences of φ. However, regarding the questions of what constitutes coercion and when actions can reasonably be viewed as free, the disagreement is considerable. The extensive discussion between compatibilists and incompatibilists in the metaphysical debate about 'responsibility and free will' essentially concerns this condition. The focal point of that debate is whether it is reasonable to hold individuals responsible if human beings are causally determined. Some philosophers in this debate argue that the kind of control necessary for responsibility requires that we have alternatives (Van Inwagen 1983, Ginet 2006, Widerker 2005, Copp 2006), whereas others disagree (cf. French, Wettstein, and Fischer 2005, Frankfurt 1969, Widerker and McKenna 2006).

In the light of free will debate, the freedom condition can be interpreted in a range of different ways. One interpretation would be only to require that the agent was not coerced to do an action. This interpretation of the freedom condition implies that when an agent chooses an action without being coerced, the freedom condition is met, even when there were no alternative actions available to the agent. Other interpretations of the freedom condition might require the availability of alternative actions. A subsequent question, in that case, is which conditions these alternatives should meet. Should there be an alternative action available to the agent that prevents the undesirable outcome, or is it enough that there is an alternative that allows the agent to withdraw herself from the (actual) causal chain leading to the undesirable outcome? (cf. Braham and van Hees 2012) If one requires the availability of alternatives, a further question is also whether the costs of these alternatives to the agent are relevant and, if so, in what sense. For example, one might only be able to prevent an undesirable outcome by putting one's life at risk. Depending on the severity of the undesirable outcome, this may be an unreasonably high price. One might, thus, want to require that not only certain kinds of alternatives are available, but that these are also available at 'reasonable' costs (cf. Nihlen Fahlquist 2009).

Thus, there is extensive discussion on the condition of freedom, its meaning, and its scope. However, few would argue that if an agent performs an act under coercion, she is responsible-as-blameworthiness; disagreement concerns when an act can be said to be free.

Wrong-Doing

When we hold agents responsible-as-blameworthy, it is usually the case that some harm has occurred or some norm has been transgressed.[14] An agent has done something that is perceived as wrong, and therefore she is blameworthy for that thing, given that she did it voluntarily and knowingly (Smiley 1992). Clearly, what counts as wrong-doing is at the core of the discipline of ethics, and utilitarian, deontological, and virtue ethics give different answers to this question. However, what is important in this context is that there is enough agreement that when we hold an agent responsible it is partly because the agent is perceived to have done something wrong, regardless of whether the argument is based on utilitarian, deontological, virtue ethics, or on some other set of ethical principles or norms.

24   *Ibo van de Poel*

1.3.2   Responsibility-as-Accountability

The ascription of responsibility-as-accountability has the following implication:

> *(Implication 2) i is responsible-as-accountable for φ implies that i should account for (the occurrence of) φ, in particular for i's role in doing, or bringing about φ, or for i's role in failing to prevent φ from happening,*

where i is some agent, and φ an action or a state-of-affairs.

Like responsibility-as-blameworthiness, the ascription of responsibility-as-accountability is based on certain conditions that need to apply in order to hold someone reasonably accountable. Our suggestion is that some of the above mentioned conditions (knowledge and freedom) for blameworthiness are possible excuses (reasons) that can be used by an agent who is accountable for something in order to show that she is not blameworthy.[15] The other three—capacity, causality, and wrong-doing—are, rather, preconditions for being accountable.

The freedom and knowledge conditions are both arguments that can be used in an account to excuse oneself.[16] Typically, both are already mentioned by Aristotle as possible reasons why someone is not to be blamed for her actions or the consequences of these (Aristotle 2000).[17] The capacity and causality conditions, on the other hand, are typically conditions for holding someone accountable. We do not hold people, or other entities, accountable if we do not have reason to believe that they have the capacity to act responsibly;[18] without this capacity, they would, in fact, not be able to provide an account at all. We also do not hold people accountable if we believe that they are completely, causally disconnected from the action or state of affairs φ we are concerned about. There should be at least a suspicion of causal involvement or the ability to causally influence φ by the agent i. Although capacity and causality are conditions for holding someone accountable, they may also function as arguments in the account given. We might suspect a causal connection, but the agent might be able to show in her account that we are wrong. Similarly, the agent might argue that she temporarily lacked, for circumstances beyond her control, the capacity to act responsibly, and therefore is not to be blamed.

How does the wrongdoing condition fit into this picture? In general, it seems that we hold people not only accountable for bad things, but also for neutral things, like a reimbursement, and even for good outcomes, for example to judge whether a certain prize would be deserved. What is common to these cases of accountability is that a judgement is made whether a certain treatment is deserved. In this case, we are interested in the question of whether blame is deserved. Such accountability for blame is sometimes called answerability. In the words of Hart:

> The original meaning of the word 'answer', like that of the Greek 'ἀποχρινέσθαι' and the Latin *respondere*, was not that of answering

Moral Responsibility 25

Table 1.3 Conditions for accountability and blameworthiness

Conditions for accountability	Possible excuses to avoid blameworthiness (if held accountable)
Capacity	Ignorance (knowledge)
Causality	Coercion (freedom)
Suspicion of	No wrongdoing
wrongdoing	(No capacity)
	(No causality)

questions, but that of answering or rebutting accusations or charges, which, if established, carried liability to punishment or blame or other adverse treatment (see O.E.D., *sub. tit. 'answer'*). . . . a person who fails to rebut a charge is liable to punishment or blame for what he has done, and a person who is liable to punishment or blame has had a charge to rebut and failed to rebut.

(Hart 1968: 265)

In order to hold someone reasonably accountable, at least a reasonable suspicion of wrongdoing needs to apply. The reason for this is that accountability shifts the burden of proof for blameworthiness. Accountability implies blameworthiness unless the accountable agent can show that a reasonable excuse applies that frees her from blameworthiness. So holding an agent i accountable shifts the burden of proof for showing that i is not blameworthy to the agent i: the agent i is now to show—by giving an account—that she is not blameworthy. Such a shift in the burden of proof seems only reasonable if there is a reasonable suspicion of wrongdoing.

To summarise: an agent i is accountable for φ if i has the capacity to act responsibly (has moral agency), is somehow causally connected to the outcome φ (by an action or omission) and there is a reasonable suspicion that agent i did somehow do something wrong. Agent i may then provide an account that she is not blameworthy. In this account, she can refer to the knowledge and freedom conditions, but possibly also to the other three conditions. Table 1.3 summarises this idea.

1.3.3 Responsibility-as-Liability

Liability is a central notion in accounts of juridical or legal responsibility. It is usually related to punishment for what one has done or caused and/ or the obligation to pay damages. Legal liability does not require moral blameworthiness, as is witnessed by legal notions like strict liability, vicarious liability, and liability without fault. Whereas the notion of legal liability

26 *Ibo van de Poel*

is relatively clear, this is far less true for moral liability. Hart has suggested that moral liability, although different in content, is similar in structure to legal liability:

> [T]he moral counterpart of the account given of legal liability-responsibility would be the following: to say that a person is morally responsible for something he has done or for some harmful outcome of his own or others' conduct, is to say that he is morally blameworthy or morally obliged to make amends for the harm.
>
> (Hart 1968: 225)

Interesting as this suggestion is, it is a bit confusing. On the one hand, it equates moral liability with blameworthiness ('to say that someone is liable is to say that he is blameworthy'); on the other hand, it suggests that moral liability is—or can (sometimes?) be—more than just blameworthiness ('morally obliged to make amends for the harm'). We think it is better to separate both elements and to restrict the notion of liability to the latter, i.e., obligation to make amends rather than blameworthiness. Hart's quote then can be read as saying that moral liability requires blameworthiness.

Although moral liability can be understood in terms of making amends or rectifying an unjust situation, we think that not every obligation to put right a wrong situation implies moral liability. For example, in the parable of the Good Samaritan, it might be argued that the Samaritan, in helping the robbed and beaten traveller, answers to an obligation—or least desirability— of turning a wrong situation (i.e. someone lying half dead along the road) right. However, this is not a case of liability because the wrong situation is by no means rooted in actions or omissions of the Samaritan. It is rather a case, we think, of responsibility-as-virtue (see section 1.4.2).

So, we take it that to speak of liability, the obligation to remedy a wrong should be somehow rooted in a past action or omission of the agent. We therefore propose the following implication of moral liability:

> *(Implication 3) i is responsible-as-morally-liable for φ implies i should remedy or compensate for (the occurrence of) φ on the basis of some past action, or omission, of i,*

where i is some agent, and φ an action or a state-of-affairs.

We can now ask under which conditions it is reasonable to ask i to remedy or compensate for (the occurrence) of φ (on the basis of some past action, or omission, of i). In the case of legal liability, these conditions are mainly laid down in the law or have been established on the basis of jurisprudence. In the case of legal liability, these conditions do not necessarily or always require moral blameworthiness, as indicated above. We believe,

Moral Responsibility 27

however, that this is different for *moral* liability. Like Hart, we will assume that moral liability requires moral blameworthiness.[19] More specifically, we will assume that moral liability can be appropriately attributed to an agent if, and only if, that agent is blameworthy.

1.4 FORWARD-LOOKING RESPONSIBILITY

It might be argued that responsibility always has a forward-looking component, in the sense that the ascription of responsibility is usually accompanied by a prescription to do something in the future. So if an agent is responsible-as-accountable, she has to give an account; if she is responsible-as-blameworthy, she has to accept blame and maybe has to feel guilty; in the case of responsibility-as-liability, compensation may be due.

Even if backward-looking responsibility has such a forward-looking component, we can still make the distinction between backward-looking and forward-looking responsibility. The distinction is this: in cases of backward-looking responsibility, the agent is responsible *for* something that happened in the past (even if this may imply an obligation in the future); in the case of forward-looking responsibility, the agent is responsible *for* something that is not yet the case or has not yet occurred (even if this forward-looking responsibility may be rooted in something in the past, like a promise). Backward-looking and forward-looking responsibility thus differ as to whether they refer to past or future state of affairs or actions in answer to the question: What is the agent responsible *for*?

We will discuss two kinds of forward-looking responsibility: responsibility-as-obligation to see to it and responsibility-as-virtue (see Table 1.1). Responsibility-as-obligation to see to it typically refers to state-of-affairs that are to be brought about, whereas responsibility-as-virtue is seen as a character trait of virtuous persons. After discussing the two varieties of forward-looking responsibility, we will discuss how agents can acquire forward-looking responsibility.

1.4.1 Responsibility-as-Obligation

In line with our discussion in 1.2.2, we might understand responsibility-as-obligation as follows:

> *(Implication 4A) i is forward-looking responsible-as-obligation for φ implies that i ought to see to it that φ*

This formulation may, however, be too broad if φ also includes actions of i. Following Goodin (1995), we might want to make a distinction between responsibility-as-obligation and duties.

28   *Ibo van de Poel*

Goodin conceives of both duties and responsibilities as prescriptions of the general form (Goodin 1995: 82):

i ought to see to it that φ,

where i is some agent, and φ is some state of affairs. For duties, φ takes the form:

i does or refrains from doing α,

where α is some specific action.

In order to distinguish responsibilities from duties, φ should, in implication 4A not refer to specific actions of i. φ can refer to states-of-the-world, to states-of-mind of i, to i possessing certain virtues, or to actions of other agents, as long as it does not include specified actions of i.

What then does it imply to see to it that φ? Goodin suggests that the exercising of forward-looking responsibility:

> require[s] certain activities of a self-supervisory nature from A. The standard form of responsibility is that i *see to it* that X [φ]. It is not enough that X occurs. i must also have 'seen to it' that X occurs. 'Seeing to it that X' requires, minimally; that i satisfy himself that there is some process (mechanism or activity) at work whereby X will be brought about; that i check from time to time to make sure that that process is still at work, and is performing as expected; and that i take steps as necessary to alter or replace processes that no longer seem likely to bring about X.
>
> (Goodin 1995: 83)

According to Goodin, these self-supervisory activities are 'genuine responsibilities' because "they are injunctions that mandate goals and very general classes of activities, rather than specific actions" (Goodin 1995: 83). For Goodin, the crucial distinction between duties and responsibilities is the discretionary component built into the latter (Goodin 1995: 84). However, most duties also have a discretionary component. Such duties do not prescribe specific actions but rather forbid general classes of actions or prescribe actions with certain properties. There are usually several ways in which one can abide by duties such as 'tell the truth' or 'do not lie'. Duties are, therefore, often best seen as constraints on actions rather than as strict prescriptions.

Nevertheless, there is a sense in which responsibilities are different from duties and it is related to the presence of a discretionary component. The difference is that responsibilities do not require the agent to achieve the outcome φ by her own actions. Responsibilities can be delegated, whereas duties cannot. If I have the duty to tell the truth it is not enough that somebody else tells the truth or that the truth surfaces in some other way. Each of these does not count as fulfilling the duty; the duty can only be fulfilled by an action of mine. This is different in the case of responsibilities. Consider the following example. Suppose that I have a forward-looking responsibility to see to it that the door of the classroom is closed before my lecture commences. Initially, I can just wait and see whether somebody closes it. If so, my responsibility has been discharged and I can start my lecture. If not, I can ask one of my students to close the door. If he indeed closes the door, my responsibility has been discharged. If not, I can decide to close the door myself in order to discharge my responsibility.

The example illustrates two points. One is that fulfilling my responsibility does not require that φ is achieved by an action of mine. The other point is that responsibility requires, as also suggested by Goodin, some action on my part of a supervisory nature: I have to see to it that φ is achieved. This supervisory activity refers, contrary to what Goodin believes, not to a responsibility, but to a duty. This is so because the supervision is to be done by me and cannot be delegated.[20]

The above is helpful in further specifying what it means to say that i did or did not fulfil her forward-looking responsibility to see to it that φ. Although this responsibility is aimed at realizing φ, the occurrence of φ is not the main criterion whether i actually fulfilled her forward-looking responsibility. The reason is that φ may occur even if i did not see to it that φ because φ may be caused by something else. So even if i did not fulfil her responsibility φ may be the case. Moreover, φ may not be realised even if i saw to it that φ; φ may, for example, come about due to circumstances that i could neither foresee nor control. The main criterion for fulfilling one's responsibility-as-obligation is therefore not whether φ actually occurred but whether i exercised her (self-)supervisory duties to see to it that φ. This can be expressed as follows:

(Implication 4B) i is forward-looking responsible-as-obligation for φ implies that i should exercise her (self-)supervisory duties to see to it that φ.

We will discuss the *conditions* under which the attribution of responsibility-as-obligation to an agent is appropriate in section 1.4.3.

1.4.2 Responsibility-as-Virtue

Williams suggests that responsibility as a virtue has the following connotations:

There is an element of reliability and commitment, of carrying on with something over time. There is a dimension of initiative and judgement: the agent can be trusted with something and to exercise some degree

30   *Ibo van de Poel*

of discretion. There is an obvious connection between the virtue and retrospective responsibility, in terms of mutual accountability. This involves a readiness to identify with and answer for past actions or omissions, and to make up for these where they have proved faulty. . . . Clearly, the virtue is closely related to consciousness in fulfilling one's responsibilities. With some circularity, one might say that responsibility suggests an agent who lives up to her, or its, position within a division of responsibilities and within relations of mutual accountability.

(Williams 2008: 459)

This suggests that a responsible agent (in the virtue sense) is one who accepts accountability ('a readiness to identify with and answer for past actions or omissions') and liability ('to make up for these where they have proved faulty') when that is due. It also suggests that responsibility-as-virtue is helpful, or even required, for fulfilling one's forward-looking responsibilities, in the sense of obligations of seeing to it that ('reliability and commitment', 'carrying on with something over time', and 'consciousness in fulfilling one's responsibilities'). Finally, it suggests that a responsible agent is an agent that consciously takes responsibilities-as-obligations ('initiative and judgement').[21]

As suggested by Williams' quote, a responsible agent is one who shows initiative, i.e., who actively takes certain responsibilities and who does so with judgement. A responsible person is then one who deliberates about which responsibilities to assume and which not. It is the kind of agent that takes the 'right' responsibilities and the 'right' amount of responsibilities, i.e., neither too many (so that one cannot live by her responsibilities) nor too few (which would imply a lack of initiative and commitment).

Williams suggests a further definition of responsibility as a virtue that can be related to judgement in assuming responsibility. His definition reads: "responsibility represents the readiness to respond to a plurality of normative demands". This readiness implies that a responsible agent assumes certain responsibilities (as obligations to see to it that) in response to normative demands and does so with judgement, because not all normative demands can usually be answered. Not only may various normative demands conflict, as Williams suggests, there may also simply be too many normative demands for an agent to answer, or to answer responsibly.

This brings us to the following implication of responsibility-as-virtue:

(Implication 5) i is responsible-as-virtue implies that i voluntarily assumes various responsibilities-as-obligations in the light of plurality of normative demands and does so with judgement.

1.4.3 Acquiring Forward-Looking Responsibility

We will distinguish three routes for acquiring forward-looking responsibility-as-obligation based on three main ethical theories: consequentialism, deontology, and virtue ethics:

1. The consequentialist route takes as starting point the desirability of certain state of affairs (as established by a consequentialist ethical theory), and hence the desirability of bringing about these state-affairs. On basis of these, responsibilities-as-obligations to bring about certain state of affairs may be established.
2. The deontological route focuses on the duty to live by one's promises and commitments. Such promises or commitments may create certain responsibilities-as-obligations.
3. The virtue routes takes as starting point that virtuous agents will assume certain responsibilities-as-obligations as we saw in section 1.4.2.

The Consequentialist Route

Consequentialism takes the desirability of certain state of affairs as point of departure for ethical deliberation. From the desirability of state of affairs the desirability of certain actions follows, in particular those actions that bring about desirable state of affairs. Consequentialism, thus, can advise an agent what to do in a given situation. However, most consequentialist ethical theories do not specify which agent is responsible for bringing about a certain desirable state of affairs. Who is responsible for reducing poverty in the world? A consequentialist theory might establish that it is desirable to eliminate or at least reduce poverty; it does usually not establish who is—primarily—responsible for achieving a reduction in poverty. Therefore, consequentialism needs to be supplemented by a theory, principle, or reasons for distributing responsibility in order to establish forward-looking responsibility-as-obligation.

The responsibility to see to it that φ may be attributed on strictly consequentialist grounds, for example, to that agent or those agents that are in the best position to bring about φ. However, consequentialism may also be supplemented by non-consequentialist or pluralist principles or reasons for distributing responsibility. Such possible principles or reasons include past causal responsibility (for 'not φ'), blameworthiness (for 'not φ'), the capacity to bring about φ, power, the relation between agent i (that ought to see to it that φ) and the agents that have a stake in φ being brought about, membership of a group, et cetera. We will not try to develop a theory here that is able to account for all these possible reasons (or that ignores some of them because we have good reasons to think that they are, after all, irrelevant). We do believe, however, that the most likely candidates for such theories are

32   *Ibo van de Poel*

what David Miller (2001) calls pluralist theories, i.e., theories that take into account a variety of reasons for distributing responsibility rather than one or two in isolation.

Any reasonable theory or principle for distributing responsibility should at least meet a minimal condition with respect to causal efficacy. Only agents who are able to see to it that φ can be responsible-as-obligation for φ. It should be noted that seeing to it does not require that the agent i also herself brings about φ. So the actual occurrence of φ is not necessarily caused by i. Moreover, as we have seen in section 1.4.1, the main criterion in fulfilling one's responsibility to see to it that φ is not whether φ actually occurred but whether i exercised her (self-) supervisory duties to see to it that φ. Still, it seems that an appropriate attribution of responsibility-as-obligation to i requires at least some minimal causal efficacy of i with respect to φ. We would like to suggest that this causal efficacy is best caught by the following conditional:

if i properly fulfils her supervisory duties to see to it that φ under normal circumstances, φ will occur.

We have added the clause 'under normal circumstances' because it is always conceivable that under some extreme and rare circumstances φ does not occur, even if i properly fulfilled her responsibility-as-obligation. It should also be noted that this conditional does not require that i herself causes φ, but only that i can ensure φ (under normal circumstances) when i lives by her supervisory duties.

The Deontological Route

Deontological ethical theories take as their point of departure the (un) desirability of actions as expressed in duties. In section 1.4.1 we distinguished duties from forward-looking responsibilities. This means that whereas deontological ethical theories can establish duties, they cannot directly establish forward-looking moral responsibilities. They can do so, however, indirectly. More specifically, the forward-looking responsibility to see to it that φ can be grounded in the general duty to live by one's promises and commitments. The reason for this is that agents can promise or commit themselves to bringing about certain state of affairs. So if an engineer commits him- or herself to designing a car that is reasonably safe, he or she obtains a moral obligation to see to it that the care designed is reasonably safe.

Nevertheless, one might wonder whether every promise or commitment to bring about a certain state-of-affair creates a responsibility-as-obligation. There seems to be at least one additional condition required, that is: the state-of-affairs that is promised to be brought about should not be morally objectionable. I can promise to see to it that someone is killed, but that does not create a moral obligation to see to it that that person is killed. The point is not that immoral promises (or commitments) can be broken at will, but rather that they should not have been made in the first place. The point, then, is that we cannot make a bad state-of-affairs good by just promising to bring it about, or can create a moral responsibility to do something bad just by promising it.

It seems, therefore, that the following two conditions can be sufficient to create a responsibility to see to it that φ for i:

1. i voluntarily committed herself to see to it that φ
2. φ is not morally objectionable
   So: i is responsible-as-obligation to see to it that φ.

The conditions above do not explicitly refer to a causality condition as a condition for assuming forward-looking responsibility.[22] In fact, people can make promises (or commitments) about state of affairs they cannot (yet) causally affect. However, as we saw in 1.4.3.1, assuming responsibility-as-obligation does not require the agent to be able to causally bring about φ herself but 'only' to be able to effectively see to it that φ. As suggested earlier this causality requirement is probably best caught in the conditional:

if i properly fulfils her supervisory duties to see to it that φ, under normal circumstances φ will occur.

What about cases in which the causality criterion is not met? What if someone makes a promise about something that is known to be impossible? Think of an engineer promising to develop a perpetuum mobile. From the law of thermodynamics, we know that a perpetuum mobile is impossible, so we have good reasons to suppose that this promise does not meet the causality criterion and can, therefore, never be met. Does, in this case, the promise still create a responsibility to develop a perpetuum mobile? The point to be made here is similar to the case of immoral promises. The point is not that promises to do the impossible or to bring about something that is entirely beyond the causal influence of the promisor can be broken at will, but rather that they should not have been made in the first place. If people know that a promise cannot be kept, they should not make it.

The above discussion suggests that we need an additional condition to establish forward-looking responsibility resulting in the following scheme:

1. i voluntarily committed herself to see to it that φ
2. φ is not morally objectionable
3. If i properly fulfils her supervisory duties to see to it that φ, under normal circumstances φ will occur
   So: i is responsible-as-obligation to see to it that φ.

34 *Ibo van de Poel*

Promises or commitments may not only concern individual state-of-affairs, but also a domain or set of forward-looking responsibilities. For example, if one accepts a certain task or role, for example by accepting a certain job, this usually implies a range of forward-looking responsibilities. Such cases might be captured by a set of conditions like the following:

1. i voluntarily committed herself to task T
2. Task T implies seeing to it that φ, ψ and χ
3. φ, ψ and χ are not morally objectionable
4. If i properly fulfils her supervisory duties to see to it that φ, ψ and χ, under normal circumstances φ, ψ and χ will occur
   So: i is responsible-as-obligation to see to it that φ, ψ and χ.

A specific case of this type of scheme is when an agent joins a profession, like the profession of engineering and so assumes certain responsibilities. Michael Davis has proposed the following definition of a profession:

> A profession is a number of individuals in the same occupation voluntarily organized to earn a living by openly serving a certain moral ideal in a morally-permissible way beyond what law, market, and morality would otherwise require.
>
> (Davis 1997: 417)

He also argues that engineering is a profession (at least in the United States). For engineering, the ideal is something like 'enhancing human welfare by developing technology'.[23] Serving this ideal involves certain duties, but obviously also forward-looking responsibilities that leave it to the discretion of engineers how to achieve the stated outcomes. This includes, for example, serving the 'health, safety and welfare of the public'.[24]

The case of agents assuming certain responsibilities by joining a profession may be summarised by a scheme like this:[25]

1. i voluntarily joined profession P
2. Membership of profession P implies the task to see to it that φ, ψ and χ
3. φ, ψ and χ are not morally objectionable
4. If i properly fulfils her supervisory duties to see to it that φ, ψ and χ, under normal circumstances φ, ψ and χ will occur
   So: i is responsible-as-obligation to see to it that φ, ψ and χ.

The Virtue Route

Virtue ethics takes the agent and her character traits as point of departure for ethical deliberation. In section 1.4.2 we discussed some of the character traits that are implied by responsibility as virtue. As we saw responsibility-as-virtue implies a willingness to actively assume certain responsibilities, and

Moral Responsibility 35

it implies initiative and judgment in taking responsibility. Typical for the virtue route to responsibility-as-obligation to see to it is that such responsibilities are actively assumed by a virtuous agent. In this sense the virtue route is somewhat similar to the deontological route where responsibility is taken on by a promise or commitment. What the virtue route adds to that is the idea that it is morally virtuous to assume certain responsibilities rather than taking on no responsibility. Moreover, it may be more virtuous to take on certain responsibilities rather than others. Which responsibilities to assume can, in this route, in contrast to the consequentialist route, not be deducted for some abstract principle, but requires judgement by the agent and wisdom. It requires, thus, a practical deliberation by the agent that takes into account the specific situation, involving not only, for example, what the agent is able to influence causally, but also her earlier commitments and assumed responsibilities. As we said, responsibility-as-virtue is the inclination to assume the 'right' responsibilities-as-obligations in response to a range of normative demands. In this way, responsibility-as-virtue may ground more specific responsibilities-as-obligations.

The Three Routes Compared

All three routes are based on a normative condition stating something about the desirability or acceptability of φ and about why i (possibly amidst others) is responsible for φ, and on a causality condition. Although, not discussed above, a capacity condition can be added to this, because in all routes we only ascribe responsibility to agents that have a capacity to act responsibly. Table 1.4 summarises this result.

Table 1.4 Routes for acquiring responsibility-as-obligation

	Consequentialist	Deontological	Virtue
Normative condition	φ ought to be (brought about) and a distribution principle that attributes responsibility for φ to i.	φ is not morally objectionable and i promised to see to it that φ.	It is virtuous to bring about φ and i has assumed the obligation-responsibility for φ on the basis of initiative and judgment.
Causality condition	If i properly fulfils her supervisory duties to see to it that φ, under normal circumstances φ will occur.	If i properly fulfils her supervisory duties to see to it that φ, under normal circumstances φ will occur.	If i properly fulfils her supervisory duties to see to it that φ, under normal circumstances φ will occur.
Capacity condition	Ability to act responsibly.	Ability to act responsibly.	Ability to act responsibly.

36 *Ibo van de Poel*

1.5 THE RELATION BETWEEN FORWARD-LOOKING AND BACKWARD-LOOKING RESPONSIBILITY

We will now look at the relation between forward-looking and backward-looking responsibility. In the literature, it has been suggested that backward-looking responsibility supposes, or requires, forward-looking responsibility (e.g Vedder 2001, Duff 2007: 30–31). It has also been suggested that forward-looking responsibility is vacuous if it is not accompanied by (potential) backward-looking responsibility (Goodin 1995: 101, Bovens 1998: 49). In this section, we will critically asses such ideas, using the conceptions of responsibility and the related conditions for responsibility we have developed in the previous sections.

For a first order answer to the question about the relation between forward-looking and backward-looking responsibility, we will look at a real-life case. The case is a brief account that Leslie Robertson, the structural engineer who designed the Twin Towers in New York, provided when he was asked whether he felt guilty about the fact that the towers did not stand longer after they had been hit by two planes in a terrorist attack on 11 September 2001:

> The responsibility for arriving at the ultimate strength of the towers was mine. The fact that they could not stand longer could be laid at my feet. Do I feel guilty about . . . the fact that they collapsed? The circumstances on September, 11 were outside of what we considered in the design. . . . If I knew then what I know now they would have stood longer, of course.[26]

The different elements of his account can be interpreted as follows:

- 'The responsibility for arriving at the ultimate strength of the towers was mine'. This refers to responsibility-as-obligation.
- 'The fact that they could not stand longer could be laid at my feet'. This can be interpreted as: It would be proper (for others) to hold me accountable for that fact.
- 'Do I feel guilty about . . . the fact that they collapsed?' This could be interpreted as: 'Would it be proper to blame me for it?'
- 'The circumstances on September, 11 were outside of what we considered in the design. . . . If I knew then what I know now they would have stood longer, of course'. This can be interpreted as giving an account (invoking certain excuses, like nonculpable ignorance) that shows why it would not be proper to blame him.[27]

This example then suggests a first order answer along the following lines:

If i is forward-looking responsible-as-obligation for some state-of-affairs φ and φ happens not to be the case, i is accountable for 'not φ'. If i is not able to give a satisfactory account for 'not φ', i is also blameworthy.

This first-order answer suggests that forward-looking responsibility can be a ground for backward-looking responsibility (accountability and liability). It does not, however, show that forward-looking responsibility is *required* for backward-looking responsibility, an issue to which we will turn in section 1.5.1. It also does not show that forward-looking responsibility necessarily or always implies backward-looking responsibility, an issue that we will discuss in section 1.5.2.

1.5.1 DOES BACKWARD-LOOKING RESPONSIBILITY REQUIRE FORWARD-LOOKING RESPONSIBILITY?

Some authors have suggested that an agent can only be backward-looking responsible (accountable or blameworthy) for a state of affairs if that agent was forward-looking responsible for preventing that state of affairs (e.g Vedder 2001, Duff 2007: 30–31). In this section, we will question this relationship.

To do so, we start with comparing the suggested relation between forward-looking responsibility and backward-looking responsibility that we distilled from the Twin Towers case with the conditions for accountability discussed in section 1.3.2. There we found the following conditions for accountability: i is accountable if i has the capacity to act responsibly, is causally involved in φ, and did something wrong. It might well be possible to combine the account in section 1.3.2 with the new suggestion. We could argue that in order for an agent to be forward-looking responsible for φ, that agent needs to possess moral agency (i.e., the capacity to act responsibly) and i needs to be able to causally influence the occurrence of φ. In addition, we could try to argue that the occurrence of φ constitutes wrongdoing, given i's responsibility to bring about 'not φ'.

Nevertheless, we think it is better not to merge the two suggestions completely. The reason for this is that it would tie accountability too closely to the notion of forward-looking responsibility-as-obligation. Typically, we do not only hold people accountable for not discharging their forward-looking responsibilities, but also for not meeting other moral obligations, preeminently for not living by their duties. One could deal with this by arguing that doing our duty is part of our responsibility-as-obligation. However, in section 1.4 we have argued that duties are to be distinguished from responsibilities-as-obligations. In line with the discussion there, it seems better to distinguish between moral obligations that refer to actions by the agent self (duties), and ones that refer to state of affairs (forward-looking responsibilities).

There is, then, not one route to accountability and blameworthiness, but rather two. One route, call it the consequentialist one, is rooted in i's

38 *Ibo van de Poel*

forward-looking responsibility for φ; the other, call it the deontic one, is rooted in some moral duty that is transgressed. On the consequentialist route, an agent is basically accountable for a state-of-affairs φ if that agent was forward-looking responsible for 'not φ' but did not see to it that 'not φ'. On the deontic route, an agent may be said to be accountable if he transgressed a duty D (and blameworthy if he was not acting under coercion or ignorance). The latter is, however, accountability for actions rather than for consequences. But suppose that the transgression of D results in φ in which φ is a undesirable state-of-affairs then it might be said that i is accountable for φ if i is a moral agent, who did an action transgressing D and this action caused, or causally contributed to, φ.

Both routes are based on the same general conditions for accountability, i.e., capacity, causality and wrong-doing, although the latter two conditions have a different meaning in the different routes. In the deontic route, wrong-doing consists in the breach of a duty D; the causality conditions boil down to this breach of D (rather than something else), causing a state-of-affairs φ (Feinberg 1970: 222). For the consequentialist route, the wrong-doing consists in the not discharging of one's supervisory duties to see to it that 'not φ'.

How does the causality condition fit in the consequentialist route? In section 1.4.3, we saw that a causality condition applies to all three routes we discussed for acquiring forward-looking responsibility-as-obligation (see also Table 1.4). So if an agent is forward-looking responsible for, say, 'not φ', this implies that: If i properly fulfils her supervisory duties to see to it that 'not φ', under normal circumstances 'not φ' will occur. In case of accountability, we already know that φ has occurred. So, the crucial question at this point of time is whether i could have prevented φ from occurring by exercising her supervisory duties. Three types of situations should be distinguished here. First, it is possible that φ occurred due to exceptional circumstances even if i exercised her supervisory duties. In such cases, it does not seem proper to hold i accountable. Second, it might be that i could have prevented φ from occurring by living by exercising her supervisory duties. In such cases, it seems proper to hold i accountable for φ. Third, i did not properly exercise her supervisory duties for not φ but if she had done so φ would still have occurred due to exceptional circumstances. We would suggest that in that case i is not accountable for φ because she could not have prevented φ. Of course, i is then still accountable for not exercising her supervisory duties, but that is another kind of accountability than accountability for φ.

Table 1.5 summarises the conditions for both routes to accountability that have been discussed. The following example further illustrates the difference between the two routes to accountability. Suppose a house has set fire because agent i lighted a cigarette (that caused the fire) and because no sprinkler installation was installed. We consider two agents: agent i who did not have a forward-looking responsibility to see to it that the house did not catch fire, but who had a moral duty, we suppose, not to light a cigarette in the house

Moral Responsibility 39

Table 1.5 Routes to accountability for φ

	Consequentialist route	Deontological route
Capacity	Ability to act responsibly	Ability to act responsibly
Suspicion of wrong-doing	Supervisory duties to see to it that 'not φ' not properly fulfilled	Transgression of duty D
Causality	If i had properly fulfilled her supervisory duties to see to it that 'not φ', under normal circumstances, φ would not have occurred	Transgression of D caused φ

(e.g., because the house was known to be susceptible to fire), and agent j, who had a forward-looking responsibility to see to it that the house did not catch fire. In this example, both agents may be considered accountable for the fire. i is accountable according to the deontological route because the transgression of the duty not to light a cigarette caused the fire. j is accountable according to the consequentialist route because by not having a sprinkler installation installed, j failed to properly fulfil her supervisory duty, and if a sprinkler installation had been installed the house would not have caught fire.

As this example suggests, the forward-looking responsibility to see to it that 'not φ' will often encompass much more than the duty not to cause φ. This is related to the distinction between forward-looking responsibilities and duties that we discussed in section 1.4.1. Duties only relate to actions of the agent herself; so the duty not to cause fire 'only' forbids certain actions; however, the responsibility to see to it that the house does not catch fire requires that the agent, in addition, also checks, and possibly controls, the action of others and of all other kind of causal paths, in which one is not actively involved as a causal agent. The causal criterion is not here whether the agent was a cause of the harm, but rather whether the agent could have prevented the fire by fulfilling her supervisory duties.

1.5.2 Does Forward-Looking Responsibility Require Backward-Looking Responsibility?

We have seen that backward-looking responsibility does not require forward-looking responsibility. What about the opposite relationship: Can there be forward-looking responsibility without backward-looking responsibility?

Some authors have suggested that forward-looking responsibility can only be meaningful or effective if it translates into backward-looking responsibility. Bovens has, for example, suggested that if people cannot be held accountable after the fact, they also do need to feel responsible beforehand (Bovens 1998, 49). Similarly, Goodin has argued:

40   *Ibo van de Poel*

It would make no sense to assign people task responsibilities if they were also not going to be held to account for how well or badly they performed those tasks and discharged those responsibilities. Therefore task responsibilities inevitably entail correlative blame-responsibilities.

(Goodin 1995: 101)

Goodin's notion of task-responsibility here refers to what we have called responsibility-as-obligation, and blame-responsibility corresponds to responsibility-as-blameworthiness.

Both Bovens and Goodin seem to believe that forward-looking responsibility, understood as the moral obligation to see to it, need to translate into backward-looking responsibility to be effective. It seems that the kind of relation Bovens and Goodin are thinking of is mainly motivational in nature: if someone knows she will not be held responsible afterwards, she will not assume or live by any forward-looking responsibility for φ.

It should be noted that this motivational link is based on behavioural assumptions. More specifically, it appears to be based on the psychological assumption that people avoid forward-looking responsibility if they will not be held responsible afterwards. This assumption would need to be confirmed empirically before it can be assumed. And even if this assumption would be proven to be true, one could wonder whether people should not take or live by forward-looking responsibilities, even if they are psychologically not inclined to do so in the absence of (potential) backward-looking responsibility.

Apart from a motivational link, there may be a conceptual link between forward-looking responsibility and backward-looking responsibility. Our analysis in section 1.5.1 suggests that if an agent i is forward-looking responsible-as-obligation for 'not φ' and φ happens to be the case then i is accountable for φ, although not necessarily blameworthy for φ. On the basis of this, one could set up the following argument:

1. If an agent i is forward-looking responsible-as-obligation for 'not φ' and φ happens to be the case then i is accountable for φ
2. φ is the case
3. i is *not* accountable for φ
   So: i is not forward-looking responsible-as-obligation for 'not φ'.

This argument is valid (modus tollens). So it seems that there is indeed a conceptual relation between forward-looking responsibility-as-obligation and backward-looking responsibility-as-accountability of the kind that Bovens is assuming. It should be noted, however, that this conceptual relation does not extend to the relation between backward-looking responsibility-as-blameworthiness and forward-looking responsibility-as-obligation, as Goodin seems to assume. The reason for that is that the accountable agent

Moral Responsibility 41

may be able to provide an account by invoking certain excuses, so that the agent is not blameworthy. One possible excuse may, for example, be that agent i properly discharged her responsibility-as-obligation but that φ nevertheless occurred for some reason beyond the control of agent i.

1.6 CONCLUSIONS

In this chapter, we have discussed the five main normative meanings of responsibility and their relations. We have also discussed the conditions under which it is reasonable to attribute the different meanings of responsibility to an individual agent, and the implications of these responsibility attributions. Table 1.6 and 1.7 summarise these findings. No conditions for responsibility-as-virtue are indicated in Table 1.5 because this kind of responsibility is usually not attributed to, but is voluntarily taken by, an agent on the basis of initiative and judgment.

To conclude this chapter, we want to summarise some of the conceptual relations we have established in this chapter between the different notions of responsibility.

The first relation is between responsibility-as-obligation to see to something and responsibility-as-accountability. From what we said in section 1.5.1, it follows that:

> *Proposition1: If agent i had a forward-looking responsibility-as-obligation for φ and φ did not occur and 'not φ' is not caused by exceptional circumstances then agent i is accountable for 'not φ'*

It should be noted that, according to the conceptualisation developed in this chapter, a lack of responsibility-as-obligation for φ does not necessarily imply that the agent is also not accountable for 'not φ'. The reason, for this, according to section 1.5.1, is that accountability can be based on a consequentialist, as well as on a deontic, route, and a lack of responsibility-as-obligation for φ only blocks the consequentialist route.

Table 1.6 Conditions for proper attribution of responsibility. (Please note that the exact content of the conditions is not necessarily the same for all kinds of responsibility.)

	Capacity	Causality	Knowledge	Freedom	Normative
Virtue					
Obligation	X	X			X
Accountability	X	X			X
Blameworthiness	X	X	X	X	X
Liability	X	X	X	X	X

42 Ibo van de Poel

Table 1.7 Implications of the attribution of responsibility and the related aims of attributing responsibility

Meaning of responsibility	Implication	Aim
Virtue	i voluntarily assumes various responsibilities-as-obligations in the light of plurality of normative demands, and does so with judgement.	Due care to others
Obligation	i should exercise her (self-)supervisory duties to see to it that φ.	Efficacy
Accountability	i should account for (the occurrence of) φ, in particular for i's role in doing, or bringing about φ, or for i's role in failing to prevent φ from happening.	Maintaining moral community
Blameworthiness	It is appropriate to adopt a blaming reactive attitude toward i in respect of φ.	Retribution
Liability	i should remedy or compensate for (the occurrence of) φ on the basis of some past action, or omission, of i.	Remediation, Justice to victims

The second relation is that between accountability and blameworthiness. From what we said in section 1.3.2, it follows that:

> *Proposition2: If agent i is accountable for φ and has no appropriate excuse why φ is the case then agent i is blameworthy for φ.*

So accountability does not yet imply blameworthiness. Conversely, in order for an agent to be blameworthy, she has to be accountable (and to have no excuse). The following, thus, is also true:

> *Proposition3: If an agent i is blameworthy for φ and φ is the case, then agent i is also accountable for φ.*

Let us finally look at the conceptual relation we established in section 1.5.2. There we found that proposition 1 above applies in the opposite direction in the following sense: If φ is not the case and i is not accountable for 'not φ', it follows that agent i did not have a forward-looking responsibility-as-obligation to see to it that φ was the case in the first place. Therefore:

Proposition 4: If agent i is not accountable for 'not φ' whereas φ is not the case and 'not φ' is not caused by exceptional circumstances then agent i had no forward-looking responsibility-as-obligation for φ.

This conceptual relation does not extend to the relation between blameworthiness and forward-looking responsibility-as-obligation. So even if an agent i is not blameworthy for 'not φ', she may still be responsible-as-obligation for φ. The reason for this is that the lack of blameworthiness may be due to the fact that the agent has an appropriate excuse rather than that the agent is not accountable.

Appendix: Responsibility and Delegation

In organisations, it is common that certain responsibilities-as-tasks are delegated, for example, by managers to employees lower in the hierarchy. Also, outside organisations, it is not uncommon that people ascribe responsibility-as-task to others. Can such delegations and ascriptions also create a (moral) obligation to see to it that φ, and of so under what conditions? In general, it seems problematic to assume that somebody has, or can acquire, certain responsibilities because somebody else says so. Still, the person making the ascription, say agent B, may be able to give good reasons why agent i is responsible or should take responsibility. It might, for example, be the case that the responsibility that is ascribed by agent B to agent i is already a moral obligation of agent i (independent of the delegation or ascription). It that case, however, the ascription seems to have little added value; it just confirms what is, basically, already the case. It might help to remind people of their responsibilities, but that is all. There is also another possibility, however: Agent j may also be able to convince i that i should assume a certain responsibility. This case, however, seems reducible to the earlier discussed route of voluntary commitment by something like the following scheme:

1. Agent j ascribes (or delegates) the responsibility for φ to agent i.
2. Agent i voluntarily accepts this ascription.
3. φ is not morally objectionable.
4. If i properly fulfils her supervisory duties to see to it that φ, under normal circumstances φ will occur.
   So i is responsible-as-obligation for φ.

Although this scheme is based on responsibility as a voluntary commitment, it should be noted that it can lead to agent i taking certain responsibilities, it would not have taken without the ascription by j.

There is still another way in which responsibility by delegation can perhaps be grounded in a voluntary commitment. Think of a scheme like this:

1. Agent i has voluntarily joined organization O.
2. Organization O is characterised by certain rules R for delegating tasks.

Moral Responsibility 45

3. Agent j delegates task T in accordance with R to i.
4. Task T implies seeing to it that φ, ψ and χ.
5. φ, ψ and χ are not morally objectionable.
6. If i properly fulfils her supervisory duties to see to it that φ, ψ and χ, under normal circumstances φ, ψ, and χ will occur.
   So i is responsible-as-obligation for φ, ψ and χ.

Like the previous scheme, this scheme is ultimately based on responsibility as a voluntary commitment; again, however, it may lead to i acquiring responsibilities it would not have acquired if i had not joined organisation O.

NOTES

1. Hart (1968: 210–237) was probably the first to distinguish four main meanings of responsibility: role-responsibility, causal-responsibility, liability-responsibility, and capacity-responsibility. The additional meanings we distinguish in addition are related to these, but have in certain respects an (importantly) different meaning as explained. All the additional meanings can indeed also be found in the literature on responsibility (Ladd 1982, Baier 1972, Bovens 1998, Lucas 1993, Zimmerman 1988, Duff 2007, Cane 2002, e.g. Casey 1971, Williams 2008, Davis 2012). Hart discusses blameworthiness as a component of moral liability, but we think that it is conceptually clearer to distinguish both meanings.
2. This is what Hart calls role-responsibility.
3. This may also be called responsibility-as-office or responsibility-as-jurisdiction. It refers to a realm in which one has the authority to make decisions, or is in charge, and for which one can be held accountable.
4. Sometimes responsibility-as-accountability may be understood in a descriptive sense, as in cases in which one is accountable on the basis of certain organisational or legal rules. In such cases, responsibility-as-accountability seems often closely related to responsibility-as-task.
5. Goodin (1995), in fact, calls such responsibilities "task-responsibilities", but— as pointed out in the text—we think there is an essential difference between task-responsibility in the sense we use the term here and a (moral) obligation to see to something.
6. According to Duff (2007: 23), responsibility-as-capacity can be explained in relational terms as "the capacities that are necessary if one is to answer for one's actions". However, this conflates the conceptual nature of responsibility-as-capacity with its being a precondition for other relational concepts of responsibility.
7. This might be expressed by: 'i is responsible as φ' in which φ is for example an engineer or a parent.
8. In fact, responsibility-as-task is also usually understood as a triadic relation.
9. In fact, we may also have different responsibilities in the different roles we have, for example, as a teacher, as a colleague, and as a parent, and these responsibilities may be conflicting.
10. This is our example. Kutz provides other examples, including examples in which it seems appropriate for the agent i to assume responsibility rather than, as in our example, there being a degree of freedom in taking responsibility or not. Our suggestion is then not that the phenomenon of taking responsibility,

46   *Ibo van de Poel*

to which we draw attention below, exhausts the relational nature of responsibility. Rather, it draws attention to an aspect of responsibility that is also not fully grasped by formulations like (4).

11. This does not necessarily hold for all versions of liability. The principle of fault liability holds that an offender can only be held liable in case of culpably careless or faulty behavior (Zweigert and Kötz 1992). Note also that some authors defend the claim that establishing someone as the cause of some undesirable event is already a way of blaming—in the sense of criticizing—the particular person; hence, also strict liability includes an element of blame, these authors argue (see e.g. Davis 2012).

12. This classification is meant for analytical clarification, and as such, it shows a somewhat simplified picture of the "ethical landscape". The use of a merit-based perspective is not applied exclusively by deontologists, neither is it impossible to think of consequences in a deontological or rights-based discourse. It should also be noted, however, that moral philosophers who take rights as their starting point should also have something to say about duties, as a right to protection or compensation cannot exist without someone else's duty to protect or compensate. However, the primary focus of the three approaches is sufficiently different to distinguish between the three. The classification does describe the moral theory *most akin* to a certain responsibility perspective.

13. It does so in two ways. First, by holding *someone* accountable we confirm that that agent is a moral agent and, hence, part of the moral community. Second, by holding someone accountable for an *undesirable* action or outcome, we confirm or restore the moral rules on basis of which an outcome or action is deemed undesirable and which ties the moral community together.

14. Of course, sometimes we hold agents responsible when they have done something good or praiseworthy. However, when discussing responsibility-as-blameworthiness, we are interested in negative outcomes.

15. A similar suggestion can be found in Hart (1968), Wallace (1994), and Duff (2007). Although Hart and Duff do not distinguish between blameworthiness and liability, they suggest a similar relation between accountability (or answerability) and liability, as we do between accountability and blameworthiness. Wallace makes a distinction between A- and B-conditions for responsibility: "B-conditions make it fair to hold people morally to blame . . . while A-conditions make it fair to hold people morally accountable" (Wallace 1994: 118) His A-conditions focus on when it is in general fair to hold people accountable (cf. Wallace 1994: 154), this is our first condition (moral agency); his account seems to assume wrongdoing implicitly (e.g Wallace 1994: 156). Our conditions for accountability also include conditions for when it is fair to hold someone accountable for a *specific outcome*.

16. Wallace (1994: 136–147) mentions four types of excuses: (1) inadvertence, mistake or accident, (2) unintentional bodily movements, (3) physical constraint and (4) coercion, necessity and duress. The first is a case of non-culpable ignorance (referring to the knowledge condition), the others of coercion (referring to the freedom condition).

17. Typically, many other authors have treated those two conditions as the conditions for being at fault, suggesting that these are conditions for blameworthiness rather than for accountability.

18. This capacity might be understood in terms of reason-responsiveness (Fischer and Ravizza 1998) or reflective self-control (Wallace 1994).

19. For an opposing opinion see, for example, Davis (2012). Davis supports his claim that moral liability does not require moral blameworthiness with an example of a cat run over in a traffic accident (Davis 2012: 19–20). We believe,

however, that what is at stake in this example is not responsibility-as-liability but rather responsibility-as-virtue.

20. It might in specific circumstances be possible to delegate some supervision, but the agent cannot delegate away all responsibility as she still has a duty to supervise the supervision, et cetera.

21. Cf. also Fingarette: "In accepting responsibility as a responsible *person*, we tacitly engage ourselves to take on a vast, and antecedently unspecifiable, range of responsibilities. The responsible person is one who has learned to identify a reasonable variety of these when he comes upon them. And he distinguishes these cases where he is antecedently committed from those very many cases where he is antecedently uncommitted. He knows the ropes, although there is no rule book" (Fingarette 1967).

22. It does also not explicitly refer to a capacity condition, but this is presupposed in the notion of voluntary commitment or promise.

23. Cf. the preamble of the codes of ethics of the American Society of Mechanical Engineering and the American Society of Civil Engineers.

24. Cf. for example the first fundamental canon of the ABET code of ethics and a number of other U.S. codes of ethics for engineers.

25. Also Larry May has suggested that joining a profession means assuming certain responsibilities, although his emphasis is a bit different: "groups such as professions derive various benefits from society, and their members must be seen as having to pay corresponding costs for their increased ability to influence the world. For this reason, group membership creates a standard of care . . . When people voluntarily join groups, they thereby increase their moral and legal duties" (May 1992: 92) .

26. Excerpt from the documentary "Why the Twin Towers Collapsed", broadcasted by Discovery Channel.

27. It is very interesting and indeed impressive that on the video of the interview Robertson starts nodding when he poses himself the question "Do I feel guilty?" One interpretation would be that in his non-verbal expressions (the nodding) he answers the question "Do I take the blame?" (He obviously feels very bad about what happened if not guilty), whereas in his verbal expressions he answers the question "Would it be proper for others to blame me?" His answer to the first question seems affirmative, and to the second, not.

REFERENCES

Aristotle. 2000. *Nicomachean ethics, Cambridge texts in the history of philosophy.* Cambridge, U.K.; New York: Cambridge University Press.

Austin, J.L. 1956–57. "A plea for excuses." *Proceedings of the Aristotelian Society.*

Baier, K. 1972. "Guilt and responsibility." In *Individual and collective responsibility: Massacre at My Lai,* edited by P.A. French, 35–61. Cambridge, MA: Schenkman.

Bovens, M. 1998. *The Quest for Responsibility. Accountability and Citizenship in Complex Organisations.* Cambridge: Cambridge University Press.

Braham, M., and M. van Hees. 2012. "An anatomy of moral responsibility." *Mind* 121(483): 601–634.

Cane, P. 2002. *Responsibility in law and morality.* Oxford: Hart Publishing.

Casey, J. 1971. "Action and consequences." In *Morality and moral reasoning: Five essays in ethics,* edited by J. Casey, 155–205. London: Methuen.

Copp, D. 2006. "'Ought' implies 'can', blameworthiness and alternate possibilitites." In *Moral responsibility and alternative possibilities: Essays on the importance of alternative possibilities,* edited by D. Widerker and M. McKenna, 265–300. Aldershot: Ashgate.

48   Ibo van de Poel

Davis, M. 1997. "Is there a profession of engineering?" *Science and Engineering Ethics* 3(4): 407–428.

Davis, M. 2012. "'Ain't no one here but us social forces': Constructing the professional responsibility of engineers." *Science and Engineering Ethics* 18(1): 13–34. doi: 10.1007/s11948-010-9225-3.

Duff, A. 2007. *Answering for crime: Responsibility and liability in the criminal law, Legal theory today*. Oxford: Hart Publishing.

Eshleman, A. 2014. "Moral responsibility". In *The Stanford encyclopedia of philosophy (Fall 2008 edition)*. (http://plato.stanford.edu/entries/moral-responsibility/)

Feinberg, J. 1970. *Doing & deserving: Essays in the theory of responsibility*. Princeton University Press.

Fingarette, H. 1967. *On responsibility*. New York: Basic Books.

Fischer, J.M., and M. Ravizza. 1998. *Responsibility and control: A theory of moral responsibility, Cambridge studies in philosophy and law*. Cambridge University Press.

Frankfurt, H. 1969. "Alternate possibilities and moral responsibility." *Journal of Philosophy* 66(23): 829–839.

French, P.A., H.K. Wettstein, and J.M. Fischer, eds. 2005. *Free will and moral responsibility, Midwest studies in philosophy*. Malden: Blackwell Publishing.

Ginet , C. 2006. "In defense of the principle of alternate possibilities: Why I don't find Frankfurt's argument convincing." In *Moral responsibility and alternative possibilities. Essays on the importance of alternative possibilities*, edited by D. Widerker and M. McKenna, 75–90. Alsdershot: Ashgate.

Goodin, R.E. 1995. *Utilitarianism as a public philosophy*. Cambridge University Press.

Hart, H.L.A. 1968. *Punishment and responsibility: Essays in the philosophy of law*. Oxford: Clarendon Press.

Honoré, T. 1999. *Responsibility and fault*. Oxford: Hart.

Johnson, D.G. 2006. "Computer systems: Moral entities but not moral agents." *Ethics and Information Technology* 8(4): 195–205.

Kutz, Ch. 2000. *Complicity: Ethics and law for a collective age, Cambridge studies in philosophy and law*. Cambridge University Press.

Ladd, J. 1982. "Philosophical remarks on professional responsibility in organizations." *International Journal of Applied Philosophy* 1(2): 58–70.

Ladd, J. 1991. "Bhopal: An essay on moral responsibility and civic virtue." *Journal of Social Philosophy* 32(1): 73–91.

Lucas, J.R. 1993. *Responsibility*. Oxford University Press.

Mackie, J.L. 1977. *Ethics : inventing right and wrong, Pelican books : Philosophy*. New York: Penguin.

Magill, K. 2000. "Blaming, understanding, and justification." In *Moral responsibility and ontology*, edited by T. van den Beld, 183–197 . Dordrecht: Kluwer Academic Publishers.

May, L. 1992. *Sharing responsibility*. University of Chicago Press.

Miller, D. 2001. "Distributing responsibilities." *The Journal of Political Philosophy* 9(4): 453–471.

Miller, David. 2004. "Holding nations responsible." *Ethics* 114(2): 240–268.

Nihlen Fahlquist, J. 2009. "Moral responsibility for environmental problems—Individual or institutional?" *Journal of Agricultural and Environmental Ethics* 22(2): 109–124. doi: 10.1007/s10806-008-9134-5.

Nozick, R. 1974. *Anarchy, state, and utopia*. New York: Basic Books.

Ransdell, J. 1971. "Rules and speech-act analysis." *Journal of Philosophy* 68(13): 385–400.

Scheffler, S. 1997. "Relationships and responsibilities." *Philosophy and Public Affairs* 26(3): 189–209.

Shapiro, P. 2006. "Moral agency in other animals." *Theoretical Medicine and Bioethics* 27(4): 357–373.

Smiley, M. 1992. *Moral esponsibility and the boundaries of community: Power and accountability from a pragmatic point of view*. Chicago University Press.

Strawson, P. 1962. "Freedom and resentment." *Proceedings of the British Academy* 48: 187–211.

Van de Poel, I.R. 2011. "The relation between forward-looking and backward-looking responsibility." In *Moral responsibility. Beyond free will and determinism*, edited by N. Vincent, I.R. van de Poel and J. van den Hoven, 37–52. Dordrecht: Springer.

Van den Hoven, J. 1998. "Moral responsibility, public office and information technology." In *Public administration in an information age*, edited by I.Th.M. Snellen and W.B.H.J. van de Donk, 97–112. Amsterdam: IOS Press.

Van Inwagen, P. 1983. *An essay on free will*. Oxford: Clarendon Press.

Vedder, A. 2001. "Accountability of internet access and service providers: Strict liability entering ethics?" *Ethics and Information Technology* 3(1): 67–74.

Wallace, R.J. 1994. *Responsibility and the moral sentiments*. Cambridge (Ma.): Harvard University Press.

Watson, G. 1996. "Two faces of responsibility." *Philosophical Topics* 24(2): 227–248.

Widerker, D. 2005. "Blameworthiness, non-robust alternatives and the principle of alternative expectations." *Midwest Studies In Philosophy* 29(1): 292–306.

Widerker, D., and M. McKenna. 2006. *Moral responsibility and alternative possibilities: Essays on the importance of alternative possibilities*. Aldershot: Ashgate.

Williams, B. 1999. *Moral luck. Philosophical papers 1973–1980*. Cambridge University Press.

Williams, G. 2008. "Responsibility as a virtue." *Ethical Theory and Moral Practice* 11(4): 455–470.

Zandvoort, H. 2000. "Codes of conduct, the law, and technological design and development." In *The empirical turn in the philosophy of technology*, edited by P. Kroes and A. Meijers, 193–205. Amsterdam: JAI (Elsevier).

Zandvoort, H. 2005a. "Globalisation, environmental harm and progress: The role of consensus and liability." *Water Science & Technology* 52(6): 43–50.

Zandvoort, H. 2005b. "Knowledge, risk, and liability: Analysis of a discussion continuing within science and technology." *Cognitive Structures in Scientific Inquiry: Essays in Debate with Theo Kuipers* 2(84): 469–501.

Zimmerman, M.J. 1988. *An essay on moral responsibility*. Totowa, NJ: Rowman & Littlefield.

Zimmerman, M.J. 2009. Responsibility, reaction and value. Paper read at International Conference on Moral Responsibility: Neuroscience, Organization & Engineering, August 24–27, 2009, at Delft University of Technology, the Netherlands.

Zweigert, K., and H. Kötz. 1992. *Introduction to comparative law*. Oxford University Press.

2 The Problem of Many Hands

Ibo van de Poel

2.1 INTRODUCTION

When harm occurs, we often ask who is to be held responsible. However, in complex situations in which many agents are involved, it is often quite difficult to pinpoint responsibility. In a review of a hundred shipping accidents, Wagenaar and Groenewegen (1987: 596) conclude: "Accidents appear to be the result of highly complex coincidences which could rarely be foreseen by the people involved. The unpredictability is due to the large number of causes and by the spread of the information over the participants". Because the ability to foresee undesirable consequences is usually seen as a condition for responsibility, this raises doubts as to whether it is reasonable to hold someone responsible for the accident that occurred.

The phenomenon that, due to the complexity of the situation and the number of actors involved, it is impossible—or at least, very difficult—to hold someone reasonably responsible is sometimes referred to as 'the problem of many hands'. Dennis Thompson, who was probably the first to use the notion in an article about the responsibility of public officials, describes it as follows: "Because many different officials contribute in many ways to decisions and policies of government, it is difficult even in principle to identify who is morally responsible for political outcomes" (Thompson 1980: 905). Helen Nissenbaum discusses the problem of many hands as one of the barriers for attributing responsibility in what she calls a 'computerized society'. Some of the barriers she describes are, however, more generally characteristic for modern technology and engineering. She characterises the problem of many hands as follows: "Where a mishap is the work of 'many hands', it may not be obvious who is to blame because frequently its most salient and immediate causal antecedents do not converge with its locus of decision-making. The conditions for blame, therefore, are not satisfied in a way normally satisfied when a single individual is held blameworthy for a harm" (Nissenbaum 1996: 29).

Nissenbaum, thus, attributes the problem of many hands to the difficulty of holding any individual responsible, because the different traditional conditions for responsibility, like intent, knowledge, and freedom of action are distributed over many different individuals, and none of them might meet all the conditions. According to Nissenbaum, "the upshot is that victims and those who represent them are left without knowing at whom to point a finger. It may not be clear even to the members of the collective itself who is accountable" (Nissenbaum 1996: 29). A similar point is made by Kutz (2000: 113) when he writes: "The most important and far-reaching harms and wrongs of contemporary life are the products of collective actions, mediated by social and institutional structures. These harms and wrongs are essentially collective products, and individual agents rarely make a difference for their occurrence. So long as individuals are only responsible for the effects they produce, then the result of this disparity between collective harm and individual effect is the disappearance of individual accountability. If no individual makes a difference, then no individual is accountable for these collective harms".

However, as Helen Nissenbaum stresses, "we should not mistakenly conclude from the observation that accountability is *obscured* due to collective action that no one is, or ought to have been, accountable" (Nissenbaum 1996: 32, emphasis in orginal). It remains unclear, however, whether Nissenbaum believes that it is always problematic if no one can reasonably be held responsible or that it is only problematic in some specific cases. Bovens (1998: 47) has made an interesting suggestion in this respect; he suggests that the problem of many hands occurs if a collective is responsible for an undesirable outcome but none of the individuals in the collective is responsible. We will take up this suggestion and will develop it further in section 2.2. In section 2.3 we look deeper into the notion of collective responsibility. In section 2.3.1 we indicate under what circumstances we consider it meaningful to attribute responsibility to collectives, and we will distinguish three types of collectives: (1) organised groups, (2) collectives involved in a joint action, and (3) occasional collections of individuals that can be reasonably expected to organise themselves into a collective. In section 2.3.2 we discuss how the conditions for responsibility we discussed in Chapter 1 translate to the collective level, and in section 2.3.3 we will look into the question whether collective responsibility can always be reduced to individual responsibility, or not as Bovens' characterisation of the problem of many hands seems to suggest that such a reduction is not always possible. In sections 2.4, 2.5, and 2.6 we discuss examples of the problem of many hands in the three types of collectives that we distinguished in section 2.3.1. Section 2.7 will draw conclusions.

2.2 A CHARACTERISATION OF THE PROBLEM OF MANY HANDS (PMH)

According to Bovens (1998: 46–49), the problem of many hands has three dimensions: a practical, a normative, and a preventive one. First, the problem of many hands can be conceived as a practical problem. It is often difficult in complex organisations or networks to identify and prove who was responsible for what, especially for outsiders. It is usually very difficult,

52   *Ibo van de Poel*

if not impossible, to know who contributed to, or could have prevented a certain action, who knew or could have known what, et cetera. So conceived, the problem of many hands is primarily an epistemological problem because the problem of identifying who is responsible for what arises from a lack of knowledge. Although this epistemological dimension is important, it does not get at the heart of the problem of many hands. This can be seen as follows. Suppose that someone, say an independent observer, had perfect knowledge of who did what, could have known what, et cetera. Now, even for this observer, it may be impossible to identify who was responsible for a certain outcome because none of the individuals meets the conditions for individual responsibility, as discussed in Chapter 1, whereas at the meantime it might be reasonable to hold the collective, as a whole, morally responsible for that outcome. We give examples in sections 2.4, 2.5, and 2.6.

This brings us to the second dimension of the problem of many hands: the normative or moral dimension. As Bovens says this dimension "raises the question whether the responsibility of the collective, the organisation, can be reduced to the individual responsibilities of discrete functionaries not just in practical but also in moral regard" (Bovens 1998: 47). Bovens suggests that the collective might sometimes be responsible whereas none of the individuals is responsible.

Third, the problem of many hands can be seen as a problem of prevention or as a problem of control, as Bovens phrases it. According to Bovens, the problem of many hands "frustrates the need for compensation and retribution on the part of victims" (Bovens 1998: 49). Moreover, the "fact that no one can be meaningfully called to account after the event also means . . . that no one need feel responsible beforehand" (Bovens 1998: 49), so that future harm cannot be prevented. Both points indicate why the occurrence of the problem of many hands is undesirable, but that does not seem to change the characterisation of the problem of many hands.

The core of the problem of many hands thus appears to be the potential gap between individual and collective responsibility. This brings us to the following general characterisation of the problem of many hands:

> *(PMH): The problem of many hands (PMH) occurs if a collective is morally responsible for φ, whereas none of the individuals making up the collective is morally responsible for φ,*

with φ some action or state-of-affairs.

There are a number of issues that need to be further detailed to make this characterisation of the PMH more precise.

First, as we have seen in Chapter 1, the meaning of 'morally responsible' is ambiguous. As 'morally responsible' refers to one of the normative meanings of responsibility, we take it that the phrase 'morally responsible' can be understood in five distinct ways (see Table 1.1 in Chapter 1): as morally accountable, morally blameworthy, morally liable, morally obliged (to see to it), and as a moral virtue. We can now, in principle, distinguish five varieties of the PMH, which may be denoted by a subscript to make clear to which variety of the PMH we are referring. So PMH_B would refer to the problem of many hands for responsibility-as-blameworthiness.

Second, we need to spell out what we mean by 'the collective'. Usually, the action or state-of-affairs φ on which we focus will determine what the relevant collection of agents is. In the case of backward-looking responsibility, for example, we might focus on the collection of agents that together caused φ, and, in cases of forward-looking responsibility, we can focus on the collection of agents that can be causally efficacious with respect to φ. (We will further elaborate this in Chapter 4.) However, not all collections of agents can be bearers of responsibility. We therefore propose the following terminological distinction. A *collection of agents* is a set of individual agents; a *collective* is a collection of agents that collectively meet the capacity condition for responsibility, i.e., it can, as a collective, be a bearer of responsibility (which does not yet mean that it is actually responsible). In section 2.3.1 we will further elaborate which conditions a collection of agents have to meet to be a collective and we will distinguish three kinds of collectives.

Third, we need to be more precise about what we mean by collective moral responsibility. Although the notion of collective moral responsibility has been defended by various authors (e.g., French 1984; May 1987; Gilbert 1989; Copp 2007; Pettit 2007), it is not uncontroversial. One way to deal with this would be to avoid the notion of collective moral responsibility altogether in the characterisation of the PMH. One could, for example, replace the phrase 'if a collective is morally responsible' by 'if a collective is causally responsible'. This seems to catch at least some of the intuitions behind the PMH because often if a collective caused some harm, we tend to believe that at least someone in the collective should be responsible, e.g., as-blameworthy, for that harm.

However, closer inspection shows that understanding the responsibility of the collective only in causal terms has its drawbacks as well. Causal responsibility refers to outcomes that have already materialised and therefore cannot be directly applied to cases where we are interested in forward-looking responsibility, because in such cases the outcome in which we are interested has not occurred yet. Perhaps, in that case, we should replace the criterion of causal responsibility by causal efficacy, i.e., whether the collective could avoid, or bring about, some outcome. There is another difficulty with a causal criterion, however. We only tend to consider it problematic that no one can be held backward-looking responsible (accountable, blameworthy, or liable) if something *undesirable* has happened. Conversely, we only consider it desirable that some individual is forward-looking responsible for seeing that an outcome occurs if that outcome is *desirable*. This suggests that a purely descriptive notion of collective responsibility, like a causal one, will not do.[1] We also need reference to a normative element to capture the idea that the PMH is undesirable.

54 *Ibo van de Poel*

For these reasons, we have chosen to refer in the characterisation of the PMH to the moral responsibility, rather than to a descriptive responsibility, of the collective. This choice leaves still open how we are to understand collective moral responsibility in terms of the five normative meanings distinguished in Chapter 1. Above we indicated that one could distinguish five varieties of the PMH depending on how *individual* moral responsibility is understood. How are we to understand collective moral responsibility in each of these cases? We have chosen here to understand collective moral responsibility in each analogously to individual moral responsibility. So PMH_B refers to individual blameworthiness and collective blameworthiness.

One of the reasons for understanding individual and collective moral responsibility analogously in the characterisation of the PMH is that the different meanings of responsibility are connected to different aims for attributing responsibility as we have seen in Chapter 1. Table 2.1 summarises the aims of attributing responsibility that we discussed in Chapter 1. So if PMH_B occurs, the aim of retribution is frustrated.

Given these choices made above, the PMH with respect to responsibility-as-blameworthiness, i.e., PMH_B, can be characterised as follows:

> *(PMH_B): The problem of many hands occurs with respect to responsibility-as-blameworthiness if a collective meets the conditions for attribution of moral responsibility-as-blameworthiness for φ (capacity, wrong-doing, causality, knowledge, and freedom), whereas none of the individuals making up the collective meets the conditions for attribution of moral responsibility-as-blameworthiness for φ.*

Similar characterisations can be given for the PMH for responsibility-as-accountability or responsibility-as-obligation.

PMH_B raises the question how we are to understand the conditions for responsibility in the case of collective moral responsibility. In the next section, we will therefore address the question how to translate the conditions for individual moral responsibility that we discussed in Chapter 1 to collective moral responsibility.

Table 2.1 Aims of attributing responsibility

Meaning of responsibility	Aim of attributing responsibility
Backward-looking	
Responsibility-as-blameworthiness	Retribution
Responsibility-as-accountability	Maintaining moral community
Responsibility-as-liability	Remediation, Justice to victims
Forward-looking	
Responsibility-as-obligation	Efficacy
Responsibility-as-virtue	Due care to others

2.3 COLLECTIVE RESPONSIBILITY

Our characterisation of the problem of many hands presupposes the notion of collective moral responsibility. This notion is, however, philosophically controversial and, among those philosophers who subscribe to it, there is considerable disagreement about how the notion should be exactly understood. In this section we will therefore look deeper into the notion of collective responsibility.

We start with giving a defence of attributing responsibility to collectives in certain circumstances (section 2.3.1). In section 2.3.2, we will then discuss how the conditions for individual moral responsibility that we discussed in Chapter 1 translate to the collective level. In section 2.3.3, we will look into the issue of whether collective responsibility is always reducible to individual responsibility or not. This issue is particularly relevant for our characterisation of the PMH because it supposes that it is possible for the collective to be responsible for φ without any of the individuals within the collective being responsible for φ. It seems that if collective responsibility is always reducible to individual responsibility, the PMH cannot occur.

2.3.1 Collective Responsibility: Three Types of Collectives

Essentially, the argument for collective responsibility runs as follows. Today, activity increasingly takes place in a complex web of individual and collective doings. It is becoming more difficult to apply traditional ethical theories, because these theories have traditionally focused on individual actions (cf. Kutz 2000). Moreover, there is the potential for greater harm when individuals join in groups (May 1992: 91). Collectives act in ways that would not be possible if there were merely individuals. Although such collective undertakings have brought substantial benefits to society, they have also increased the possibilities to create harm. Individuals, however, often lack the means to prevent such harms and it may therefore not be reasonable to hold them responsible for such harm. In the meantime, the collective that designs and builds, for example, an airplane or skyscraper may be able to prevent certain harm, provided that the individuals in that collective would cooperate in a certain way.

A crucial question, however, is whether collectives can meet the capacity condition for moral responsibility. One common objection to the idea that collectives can meet this condition is that collectives do not have intentions. In the literature, a large range of proposals can be found about how we are to understand the notion of 'collective intention' and under what conditions we can ascribe an intention to a certain collective (e.g., Tuomela and Miller 1988; Gilbert 1989; Searle 1995; Bratman 1999; Kutz 2000).

Although some authors have defended a notion of 'collective intentionality' that is similar in structure to individual intentionality, most authors hold

56   Ibo van de Poel

that collective intentionality is somewhat different from individual intentionality because collectives do not have a mind. To avoid the suggestion that collectives have a mind, we therefore prefer to talk about collective aims, rather than collective intentions. A collective aim is an aim in the minds of individuals, but its content may be irreducibly collective in the sense that it refers to things that can only be collectively achieved and not by individuals in isolation (cf. Kutz 2000: 85–89).

We propose to make a distinction here between three types of collectives. The distinguishing feature we focus on is whether we can speak of a collective aim and, if so, how that collective aim is formed:

1. Organised groups (also sometimes called 'corporate agents') that can formulate and adopt collective aims by a collective (decision) procedure;
2. Collectives involved in a joint action. The joint action is characterised by a collective aim that is in some sense (to be specified further below) shared by the members of the collective;
3. Occasional collections of individuals that lack a collective aim but that nevertheless can be reasonably expected to form a collective in one of the two above senses to avoid harm or to do good.

For collectives of the first and second kind, it seems unproblematic to assume that the capacity condition for collective responsibility is met because we can in some sense speak of a collective aim. For occasional collections of individuals, it seems more problematic to speak about collective responsibility. Nevertheless, it can, and has, been argued by several authors that under certain conditions we can meaningfully and appropriately ascribe responsibility to such collections of agents (Feinberg 1968; Held 1970; May 1987: 73–83), especially if it is reasonable to expect of the occasional collections of individuals to organise itself or to undertake a joint action.

Below we will discuss the minimal conditions that are to be met for these three types of collectives and for the meaningful ascription of responsibility in each of these cases (see Table 2.2).

Organised Groups

In our society, a large variety of organised groups and corporate agents can be found including corporations, states, state agencies, universities, non-governmental organisations (NGOs), sport and leisure clubs, design firms, R&D institutes, and so on. These organisations are often characterised by certain institutional rules, including rules for membership, and certain roles within the organisation. Often these organisations persist over time, even if individual membership may be changing.

Here we are interested in the minimal conditions that have to be met to speak of an organised group and for the legitimacy of ascribing responsibility to such collectives. We propose the following condition: there should be a

The Problem of Many Hands 57

Table 2.2 Three types of collectives

Type of collective	Conditions for meaningful ascription of responsibility (capacity condition)	Examples
Organised group	• Collective aim • (Decision) procedure or institutional rule that authoritatively represents certain actions or aims as the actions and aims of the collective	States, companies, universities, United Nations, etc.
Joint action	• Collective aim • Individual participatory intention to contribute to joint action	Bank robbery, chess playing, traveling together, R&D project
Occasional collection of individuals that jointly caused a harm or jointly could prevent a harm from occurring	It is reasonable to expect from the occasional collection of individuals that it undertakes a joint action or organises itself in such a way that harm is jointly prevented or good is achieved.	Climate change, drowning child, train robbery, plane hijacking

(decision) procedure by which certain actions or aims can be authoritatively represented as the actions or aims of the collective.[2] This procedure can be a voting or decision procedure, like in the case that the members of a political party vote who is going to be the party's candidate for the next presidential elections. It can also be an institutional rule that authorises a certain person to speak and act on behalf of the organisation. For example, Philips' CEO may be said to speak and act on behalf of Philips. It may also be a combination of an institutional rule and a voting procedure, like in the case that the members of the board of the university vote on what to do on behalf of the university. What is important is that, in all these cases, the members of the organisations need to see the (decision) procedure as legitimate, and as resulting in an authoritative decision as to how to act as an organisation or what to aim for, even if they may personally disagree. So the member of the political party who prefers candidate X may accept that her party has nevertheless chosen candidate Y to run for the presidential elections because that decision was the result of a legitimate decision procedure within the organisation. Employees of Philips may accept that the corporate policy in certain issues is set by the CEO, even if they personally disagree with it.

58   Ibo van de Poel

Two things are to be noticed about this account. First, nothing in this account contradicts a methodological individualist account of collective actions or aims. What we said does not rule out that, in the end, all collective actions and aims can be understood in terms of individual actions and intentions.[3] Second, this account leaves open the possibility that there is a discrepancy between the intentions, aims, and preferences of individuals within a collective, and that of the collective. Remember the party member voting for candidate X, whereas Y is chosen by her party. Cases like this raise interesting questions about responsibility. Whereas it seems unproblematic to say that the party is collectively responsible for the choice for candidate Y (over X), it is unclear how this responsibility exactly distributes over individual members. Are members that voted for X not responsible for their party's decision? As we will see in section 2.4, there are cases in which no individual seems to be responsible for the collective decision, paradoxically as this may sound.

Joint Action

A joint action may be understood as an action that is undertaken by a number of individuals jointly to achieve a collective aim. The collective aim is often understood as an aim that is shared by the individuals participating in the joint action (although this is not necessary, as we will see). On some accounts the collective aim is just an individual aim that is shared among individuals (Miller 2010). Other have posed that joint actions require we- or group-intentions, i.e., intentions that belong to the group rather than to individuals (Searle 1995; Bratman 1999).

Here we will follow an account of joint action that has been proposed by Christopher Kutz (2000). There are three main reasons for adopting Kutz' account. First, his proposal is tailored to issues of responsibility (he speaks of accountability) and that is also our main interest. Second, he aims to provide a *minimal* account of joint action. Whereas he recognises that some forms of joint action require more than the minimal conditions he sets out, his interest lies in identifying the minimal forms of joint action that allow for the allocation of collective responsibility. Third, his account does not contradict a methodological individualist analysis of collective action. Whereas the content of the aims that play a role in joint action may be collective (i.e., they may refer to collective aims that cannot be reduced to individual aims), it is individualistic in structure in the sense that, in the final analysis, collectives do not have intentions apart from the intentions of individuals.

According to (Kutz 2000: 89) "Jointly intentional action is fundamentally the action of individuals who intend to play a part in producing the group outcome". Therefore, "[j]oint action as such requires only agents who act on overlapping participatory intentions. The intrinsic complexity of many kinds of collective acts will, of course, require far more coordination, but those are act-specific requirements, and inessential to the concept at the root of cooperation. Whereas collective acts are just the acts of intentional

The Problem of Many Hands   59

participants, intentional participation is just the action of individuals who understand themselves to be promoting a collective act" (Kutz 2000: 255).

Kutz proposes the following condition for a joint action:

> A set of individuals jointly G when the members of that set intentionally contribute to G's occurrence by doing particular parts, and their conceptions of G sufficiently and actually overlap.
>
> (Kutz 2000: 103)

This condition is as interesting for what it requires as for what it *not* requires. It does not require that all the individuals intend G but just that they intend to contribute to G. Like the party member that by voting for candidate X also in some sense intentionally contributes to the election of candidate Y because by voting (even if it is for another candidate) the party member contributes to the election and affirms the authority of the election procedure, both of which contribute to the election of Y.

The condition also does not require that the participants have exactly the same understanding or description of G. This is important because intention is description-relative. So whereas it is true that Oedipus intentionally killed the man who was his father (as he later found out), it is not true that he intentionally killed his father. Kutz, then, allows for the fact that the different participants in a joint action may have different conceptions of the exact aim of the joint action, although there should be a 'sufficient' degree of overlap between these conceptions.

Occasional Collection of Individuals

Occasional collections of individuals lack a collective aim. They also do not act jointly. Still, in some cases it seems meaningful and appropriate to ascribe collective responsibility to such collectives. We especially seem to do so in cases in which an occasional collection of individuals jointly causes harm, or jointly could prevent a harm (or achieve a good). It should be noted that in such cases, we tend to identify the collective along causal lines. We include those agents in the collective that jointly causes harm or jointly could prevent it, even if they individually may not make a causal difference for the occurrence of the harm, or individually could not prevent it from happening.

One prototypical situation in which we may ascribe collective responsibility to an occasional collection of individuals that jointly could prevent harm has been described by Joel Feinberg (1968). He discusses a variety of collective responsibility that he calls *contributory group fault, collective but not distributive*. He provides the following example:

> Consider the case of the Jesse James train robbery. One armed man holds up an entire car full of passengers. If the passengers had risen up as one man and rushed at the robber, one or two of them, perhaps,

60   *Ibo van de Poel*

would have been shot; but collectively they would have overwhelmed him, disarmed him, and saved their property. Yet they all meekly submitted. How responsible were they for their own losses? Not very. In a situation like this only heroes could be expected to lead the self-sacrificial charge, so no individual in the group was at fault for not resisting. The whole group, however, had it within its power to resist successfully. Shall we say then that the group was collectively but not distributively at fault? Can the responsibility of a group be more than the sum of the responsibility of its members? There is surely a point in affirming so. There was, after all, a flaw in the way the group of passengers was organized (or unorganized) that made the robbery possible.

(Feinberg 1968: 687)

There is an interesting, more recent case that seems to fit Feinberg's example: the passengers on one of the 9/11 hijacked planes that jointly decided to try to regain control over the plane after it had been hijacked.[4] They did so when they had heard that the other hijacked planes had been intentionally crashed into the Twin Towers and the Pentagon by terrorists and after taking a vote among the passengers about whether to undertake action or not. The eventual result of their attempt was that the plane crashed killing all terrorists and passengers but killing nobody on the ground. Although the actions of the passengers may be called heroic and, therefore, beyond what morality requires, the example is nevertheless illustrative in two senses. First, it shows that even if an action is not morally required, an occasional collection of individuals may sense a collective or shared responsibility to jointly undertake an action, or to organise themselves by taking a vote. Second, it shows that occasional collections of individuals can, at least in some circumstances, effectively undertake joint actions and organise themselves.

Virginia Held has argued that what she calls random collections of individuals can be morally responsible for not acting in a situation in which it is "obvious to the reasonable person" that a certain action is called for (Held 1970: 94). Accordingly, in cases where it is not obvious to a reasonable person that something should be done, a random collection of individuals should not be held responsible. However, if it was obvious to the reasonable person that one of the mutually exclusive actions a, b, or c ought to be done and the random collection did not act, the random collection can be held responsible for failing to adopt a decision method to choose between a, b, and c, i.e., it can be blamed for not forming a more organised group.

Both Feinberg and Held then suggest that the legitimacy of ascribing collective responsibility to an occasional collection of individuals does not depend on whether the group has acted jointly or is organised, but rather on whether it is realistic or reasonable to ask the group to organise itself, or to act jointly in order to prevent harm. This suggests that the capacity condition for collective responsibility is not just descriptive, but also has a normative component. We therefore suggest that occasional collections of individuals can be collectively, although not necessarily individually, responsible if the following capacity condition is met:

> *It is reasonable to expect from the occasional collection of individuals that it undertakes a joint action or organises itself in such a way that harm is jointly prevented or good is achieved.*

2.3.2 The Responsibility Conditions for Collectives

In Chapter 1, we discussed a range of conditions that play a role in the ascription of moral responsibility to individuals. Some of these conditions can rather straightforwardly be applied to collectives as well. Others are more complicated or even controversial. In the previous section, we already discussed the probably most controversial condition for collectives: the capacity condition. Table 2.3 lists the other main conditions for the ascription of three main kinds of moral responsibility that we discussed in Chapter 1. Responsibility-as-liability is basically based on the same conditions as responsibility-as-blameworthiness and is therefore not separately mentioned. Responsibility-as-virtue is usually not understood in terms of conditions and is for that reason not mentioned.

Causality
For backward-looking responsibility, the causality condition entails that the agent played a causal role in the action or outcome for which she is held responsible. This condition can rather straightforwardly be applied to collectives; the question is whether the collective, or the joint action, played a causal role in bringing about the φ for which the collective is held responsible.

For forward-looking responsibility, this condition focuses on causal efficacy, rather than on past causal contribution. Causal efficacy relates to what actions a collective can undertake and what outcomes it can achieve or

Table 2.3 Conditions for three main kinds of responsibility. (Please note that the exact content of the conditions is not necessarily the same for all kinds of responsibility.)

	Responsibility-as-obligation	Responsibility-as-accountability	Responsibility-as-blameworthiness
Capacity	X	X	X
Causality	X	X	X
Knowledge			X
Freedom			X
Normative	X	X	X

62   *Ibo van de Poel*

avoid. In general, a collective action and its consequences are the result of the actions of the individuals participating in the collective. The collective action and its consequences will thus depend on the choices of individuals, but also on the way these individuals cooperate (or fail to do so). Therefore, the actions a collective can do and the outcomes they can avoid (or achieve) are those that are available to them collectively if they would cooperate fully and coordinate their actions optimally. Of course, not all collective actions require the full cooperation of all members of the collective or require coordination. Therefore, these actions that a collective can do, and those outcomes that a collective can achieve, without full cooperation and coordination among the members of the collective, also belong to what the collective can causally affect.

Knowledge

The knowledge condition requires an answer to the question of how we are to understand the knowledge of a group, which is a complicated issue. At one extreme, one might say that the knowledge of the group is only that knowledge that all group members share and of which they also know that the other members know it. At the other extreme, one might say that the knowledge of the group is the knowledge that would become known if all group members shared their knowledge effectively with all other members. We will adopt here the second, strong, understanding of the knowledge condition. The reason for this interpretation is that, as we have seen in Chapter 1, the knowledge condition is not just a descriptive condition about what the agent actually knows, but it is normative; it is about what the agent should know or can reasonably be expected to know. We will assume that it is reasonable for a collective to share knowledge, or at least that knowledge that is crucial to exercise certain responsibilities.

Freedom

Applying the freedom condition to collectives is controversial because the condition is usually understood in terms of free intentional acting and it is controversial whether collectives can intentionally act. In fact, in the previous section we have rejected the idea that collectives have a mind and have chosen to talk about collective aims rather than about collective intentions. So how can a collective be free if it does not have a mind and has no intentions of its own? We think collective freedom can best be understood in terms of what the members of a collective can jointly freely do. Although collective freedom, so understood, is essentially based on individual freedom; collectives can freely do actions or adopt aims that individual members of the collective cannot freely do, as we will see below.

In Chapter 1, we have seen that there are different possibilities to understand the (individual) freedom condition. One weak understanding is the absence of coercion. For a collective to be free, it should be able to choose, for example through a decision procedure, its actions and aims, rather than being coerced by some outside force. It might seem that absence of collective coercion requires that each of the individuals in the collective can act without coercion, but that is actually not the case. Take a corporation that is strictly run along hierarchical lines. Let us suppose for the sake of the argument that all decisions are made by the CEO of the corporation (and that this is accepted as legitimate by all employees). In that case, the only thing that is required for collective freedom is that the CEO can act and adopt aims on behalf of the company without coercion. Even if all other employees are mere cogs in the machine, the collective is free from coercion. Although this is maybe an extreme example, it shows that the freedom of the collective does not require that all members of the collective are free.

On some understandings of the freedom condition it requires not just a lack of coercion, but also the possibility to act differently, or the possibility to avoid certain outcomes. Again, it might seem attractive to pose that a collective is free to do an action or to avoid an outcome if all of the members in the organisation are free to do their part of what is required to do the joint action or to avoid an outcome. However, as pointed out by Hindriks (2008), the relation between individual freedom and collective freedom is more complicated. Individual freedom to do one's part is sometimes not sufficient for collective freedom. Hindriks mentions the case of a football team that has a solo canoe available to leave an island. Whereas each individual member of the team has the freedom to use the boat to leave the island, the collective does not have that freedom, because only one person can be carried by the canoe. Conversely, individual freedom to do one's part is not always necessary for collective freedom. Many collective actions do not require the cooperation of all agents in the collective; usually it is enough if a subset of agents does its part and jointly does the collective action. So even if some individuals are not free to do their part, the collective might still be free to do the collective action or to avoid an outcome collectively.

The Normative Condition

For backward-looking responsibility, the normative condition refers to some kind of wrong-doing. Let us look briefly here at three main types of ethical theories (consequentialism, deontology, virtue ethics) and let us ask whether it makes sense to talk about collective wrong-doing in each of these cases. For consequentialism, wrong-doing relates to bringing about bad consequences; obviously this criterion can be applied to harm caused by collectives as well; think, for example, of climate change as a collectively caused harm. For deontological theories, wrong-doing would primarily be judged by the wrongness of collective acts and intentions. In some cases, this applies also to collectives, for example, a terrorist group that shares the aim to kill innocent people in a terrorist attack and that acts on that aim. It is more questionable whether collective acts can also be called wrong if there is not a shared aim. However, as for example Kutz has suggested participatory intentions may sometimes be enough. If an individual knowingly and

64   *Ibo van de Poel*

intentionally participates in a collective action that causes harm, she may be responsible for that harm, even if she did not intend that harm. The case is here somewhat similar to the individual who undertakes an action of which she knows that it will harm someone else even if it is not her intention to harm that person (the action may be done for other reasons, for example to make a profit). At least in some cases this would be an instance of wrong-doing, even if there is no intention to harm.

Virtue ethics may be more difficult to apply to collectives. The reason for this is that virtues are usually understood as character traits and it is not so clear how a collective can have a character, other than in a metaphorical sense. Still, some organisations, like certain companies, have committed themselves to certain virtues like integrity or honesty. Moreover, collective or joint actions can be judged by the degree to which they comply with certain virtues. For these reasons, a virtue ethics assessment of collective actions does not seem impossible although it seems to require a different understanding of virtues than just personal character traits.

For forward-looking responsibility, the normative condition refers not to wrong-doing but to moral obligations, which may be grounded in different ways. Again, the three main ethical theories are relevant here (see also Table 1.4 in Chapter 1). For the consequentialist route, one needs to establish that it is desirable to achieve a certain state-of-affairs. This task is not different at the collective level than at the individual level. In addition, a distribution principle is required. Such distribution principles can, however, both be used to distribute responsibility among individuals as well as among collectives; so collective responsibility does not introduce additional complications here. For the deontological route, one needs to establish that collectives can make promises or commitments. If a collective has a (decision) procedure that is accepted as authoritative by all members of the collective, this does not seem a problematic assumption. For this reason, organised groups are able to make commitments or promises. However, for collectives involved in a joint action, this is much more doubtful because such lack a procedure for establishing collective aims (apart from intentional participation in a joint action). For the virtue ethics route, the question arises again whether collectives can act in virtue sense with judgement. This may be a problematic assumption as we have seen.

2.3.3   Can Collective Responsibility Be Reduced to Individual Responsibilities?

Some authors claim that collective responsibility is sometimes irreducible to individual responsibility, i.e., that a collective can be responsible without any of its members being responsible (French 1984; Gilbert 1989; Copp 2007; Pettit 2007). Other claims that collective responsibility is, in the end, analysable only in terms of individual responsibility (Miller 2007, 2010). The collective responsibility of the government might, for example, be understood as the joint responsibility of the prime minster (as prime minister), other members of the government, members of the Parliament and, maybe, civil servants.

It should be noted that proponents of the irreducibility thesis do usually not claim that there is necessarily or always a discrepancy between collective and individual responsibility. As Peter French has expressed it: "[I]t should be noted that from 'Collectivity A is blameworthy for event n, and A is composed of x, y, and z,' it would be presumptuous to conclude that x, y, and z do not warrant any blame for n, or that x, y, or z is not himself blameworthy in the case of n. My point is that such judgments assessed on members of the collectivity do not follow necessarily from judgments of collective blame" (French 1998: 25).

Rather, proponents of the irreducibility thesis claim two things. First, they claim that collective responsibility usually does not directly translate into, or correspond to, individual responsibility and, second, that it might very well be possible, in some situations, that the collective is responsible for φ, whereas none of its individual members is responsible for φ. The second is especially relevant in relation to the PMH because it implies that the PMH might indeed occur.

Here, we want to investigate the consequences for our characterisation of the PMH if we would accept the reducibility thesis about collective responsibility. To this end, we propose to understand the reducibility thesis as follows:

(RT) Reducibility thesis: Collective responsibility can always be analysed in terms of individual responsibilities.

Now suppose that this reducibility thesis is indeed true, does it follow that the PMH cannot occur? That is not obvious. Let us look at an abstract hypothetical example. In section 2.5, we will give a concrete example that fleshes out this abstract example.

Suppose three agents together cause φ by each doing their part α, β, and γ. So agent i does α, agent j does β, and agent k does γ and α, β and γ together cause φ. Now suppose that the collective meets all conditions for responsibility-as-blameworthiness for φ but that the individual agents i, j, and k do not individually meet all conditions for responsibility for blameworthiness for φ, for example, each of them individually could not have reasonably foreseen that their individual action would result in φ eventually, although they together could have foreseen this. We will also assume that each agent is, nevertheless, responsible-as-blameworthiness for its own part (i for α, j for β and k for γ).

In this case, the collective responsibility for φ can be analysed in terms of individual responsibilities as follows:

1. i is responsible (as-blameworthy) for α.
2. j is responsible (as-blameworthy) for β.
3. k is responsible (as-blameworthy) for γ.

4. These three responsibilities together establish (in combination with what else is known about the case) that the three individuals are collectively (or jointly) responsible (as-blameworthy) for φ.

This analysis of the hypothetical case meets RT because the collective responsibility is understood (analysed) in terms of individual responsibilities. However, it is also an example of the PMH because whereas the collective is responsible for φ, none of the individuals is responsible for φ. As individuals they are responsible for their part but none of them is individually responsible for the collective effect. They are only jointly, or collectively, responsible for the joint effect φ.

Now, it might be objected that if the three individuals are collectively (jointly) responsible for φ, each of them is also individually *as member of the collective* responsible for φ. This argument, however, presupposes a stronger version of the reducibility thesis that might be formulated as follows:

> *(SRT) Strong reducibility thesis: If a collective is responsible for φ, all members of the collective are individually responsible for φ as member of the collective.*

If we accept SRT, it follows that the problem of many hands (PMH) cannot occur. However, if we reject SRT while still accepting RT, the PMH can occur. So we can accept RT without the need to reject PMH.

We conclude therefore that proponents of the reducibility thesis about collective responsibility need not reject our characterisation of the PMH. They only have to do so if they accept the strong version of the reducibility thesis (SRT). If they adopt a weaker version of the reducibility thesis, like RT, they can still maintain that collective responsibility can always be analysed in terms of individual responsibility, while admitting that there might be a gap between the collective responsibility for a specific φ, and individual responsibilities for that specific φ as worded in PMH.

2.4 THE PMH IN ORGANISED GROUPS: THE DISCURSIVE DILEMMA

As we have seen in section 2.2, an organised group is characterised by a (decision) procedure, which is recognised as legitimate by the group members for collective decisions as how to act and what to aim for. In illustrating the PMH in organised groups, we focus on a category of examples that is especially relevant in the case of a collective decision procedure. This category of examples is referred to as voting paradoxes or discursive dilemmas. Voting paradoxes are situations in which the collective outcome of a voting procedure is (seemingly) paradoxical given the preferences of the voting individuals. If, for example, all individuals prefer option A over B

The Problem of Many Hands 67

it would be paradoxical if the collective would, as a result of the voting procedure, prefer B over A. Discursive dilemmas are somewhat comparable to voting paradoxes, but they concern situations in which the items over which individuals (may) vote are logically related. For example, we might agree that someone is the thief (C) if the person took away the stolen object (A) and is not the owner of that object (B). In this case, the three statements A, B, and C are related as follows: $A \wedge B \rightarrow C$. In some cases voting about A and B and then deriving C will give different results than directly voting about C (we will see an example below). This is known as a discursive dilemma. In a discursive dilemma beliefs about the world are at stake rather than just preferences.

Philip Pettit (2007) has argued that due to voting paradoxes or discursive dilemmas, sometimes no individual can properly be held morally responsible (as-blameworthy) for undesirable collective outcomes. Pettit gives the following example. Suppose that three employees (A, B, and C) of a company need to decide together whether a certain safety device should be installed and suppose that they agree that this should only be done if (1) there is a serious danger (p), (2) the device is effective with respect to the danger (q), and (3) the costs are bearable (r). If, and only if, all three conditions are met ($p \wedge q \wedge r$), then the device has to be installed implying a pay sacrifice (s) for all three employees. Now suppose that the judgments of the three individuals on p, q, r, and s are as indicated in the table below. Also suppose that the collective decision is made by majority decision on the individual issues p, q, and r and then deducing s from ($p \wedge q \wedge r$). The result would be that the device is installed and that they all have to accept a pay sacrifice. But who is responsible for this outcome? According to Pettit neither A, B, or C can be properly be held responsible for the decision because each of them believed that the safety device was not worth the pay sacrifice and voted accordingly as can be seen from the table (based on the matrix in Pettit 2007: 197). Pettit believes that in cases like this the collective can be held responsible-as-blameworthy even if no individual can properly be held responsible-as-blameworthy. This is thus an illustration of the PMH_B for an organised group.

Table 2.4 Employee Safety (based on Pettit 2007)

	Serious danger? (p)	Effective measure? (q)	Bearable costs? (r)	Pay sacrifices ($p \wedge q \wedge r$)
A	No	Yes	Yes	No
B	Yes	No	Yes	No
C	Yes	Yes	No	No
Majority	Yes	Yes	Yes	[Yes] no

68   *Ibo van de Poel*

As Hindriks (2009: 166) has pointed out, Pettit in his argument relies on the following excuse condition for responsibility-as-blameworthiness:

[E] An individual member of an organisation cannot be blamed for a decision made by that organisation if s/he disagrees with it.

This condition can be seen as a filling out of the freedom condition. As we saw in Chapter 1, the freedom condition can be interpreted in a number of ways; one possible interpretation is that one should have options available that avoid the undesirable outcome. Pettit seems to suggest that such options are lacking as the agents A, B, and C vote sincerely and produce and outcome that none of them intends. But are such options indeed lacking? It may be doubted.

First, as Braham and Van Hees (2012) have pointed out, each of the agents can avoid the undesirable outcome by strategically voting; they can misrepresent their beliefs and simply vote 'no' on each of the issues; if only one of them did so, the collective decision would be not to pay the sacrifice, the outcome they all prefer. So, there is an action available to all three agents by which they can individually prevent the undesirable collective outcome. However, the question is whether this option is eligible. As Braham and Van Hees point out, in the discursive dilemma, not just preferences but beliefs about the world are at stake, and misrepresenting one's beliefs is often seen as immoral. Even if it would be morally allowed to misrepresent one's beliefs in this case, it may be doubted whether the agents are morally required to do so in order to achieve the collectively desirable outcome. It might thus be argued that whereas the agents have an option available that avoids the undesirable outcome this option is not reasonable, as it involves a misrepresentation of their beliefs.

There is, however, another option to avoid the collective outcome: to change the decision procedure as pointed out by Miller (2007) in relation to a similar example as Employee Safety. As Miller sees it, the decision procedure is flawed because it produces a result that is not intended by any of the agents. The decision procedure itself is, however, the result of an earlier decision. Now, even if agents A, B, and C were not in charge of choosing the decision procedure, at least one agent in the larger organisation is, and that agent can be held responsible for the decision procedure and the flawed result. The problem with this argument is that it seems to presuppose that there is an appropriate decision procedure available. However, the literature on social choice and discursive dilemmas (Arrow 1950; Sen 1970; List and Pettit 2002) strongly suggests that any decision procedure will have flaws. An alternative procedure may produce a desirable result in the specific case of Employee Safety, but it will likely produce undesirable results in other cases. It seems hard to hold anyone responsible for the fact that all decision procedures have flaws (as far as we know from the literature on the subject).

Hindriks (2009) himself points out that mere disagreement with the collective decision is not enough to excuse agents, as an agent should disagree with the collective decision for the *right reasons*. The argument goes as follows. Suppose some person achieves a highly desirable outcome by mere luck. We would then not be inclined to praise this person because the outcome is the result of luck rather than of the intentional actions of that person. Now suppose a person disagrees with a collective decision for the wrong reasons, for example he objects because the voting pencil was blue rather than red. In such a case, we would not excuse the person because he cites the wrong reasons for disagreeing with the collective decision. This is even the case if the person citing the wrong reasons for his disagreement could not have prevented the undesirable outcome by acting for the right reasons. Hindriks (2009: 169) therefore proposes the following alternative excuse condition:

[E*] An individual's disagreement with the decision the organisation of which s/he is a member affects the extent to which s/he can be blamed for that decision only if s/he disagrees with it for the right reasons.

He proposes a two-step procedure for distributing responsibility in cases like Employee Safety. The first step is "to determine whether the case at hand is one of faulty self-governance. If not, no one is to be blamed" (Hindriks 2009: 172). The crucial question here is whether the collective can be fittingly held responsible-as-blameworthy. The second step, which is only to be carried out if the collective is indeed responsible-as-blameworthy, is "to identify those individuals who contributed to the corporate agent's faulty assessment of the normative issues involved, the one who . . . are guilty of faulty self-governance" (Hindriks 2009: 172). If no such individual can be identified, whereas the collective is responsible-as-blameworthy, the PMH occurs, as can be easily seen.

Hindriks assumes that in the case of Employee Safety agents A and B acted for the wrong reasons. He takes it that r ('bearable costs?') is the normative premise here, and that the costs are not bearable, so that A and B made a wrong normative assessment and, hence, can be held responsible-as-blameworthy. According to Hindriks, then, the PMH_B does not occur in the case of the Employee Safety. As he recognises, however, this does not show that the situation referred to in PMH_B can never occur.

2.5 THE PMH AND JOINT ACTION: THE CITICORP CASE[5]

We now want to look at an example of PMH in the case of a joint action in the absence of an organised group. The joint action we will consider is the design and construction of the Citibank Headquarters in midtown New York. This is a joint action because a large number of individuals

70   *Ibo van de Poel*

and collectives-as-organised-groups (corporate agents) were involved in the design and construction of this building. Each of these agents intentionally contributed to the design and construction of the building by doing its part. Although it is known from the literature on design that the different participants in the design process may have somewhat different conceptions of what it is that is being designed (Bucciarelli 1994), it seems sensible to say that these conceptions at least overlap to such a degree that we can speak of the collective aim to design and construct the Citibank Headquarters in midtown New York.

The 59-story building was completed in 1977. LeMessurier, a renowned structural engineer, had been in charge of the structural design of the tower. In 1978, LeMessurier learned due to a series of serendipitous events that the tower's steel frame was structurally deficient. An announcement of the building's vulnerability could possibly have costed LeMessurier his career and reputation as a structural engineer. Moreover, it would also have considerable financial implications. Nevertheless, he undertook efforts to correct the vulnerability without making it public and eventually succeeded in doing so; the story did not become public until 1995. In the engineering ethics literature, the actions that LeMessurier undertook after discovering the structural deficiency are usually described as morally praiseworthy (Whitbeck 1998; Pritchard 2001; Martin and Schinzinger 2005; Harris, Pritchard, and Rabins 2008). We do not want to dispute this conventional interpretation of the case. Instead, we focus on the situation in 1977 before LeMessurier discovered the flaw in the building. Apparently, the building was structurally deficient at that time, although nobody knew that. So the φ we focus on is the structural deficiency of the building in 1977.

Because we focus on responsibility-as-blameworthiness, our question is: who can reasonably be held responsible-as-blameworthy for φ? To answer this question, we start by briefly sketching the main causes of the structural deficiency of the building. We then focus on the three main actors that causally contributed to this structural deficiency:

1. LeMessurier who designed the building,
2. The contractor who during construction decided to replace the welded joints by bolted joints and
3. The employee at LeMessurier's firm who approved this change but did not inform LeMessurier about it (the 'approver').

We will suggest that it might be argued that none of these actors can reasonably be held individually responsible for the building being structurally deficient in 1977, whereas they may be collectively held reasonably responsible-as-blameworthy for φ.

The structural deficiency of the CitiCorp building was mainly caused by a combination of two factors.[6] One was the peculiar design of the building, the other the change from welded to bolded joints. It was the combination of

The Problem of Many Hands 71

these two factors that made the building structurally deficient. Each of these factors considered in isolation did not jeopardise the structural strength of the building. The design was peculiar because the first floor was several stories above ground, with the ground support of the building being four pillars placed in between the four corners of the structure rather than at the corners themselves. The reason for this construction was that there had been a church on the building site and it had been agreed that this church would be reconstructed beneath the building after its completion. The change from welded to bolted joints was made on request of the contractor, who requested this change because it would ease construction. A change of this kind was not uncommon in the construction of this kind of buildings. This change was approved (and stamped) by an employee at LeMessurier's firm (the approver).

In 1978, LeMessurier found out that the combination of the peculiar design and the bolded connections made the structure vulnerable to high winds that strike the building diagonally at a 45 degree angle. Based on the New York weather records, a storm with a probability of occurrence once every 16 years (a so-called '16-year storm') would be sufficient to cause total structural failure.[7]

Now that we have some insight in the causes of the structural deficiency of the CitiCorp building, let us see whether each of the three mentioned individual agents can reasonably be held responsible: LeMessurier, the contractor and the approver. In doing so, we will apply the conditions for individual moral responsibility-as-blameworthiness that were presented in Chapter 1 (section 1.3.1). An individual is thus morally responsible for the structural deficiency if:

1. He is a moral agent that has the capacity to act responsibly (capacity);
2. A causal connection is present between the action of the agent and the structural deficiency (causality);
3. He could with reasonable efforts have known that the building was structurally deficient (knowledge);
4. He did not act under coercion and could have acted differently to avoid the harm (freedom);
5. He did something wrong (wrong-doing)

The first condition is met because all three persons are moral agents. The second condition is also met: each of them made a causal contribution to the structural deficiency, i.e., by changing the design from welded to bolded joints (the contractor), by approving the design change (the approver) and by choosing this particular design (LeMessurier). None of the three agents was coerced to do make this causal contribution. Moreover, each could have prevented φ (the structural deficiency of the building) by individually doing a different action. If the contractor would not have changed the joints, the building would not have been structurally deficient; similarly,

72   *Ibo van de Poel*

also the contractor and LeMessurier could have individually prevented φ. So all three agents also meet the freedom condition.

The crucial responsibility conditions here are therefore the knowledge condition (the person could reasonably have known of the deficiency) and the wrong-doing condition. We will focus here on the knowledge condition and will present an interpretation of the case on which none of the three mentioned agents meets the knowledge condition. We do not want to claim that our interpretation is the only possible interpretation, but we maintain that it is at least plausible enough to claim that in a situation similar to this one, the problem of many hands might occur.

If we focus on the knowledge condition, the following picture arises. LeMessurier cannot reasonably be held responsible in 1977, because he then did not know of the change from welded to bolted joints, which was crucial to foresee the structural deficiency of the building. The contractor, of course, knew about the change and probably also about the peculiar design, but it seems reasonable to say that the contractor could not have known that the combination of these two factors would lead to structural deficiency. There are two reasons why the contractor could not or should not have known this. First, in normal circumstances it would not have been a problem to change from welded to bolted joints. Second, the contractor, not being a structural engineer like LeMessurier, lacked the knowledge and expertise that was required to foresee this particular structural deficiency. Consequently, also the contractor cannot reasonably be held responsible.

What about the approver? Could or should he have foreseen the structural deficiency before approving the change? And if so, did he act wrongly in approving the change? According to Morgenstern, LeMessurier argued that the "choice of bolted joints was technically sound and professionally correct" (Morgenstern 1995). Furthermore, it took LeMessurier several weeks in 1978 after hearing about the change in joints and being asked by a student about the structural strength to find out the vulnerability to 45-degree winds. Even if LeMessurier could, and possibly should, have foreseen the structural deficiency if he had known about the change from bolded to welded joints (which he did not), it seems reasonable to assume that the approver could not have foreseen the structural deficiency. The reason for that is that the approver is likely to have had considerably less experience and knowledge about the rationale for the design compared to LeMessurier. Hence, it is not reasonable to hold the approver responsible. It then turns out that none of the actors can reasonably be held responsible.

To show that this is a problem of many hands, we also need to show that the collective can reasonably be held responsible in this case, a task to which we turn now. In the CitiCorp case, the relevant collective consist in all the individuals (and collectives) that are involved in the joint action of designing and constructing the CitiCorp building. For the moment, we will, however, focus on the sub-collective that was (causally) most directly involved in φ, i.e., the collective consisting of LeMessurier, the contractor

The Problem of Many Hands 73

and the approver together. We assume that these three people can cooperate and share information. Because the collective undertook a joint action (the design and construction of the CiticiCorp Tower) it meets the capacity condition (condition 1 above). The collective also made a causal contribution to the structural deficiency (condition 2 above). The collective was also not coerced to act in a certain way and, moreover, it had actions available collectively to avoid the structural deficiency. So also the freedom condition is met (condition 4 above). It is less clear whether the collective also meets the knowledge and wrong-doing condition.

An important argument why the collective meets the knowledge condition is that if they had shared their knowledge and expertise they could have known that the building was structurally deficient. LeMessurier in fact drew this conclusion in 1978 after being informed about the change from welded to bolded joints.

Is the wrong-doing condition also met? From a consequentialist point of view, it obviously is: structural failure once in the 16 years is unacceptably high; no engineer would contest that. One possible counter-argument is that the building still met the New York City building code because that code only requires taking into account 90-degree winds and not 45-degree winds and the building was only structurally deficient for the latter. Nevertheless, the effect of quartering winds was known long before the 1970s—the city's building code of 1899 already required to take all possible directions into account, although some later codes did not (Kremer 2002). Therefore, given the innovative design of the structure, it seems reasonable to require the engineers to take into account 45-degree winds (cf. Kremer 2002). It thus seems reasonable to hold the collective in 1977 responsible-as-blameworthy for the structural deficiency of the CitiCorp building.

To conclude: there is at least one, not implausible, reading of the case, in which the collective is responsible (as-blameworthy) for the structural deficiency of the building, whereas none of the involved individuals (LeMessurier, the contractor and the approver) is responsible (as-blameworthy) for the structural deficiency. This reading does not imply that there are no individual responsibilities in this case or that the collective responsibility cannot be understood or analysed in terms of individual responsibilities. In fact, we think it can in the following way:

1. LeMessurier is responsible (as-blameworthy) for not properly informing the approver and the contractor about the peculiarities of the design and the importance (at least in this case) to have all changes in the design approved.
2. The contractor is responsible (as-blameworthy) for not making sure that the change is communicated to and approved by LeMessurier himself instead of just by the approver.
3. The approver is responsible (as-blameworthy) for not communicating the change in design to LeMessurier himself.

74 *Ibo van de Poel*

4. These three responsibilities together establish (in combination with what else is known about the case,) that the three individuals are collectively (or jointly) responsible (as-blameworthy) for the structural deficiency of the building.

It should be noted that this attribution of individual responsibility does *not* contradict the occurrence of a PMH in this case. The reason is that PMH occurs with respect to the responsibility *for the structural deficiency*. According to the above analysis, each individual is responsible for some contributing factor but none of them is *individually* responsible for the overall effect (the structural deficiency). In addition to these individual responsibilities, there is a joint or collective responsibility that is established by the combination of individual responsibilities, and which refers to the structural deficiency.

2.6 THE PMH AND OCCASIONAL COLLECTIONS OF INDIVIDUALS: CLIMATE CHANGE

We will now look at climate change as an example of a situation in which the problem of many hands occurs with respect to an 'occasional collections of individuals.' The occasional collection we focus on in this case is the world population. The world population does not qualify as an 'organised group', despite the existence of the United Nations (UN) and its institutions. The UN has created some representation and decision procedures at world scale, but not enough, it seems, to speak of an organised group because these mechanisms are in many cases rather ineffective or are not considered binding for the member states of the UN. International agreements, like the Kyoto Protocol for example, have to be ratified by individual states before they become binding for such states. There is also not a joint action in which the entire world population participates and which creates the (increased) greenhouse effect as by-product. The activities that contribute to greenhouse warming are too diverse to speak of such a joint action.

Although the world population in relation to climate change is best conceived as an 'occasional collections of individuals' some reasons may be cited which make it reasonable to believe that this collection of individuals should organise itself to prevent, or at least mitigate climate change. One reason is the expected effects of climate change. Another reason is that at least some institutions already exist that could be used to organise collective action to mitigate climate change. In fact, the UN Framework Convention that was signed by 152 countries at Rio de Janeiro in 1992 says that nations should "protect the climate system for the benefit of present and future generations of mankind, on the basis of equity and in accordance with their common but differentiated responsibilities and respective capabilities" (United Nations 1992: 9).

We will discuss the problem of many hands with respect to responsibility-as-obligation and responsibility-as-blameworthiness. We will proceed as follows. First, we will discuss the conditions for both kinds of responsibility at the collective level (2.6.1). Then we will discuss the attribution of responsibility-as-obligation and responsibility-as-blameworthiness to the relevant collective, i.e., the world population (2.6.2). We will then repeat this procedure with respect to individual responsibility (sections 2.6.3 and 2.6.4). In the final section, we will briefly draw conclusions with respect to the occurrence of the problem of many hands (section 2.6.5).

Responsibility for climate change is obviously, both at the individual and the collective level, complicated and contested. Various philosophers, and others, have come to opposing conclusions on how responsibility should be attributed in this case (e.g., Caney 2005; Sinnott-Armstrong 2005; Miller 2009; Jamieson 2010; Miller 2011; Vanderheiden 2011). Our aim here is not to end these debates; rather, we want to show that on some plausible interpretation, it would be reasonable to maintain that no individual is (in some sense) responsible for climate change whereas the world population is collectively responsible and, therefore, the case may be seen as an example of the problem of many hands.

2.6.1 Conditions for Collective Responsibility for Climate Change

To appropriately attribute collective moral responsibility-as-obligation and responsibility-as-blameworthiness to the world population for climate change, the conditions for such an attribution need to be fulfilled. We will discuss these conditions below.

Capacity
The world population is, with respect to climate change, an occasional collection of individuals as argued above. The crucial question is therefore whether this collection can be expected to organise itself in such a way that it avoids the harm of climate change, in particular that it makes sure that effective measures are taken to mitigate climate change. In the introduction to this case, we already cited some reasons why we believe this to be the case. However, this viewpoint is not uncontroversial. Seumas Miller, for example, believes "that between 1990 and 2010 each (or most) of the (relevant) millions could not reasonably be expected to have, jointly with the others, formed the requisite collective end [i.e., mitigating climate change], and designed and implemented the technological and institutional means to realize it" (Miller 2011: 240). Miller might be right if we conceive of the world population as just a collection of individuals. However, if we take into account that a host of institutions and collective agents, including for example nations, exist it may not be unreasonable to expect that, at the level of the world as a whole, attempts are made to formulate a collective aim to mitigate climate change. In fact, such attempts have been made by nation states as witnessed by the above cited Rio Declaration and the Kyoto Protocol that was signed in 1997 (United Nations 1992, 1998). Although the Kyoto Protocol may be considered an insufficient and ineffective agreement

76 Ibo van de Poel

to mitigate climate change, the fact that it was drawn up and signed by a large number of countries (although not by the United States) seems a clear sign that many nations consider it reasonable to organise collective action at the level of the world to mitigate climate change.

The formulation of a collective aim and the adoption of means to mitigate climate change at the level of the world are, then, best seen as a process that occurs in two stages or at two levels. At the international level, nation states may be reasonably expected to formulate a collective aim to mitigate climate change as witnessed by the Rio Declaration and the Kyoto protocol. This will most likely result in aims and policies that have, in a next step, to be implemented at the national level. It is the responsibility (as-obligation) of national governments to effectively implement such policies. Whereas individual citizens may not have a responsibility (as-obligation) to organise the world population into an organised collective with respect to climate change, they do have responsibilities (as-obligation) to see to it that their governments support international action and that their governments translate international agreements into effective national policies.

We conclude that it seems reasonable to expect the world population to formulate a collective aim to mitigate climate change, albeit it not through direct international actions by individual citizens but rather through the use of existing collective agents, especially nation states, and existing institutional mechanisms and organisations like the UN.

Causality

It does not seem very controversial that the world population in the aggregate is a cause, or even the main cause, of climate change unless one wants to deny that anthropogenic emissions contribute to the occurrence of an increased greenhouse effect. Although there are still some climate sceptics who hold that position, the majority of scientists believe that climate change is at least for a considerable part caused by humans. We will therefore also adopt that assumption and we take it that the causality condition is met at the collective level.

For responsibility-as-obligation, the causality condition relates to causal efficacy. On the assumption that human greenhouse gas emissions cause an increased greenhouse effect, it seems that the world population can be causally efficacious. It might, however, be argued that the point in time has passed (or will pass in the future) at which climate change can still be avoided. Even then, it seems that the world population can still be causally efficacious in mitigating climate change to a degree that might be considered morally acceptable, i.e., to a degree at which adaption is still possible and no major irreversible catastrophe has yet occurred.

Knowledge

Despite the existence of climate sceptics, we will assume that the occurrence of climate change, and the role of humans in it, is an established scientific fact. Because we defined the knowledge condition at the collective level as

The Problem of Many Hands   77

what the collective can know if it shared all relevant knowledge (see section 2.3.2), it follows that the collective can reasonably know that human greenhouse emissions contribute to global warming. A point of debate is, however, still as of when it was known that human greenhouse emissions contribute to global warming. David Miller mentions the mid-1980s as the point in time when it became unreasonable to deny the link between human gas emissions and climate change (Miller 2009, 129), Seumas Miller takes 1990, when the first IPCC report appeared, to be the cut-off point (Miller 2011: 237).

Freedom
The freedom condition requires that the collective is not coerced and may, additionally, require that a reasonable course of action is available with which the harm can be prevented. Such a course of action seems available. According to estimates, effective measure to mitigate climate change to an acceptable degree would cost about 1.4% of the world's GDP (with an uncertainty bar between 1% and 3.5% decrease in GDP) (Stern 2006, 233).

Wrong-doing
There seems widespread agreement that if human greenhouse gases continue at the current level this will result in unacceptable harm. From a consequentialist point of view, continuing emissions at the current level would therefore constitute wrong-doing. In terms of forward-looking responsibility, mitigation of climate change seems not just morally desirable but morally mandatory given the expected harm.

2.6.2   Attributing Collective Responsibility for Climate Change

Before attributing collective responsibility for climate change, we first need to specify the relevant φ and we need to specify the point in time we are considering. For responsibility-as-obligation we will consider the responsibility to mitigate climate change to an acceptable degree in the period 2000–2014. For responsibility-as-blameworthiness we will consider the harm that will result from the failure to effective mitigate climate change to an acceptable degree in the period 2000–2014. These dates and φ-s have been chosen in such a way that the failure to live by the responsibility-as-obligation in the period 2000–2014 could be a ground for attributing the responsibility-as-blameworthiness.

For responsibility-as-obligation, the relevant conditions are capacity, causal efficacy, and the normative condition. The relevant normative condition is consequentialist, as we saw in the previous section; we therefore also need a distribution principle. Because at the collective level that we are considering, the world population, there is only one collective, the distribution principle is straightforward: It selects the only available collective. It

78 *Ibo van de Poel*

should further be noted that in or before the period we are considering, 2000–2014, already efforts had been undertaken at the global level to come to collective action (e.g. 1992 Rio Declaration and 1997 Kyoto Protocol); so we take it that the capacity condition is met. Although global warming might no longer have been completely avoidable in 2000, and later, it would still be possible in the period under consideration to mitigate climate change to an acceptable degree. So the causal efficacy criterion is also met. So we take it that we can reasonably attribute collective responsibility to mitigate climate change to an acceptable degree in the period 2000–2014 to the world population.

Let us now look at responsibility-as-blameworthiness. Usually we consider responsibility-as-blameworthiness if and when the harm has already occurred. In this case, the harm probably still has to occur (although it may already have been partly realised). So we will assume that at some time in the future, say 2020 or 2030, harm will occur as a result of the failure to effectively mitigate climate change to an acceptable degree in the period 2000–2014. It will scientifically be very hard to establish what this harm exactly is. Because even it is clear in, for example, in 2020 or 2030, what harm global warming then has caused; this harm will partly result from emissions before 2000, and partly from emissions after 2014. Moreover, we are not interested in the harm done by all emissions between 2000 and 2014, but only in the harm from those emissions that result from the failure to effectively mitigate global warming in this period. Despite these difficulties, it seems likely that there will be harm at some point in the future, due to the failure to effective mitigate climate change to an acceptable degree in the period 2000–2014. So, we will assume that in the period 2000–2014, inadequate measures have been taken to mitigate global warming, and at some point in the future harm will occur.

We will take the wrong-doing, which is the basis of the collective blameworthiness, to be the failure to fulfil the-responsibility-as-obligation that existed in the period 2000–2014. To show that this is a case of wrong-doing, we do not only need to show that the object of this responsibility, i.e., effective mitigation of global warming, was not achieved, but also that the supervisory duties that come with this responsibility-as-obligation were not lived by. The best evidence is perhaps the failure to come to a new agreement, or even the framework for a new agreement as follow-up of the Kyoto Protocol, which was already known to be insufficient as means to mitigate global warming. We take it then that the wrong-doing condition for collective moral responsibility-as-blameworthiness is also met.

If we take the failure to live by the responsibility-as-obligation as the wrong-doing, the relevant causal condition is whether the collective would have been causally efficacious if it had lived by this responsibility (see Table 1.5 in Chapter 1). Although this counterfactual is hard to establish with certainty, it seems at least likely that global warming could have been mitigated to an acceptable degree if adequate measures had been taken at world scale between 2000 and 2014. We therefore also assume that the causality condition is met.

Other relevant conditions for responsibility-as-blameworthiness are capacity, knowledge, and freedom. According to our analysis in 2.6.1, these conditions are also met. There is, however, one possible objection to the attribution of collective responsibility-as-blameworthiness that we briefly want to consider. This is the objection, or excuse, that it was impossible to come to an effective global agreement on mitigating climate change due to the persistent resistance of some crucial countries, especially the United States, to come to such an agreement. This objection can be seen as employing the freedom condition. It says that the collective is not free to undertake the relevant actions, as some members of the collective can effectively block this action. This objection certainly makes sense. We also think that it is a proper excuse for nations and states that made serious efforts to come to an international agreement and that effectively lived by their obligations set by the Kyoto Protocol; such countries can probably not be blamed for the collective failure to come to an effective new agreement. It is, however, not obvious that it is also an appropriate excuse for the collective in its entirety. We are inclined to think that it is not. What is relevant here is that we do not necessarily conceive of collective responsibility as distributive. Thus, we might blame the collective without necessarily blaming all countries, let alone all citizens, that are part of the collective.

In sum, we take it that the world population can collectively be reasonably held responsibility-as-blameworthiness for the harm that will result from the failure to effectively mitigate climate change to an acceptable degree between 2000 and 2014.

2.6.3 Conditions for Individual Responsibility for Climate Change

Capacity

In relation to individual responsibility for climate change, capacity is not an issue. Most individuals whom we possibly want to hold responsible for climate change have the right capacities to qualify as moral agents.

Causality

Causality is a more contentious issue. Sinnott-Armstrong asks whether I can be reasonably held responsible for global warming if I drive for fun on Sundays, so causally contributing, albeit to a very small degree, to global warming. He starts with noting that "my individual act is neither necessary nor sufficient for global warming" (Sinnott-Armstrong 2005: 289). As he admits, however, there are "special circumstances in which an act causes harm without being either necessary or sufficient for the harm"

80　*Ibo van de Poel*

(Sinnott-Armstrong 2005: 289). However, he maintains, that in such cases the act, to be properly called a cause either needs to be intentionally aimed at the harm or to be 'unusual'. As he explains, we do not usually call oxygen a cause of fire, because oxygen is in normal circumstances present; however, we might call the striking of a match the cause because it is unusual (Sinnott-Armstrong 2005: 290). He concludes that "we should not hold people responsible for harms by calling their acts causes of harm when their acts are not at all unusual, assuming that they did not intend the harm" (Sinnott-Armstrong 2005: 290).[8] Because driving for fun on Sunday is, according to Sinnot-Armstrong, neither unusual nor does it do *intentional* harm, it cannot be considered a cause of global warming. He also argues that another argument leads to the same conclusion: "Greenhouse gases (such as carbon dioxide and water vapour) are perfectly fine in small quantities. They help plants grow. The problem emerges only when there is too much of them. But my joyride by itself does not cause the massive quantities that are harmful" (Sinnott-Armstrong 2005: 290).[9]

David Miller distinguishes three possible accounts for the causal relation between individual greenhouse gas emissions and the harm these emissions cause in the aggregate: (1) a linear relation between emissions and a harm, (2) a progressive relation: each additional emission causes slightly more damage than the one before, and (3) a threshold effect: only above a certain level there is harm at all (Miller 2009: 130–131). Only if account 1 holds there is a clear causal relation between individual emissions and the harm done, even if the individual contribution is very small. However, from climate science we know that it is very unlikely that account 1 holds; a combination of account 2 and 3 is much more likely. This obviously makes it more difficult to establish a causal relation between individual emissions and the harm done.[10]

Knowledge

When discussing collective responsibility for climate change, we said that we collectively could have known of the relation between human emissions of greenhouse gases and climate change since at least 1990. Does this also apply to individual citizens? Not necessarily, as we defined the knowledge condition at the collective level as what we could know if all relevant knowledge is shared, collective knowledge does not imply individual knowledge. Dale Jamieson, for example argues:

> According to a recent Rasmussen Report, 44% of American voters say that climate change is primarily caused by long-term planetary trends rather than human activity. . . . It could be argued that these Americans are culpable in their ignorance of the relation between human action and climate change, but when prominent public figures are climate change deniers and science education is so obviously inadequate it is difficult to make this case.
>
> (Jamieson 2010: 437, footnote 11)[11]

The Problem of Many Hands 81

Whether global warming is really a case of excusable ignorance seems debatable, but one should be aware that even if at the collective level the link between human emissions and global warming can be reasonably known, it is not obvious that all individual citizens can reasonably be expected to know this link.

Freedom

Some contributions to global warming might be considered unavoidable or involuntary, like breathing, which produces carbon dioxide. Usually discussions about individual responsibility for climate change, therefore, focus on luxury emissions rather than on subsistence emissions (Shue 1993). But even in the case of luxury emissions, absence of coercion may not be enough to call an act voluntary. Nihlén Fahlquist (2009) has argued that people should have reasonable alternatives in order to be reasonably held responsible for environmental problems. What alternatives are reasonable might thereby depend on contextual and situational features; alternatives that are reasonable for rich people may not be reasonable for less prosperous people.

The Normative Condition

Let us, finally, look at the normative condition. It seems undeniable that it would be morally praiseworthy or morally virtuous if citizens voluntarily help curb greenhouse gas emissions. This means that citizens can voluntarily assume a responsibility-as-obligation to contribute to mitigating global warming on basis of the deontological, or virtue-ethical, route that we distinguished in Chapter 1. Here, we will mainly focus on the question whether individual citizens also have a moral obligation to curb their greenhouse gas emissions.

Moral obligations can either be moral duties or moral responsibilities-as-obligations. The first refer to constraints on actions, the second to state-of-affairs that an agent should see to that they obtain without necessarily bringing about the state-of-affairs herself. Below we will first consider moral duties of individual citizens and then responsibilities-as-obligations.

Moral Duties

Although it is often believed that citizens have a moral duty to restrain their greenhouse gas emissions even in the absence of effective national or international policy to abate greenhouse warming, this moral duty is vehemently denied by both Sinnott-Armstrong (2005) and Johnson (2003). Sinnott-Armstrong discusses a large number of possible moral principles (including the harm principle, the indirect harm principle, the contribution principle, the risk principle, the universalizability principle, the virtue principle, the ideal law principle, the group principle, and several others) on basis of which individuals may have a moral duty to avoid global warming as individuals; he rejects, however, all of them.

Also Johnson argues that, despite what many people believe, individuals do not have a moral duty to restrain themselves to a sustainable level

82   Ibo van de Poel

of consumption in a tragedy of the commons. The main reasons for her to believe that such an obligation is absent is that she believes:

1. That it is not reasonable to expect that unilateral restrictions of consumption by individuals are likely to be effective in avoiding a tragedy of the commons.
2. That unilaterally restricting one's consumption would entail a sacrifice and that "a *prima facie* moral duty can be overridden by the sacrifice it would entail" (Johnson 2003: 281). So even if it might prima facie seem a moral duty to cut one's greenhouse emissions, the sacrifice that such a reduction requires may override this moral duty, and
3. That there is "nothing wrong with any one person's use of the commons" in a typical tragedy of the commons because no "one person's use is large enough to harm the commons" (Johnson 2003: 277).

Crucial in Johnson's argument is the absence of an effective collective agreement. As she argues:

> There is a vast difference between (a) free riding or otherwise failing to live up to an existing (and functioning) collective agreement that produces benefits, and (b) refusing to act unilaterally in the way one would like to see universalised when that is costly to oneself and cannot reasonably be expected to produce the outcome whose pursuit justifies one's action. The former is a paradigm of unethical behaviour. . . . By contrast, in the absence of the collective agreement that would give one's restraint a chance of securing its object, there is no point and no obligation to make the sacrifice that restraint entails.
>
> (Johnson 2003: 282)

It should be noted that Johnson is not arguing here that we should not strive for collective agreements; in fact, she believes that there is a genuine moral obligation for individuals to do so. Rather, her argument should be understood in terms of the moral obligations that individuals have if a collective agreement is *de facto* absent.

Johnson's focus is on moral duties in a tragedy of the commons and not on climate change, and whereas there seem to be good reasons to conceive of climate change as a tragedy of the commons, one might wonder whether in the case of climate change there is an effective collective agreement that would create moral obligations for individual citizens. The best candidate is perhaps the Kyoto Protocol under which a large number of industrialised countries have committed themselves to a reduction in greenhouse gases. It may, however, be doubted whether the Kyoto Protocol creates moral obligations for individual citizens. First, the Protocol is an agreement between nations, or their governments, and it might be argued that unless national governments have translated the Kyoto reduction goals into effective national policy, citizens of those countries have no individual moral obligations to reduce greenhouse gases unilaterally. This is not to deny that governments have a moral obligation to device such national policies; the argument only states that, in the actual absence of such policies, individual citizens may not have moral obligations to restrict their own emissions. Second, the United States is not a party to the Kyoto Protocol and, hence, it seems that, at least on Johnson's argument, the treaty cannot create moral obligations for U.S. citizens. Again, the point is not that the U.S. government does not have a moral obligation to sign the Kyoto Protocol, but that individual citizens in the United States can have no moral obligations on basis of the protocol as long as the United States is not actually committed to it.

To better understand the above argument, it is useful to distinguish between the following five moral obligations that individual citizens may have:[12]

1. The moral responsibility-as-obligation to see to it that their governments come to effective and fair international agreements to mitigate global warming.
2. The moral responsibility-as-obligation to see to it that their national governments translate international agreements they have signed into effective and fair national policies to mitigate global warming.
3. The moral duty to live by the emissions targets set by their governments as part of a fair and effective national policy to implement a fair and effective international agreement to mitigate climate change.
4. The moral duty to restrict their individual greenhouse gas emissions in the absence of a fair and effective international agreement that has been signed by their government.
5. The moral duty to restrict their individual greenhouse gas emissions in the absence of fair and effective national policies to implement a fair and effective international agreement that has been signed by their government.

Johnson does not deny the existence of moral obligations 1, 2, or 3, she denies moral obligations 4 and 5. The crucial point in both cases is that the *de facto* absence of international agreement that has been signed by one's national government or the *de facto* absence of national policies makes a moral difference even if the *de facto* absence of such an agreement or such policies is morally undesirable. Although citizens can still be expected to see to it that such international agreements are signed or national policies are designed (moral obligations 1 and 2), they do not have an obligation to unilaterally cut their emissions as long as such collective arrangements are still absent (moral obligations 4 and 5). There are three related reasons why they do not have this moral obligations: (1) their individual emissions, considered in isolation, are not harmful (cf. the discussion of the causality condition above), (2) individual cuts in emissions entail a sacrifice for (most) individuals which is not justified because (3) individual cuts in emissions

84 *Ibo van de Poel*

are unlikely to be effective in mitigating global warming. The reason for 3 is that in the absence of a collective agreement, and hence the absence of effective coordination between individuals, it is very difficult for individuals to decide what individual restrains they should apply to collectively avoid climate change (or limit it to a manageable degree). One might argue that each individual should do what is reasonable possible for her. It is, however, far from clear whether, if every individual lived by such a moral obligation in isolation, the collective effect would be the prevention of climate change. Rather it seems likely that *effectively* abating global warming requires *coordinated* efforts.[13]

Moral Responsibility-as-Obligation

As we have already seen, citizens have certain moral responsibilities-as-obligations with respect to climate change as worded in moral obligation 1 and 2 above. But do they also have a responsibility-as-obligation to see to that global warming is mitigated to an acceptable degree (the φ we formulated for collective responsibility-as-obligation in 2.6.1)? A first thing to note here is that mitigating climate change to an acceptable level is outside the causal efficacy of individuals; this requires a collective action. This makes it very doubtful whether citizens have this responsibility.

In addition to causal efficacy, the consequentialist route to responsibility-as-obligation requires a distribution principle. Such principles have been discussed for the distribution of the collective responsibility to abate climate change among nation states (e.g., Miller 2009). However, these distribution principles do usually not distribute up to the individual level. David Miller, for example, who discusses the plausibility of various distribution principles for distribution among nations, holds that:

> We should want our climate change-policies to encroach as little as possible on national self-determination. Rather than imposing policy solutions from above, it is far better to agree upon targets for each nation, and then to allow policies for meeting those targets to be decided internally, ideally through a process of democratic debate.
> (Miller 2009: 121–122)

So if there would be a morally fair distribution principle that would apply to the distribution of responsibility among nations, it would not distribute responsibility down to the individual level. So again the conclusions is that individuals do not have a responsibility-as-obligation to see to that global warming is mitigated to an acceptable degree in the absence of a collective agreement.

2.6.4 Attributing Individual Responsibility for Climate Change

Let us first look at responsibility-as-obligation. From what we said in the previous section, it immediately follows that:

The Problem of Many Hands 85

Statement 1
Individuals did not have a responsibility-as-obligation to see to it that global warming was mitigated to an acceptable degree in the period 2000–2014.

Many believe, however, that individual citizens have a responsibility to do what is in their causal powers and what they are free to do. Nevertheless, as we have seen, both Sinnott-Armstrong and Johnson believe that citizens do not have a moral duty to reduce their individual emissions as long as an effective collective agreement is absent. So both Sinnott-Armstrong and Johnson seem to subscribe to the following statement:[14]

Statement 2
Individuals do not have a moral duty to unilaterally restrict their emissions of greenhouse gases to help mitigate global warming

Still, both Sinnott-Armstrong and Johnson believe that individuals as citizens have a forward-looking responsibility-as-moral-obligation to see to it that their governments take adequate measures against global warming. Sinnott-Armstrong, for example, writes that individuals have certain "real moral obligations, which are to get governments to do their job to prevent the disaster of excessive global warming" (Sinnott-Armstrong 2005: 304). Similarly, Johnson states that citizens have an obligation "to 'do the right thing' without waiting for others. 'The right thing' is not, however, a fruitless, unilateral reduction in one's use of the commons, but an attempt to promote an effective collective agreement that will coordinate reductions in commons use and therefore avert aggregate harm" (Johnson 2003: 284). Both thus subscribe to:

Statement 3
Individuals have a responsibility-as-obligation to see to it that collective agreements are achieved, which effectively mitigate global warming.

More precisely, this can be divided in two partial responsibilities, as we have seen above (sections 2.6.1 and 2.6.2):

Statement 3a
Individuals have a responsibility-as-obligation to see to it that their governments come to effective and fair international agreements to mitigate global warming.

Statement 3b
Individuals have a responsibility-as-obligation to see to it that their national governments translate international agreements that they have signed into effective and fair national policies to mitigate global warming.

This break-down is important because, as we argued in section 2.6.1, individual citizens cannot be expected to see to it that collective agreements are achieved without the use of existing institutions like nation states and the UN.

86 *Ibo van de Poel*

Both Sinnott-Armstrong and Johnson further maintain that individuals can voluntarily take the responsibility to unilaterally reduce their emissions, although they are not obliged to do so. Johnson, for example, argues that "individual reductions are surely morally permissible and perhaps even praiseworthy as supererogatory acts" (Johnson 2003: 285). And Sinnott-Armstrong says that "it is still morally better or morally ideal for individuals not to waste gas. We can and should praise those who save fuel" (Sinnott-Armstrong 2005: 303). This refers to what we have called responsibility-as-virtue in Chapter 1 (section 1.4.2), and both therefore subscribe to:

Statement 4
Individuals can voluntarily assume a responsibility-as-virtue to unilaterally restrict their emissions of greenhouse gases to help mitigate global warming and it is morally praiseworthy if they do so.

What does the above discussion imply for the attribution of responsibility-as-blameworthiness to individuals? As we have seen in Chapter 1, a reasonable attribution of such a responsibility requires wrong-doing, and, hence, a breach of some moral obligation. Now obviously statement 1 and 2 denies that people's direct individual contribution to global warming amounts to wrong-doing.[15] Hence, direct individual contributions cannot be the ground for proper blame. Statement 4 says people can assume responsibility for their individual contributions, and maybe if they have actually done so and have not lived up to this assumed responsibility they may be properly blamed. However, statement 4 leaves open the possibility that nobody actually assumes this individual responsibility and in that case nobody can be reasonably held blameworthy for their direct contribution to global warming as assuming responsibility-as-virtue, at least according to statement 4, is voluntary and not obligatory.

The best ground for possible individual blameworthiness then seems to be the moral obligation expressed in statement 3. Not living up to this responsibility may be said to contribute *indirectly* to global warming. Does this imply that individuals are also blameworthy? Not if they have a proper excuse for the absence of such an agreement. More specifically, it seems conceivable that all individuals have properly discharged their individual responsibility expressed in statement 3 without an effective collective agreement being achieved. One reason why this is possible is that a collective agreement may be achieved that turns out to be ineffective for reasons that could not have been reasonably foreseen. This would be a case of inculpable ignorance and, as we have seen, this is an excusing condition for blameworthiness. This suggests the following:

Statement 5
It is possible that no individual can be reasonably held responsible-as-blameworthy for the failure to achieve a collective agreement to effectively mitigate climate change.

It might be objected to statement 5 that at least some individuals, in particular politicians of those countries that blocked an effective collective agreement, can be blamed for the failure to achieve a collective agreement. However, that does not necessarily make these individuals responsible for the harm that will result from this failure. Seumas Miller writes about this:

> [A]rguably the members of these governments are collectively morally responsible for failing to put in place policies to avert or substantially ameliorate the harm done (or about to be done) by 1990–2010 luxury carbon emissions. However, the members of the governments in questions are not morally responsible for the harm itself; a few thousand politicians did not produce a quantum of luxury carbon emissions sufficient to cause the massive harm in question.
>
> (Miller 2011: 241)

Miller assumes here that the relevant causal condition is whether the members of the governments caused the harm. If we follow our analysis in Chapter 1, however, in case of a failure to live by a responsibility-of-obligation, the relevant causal condition is whether the harm could have been prevented if the responsibility-as-obligation had been lived by. This condition is probably met by the members of governments *collectively*. However, it is not met by the members of governments *individually*; on their own, none of them could have been causally efficacious in bringing about the required collective agreement and in avoiding the harm. This brings us to the following statement:

Statement 6

No individual can be reasonably held responsible-as-blameworthy for the harm that will result from the failure to effectively mitigate climate change to an acceptable degree in the period 2000–2014.

Of course, this result depends on various assumptions. One assumption is that the statements 1, 2, and 3 cover all the relevant moral obligations in this case.[16] Another assumption is that certain moral obligations do not exist for individuals, as worded in statement 1 and 2. The strongest assumption is here the one worded in statement 2. This statement has, as we have seen, been defended in detail by both Sinnott-Armstrong and Johnson. We think, however, that 6 might be established even if statement 2 is false. One reason is the failure to curb one's emissions can make an individual blameworthy for the harm from one's own emissions, but not for the harm from the emissions of others and statement 6 refers to the harm done by the aggregate of all emissions. More generally, wrong-doing, the condition for responsibility-as-blameworthiness to which statement 2 refers, is only one of the conditions for responsibility-as-blameworthiness. As we have seen also the four other conditions (capacity, causality, knowledge and freedom) have to apply. Whereas capacity is usually not at issue in debates about

88 *Ibo van de Poel*

responsibility for climate change, each of the other conditions has been mentioned by at least some philosophers as a possible reason why citizens cannot reasonably be held responsible-as-blameworthy for the harm done by climate change.

2.6.5 The Problem of Many Hands for Climate Change

From statement 1 in section 2.6.4 and what we said about collective responsibility-as-obligation in section 2.6.2, it follows that the problem of many hands occurs with respect to the responsibility-as-obligation to see to it that climate change is mitigated to an acceptable degree in the period 2000–2014.

Is the occurrence of this problem of many hands also problematic? A first thing to note is that our analysis shows that there is not a complete disconnect between individual responsibility-as-obligation and collective responsibility-as-obligation. Individuals, and in particular politicians and members of government, still have the responsibility-as-obligation to see that it that effective collective agreements are achieved (statement 3 in section 2.6.4).

Still the problem of many hands frustrates the effective mitigation of global warming. It does so because the absence of a collective agreement also results in the absence of individual moral duties to restrain one's greenhouse gas emission (statement 2 in section 2.6.4). This means that as long as the collective responsibility-as-obligation to mitigate global warming is not translated into individual responsibilities and duties, global warming will not be effectively abated. What is needed then is a way to distribute the collective responsibilities over individuals. David Miller (2009) has discussed principles that would help to achieve such a distribution. In Chapter 5, we will be looking for a procedural solution to achieve a fair distribution of responsibilities-as-obligation in cases where the problem of many hands occurs, or is likely to occur, with respect to responsibility-as-obligation.

Let us now look at responsibility-as-blameworthiness. From statement 6 in section 2.6.4 and what we said about collective responsibility-as-blameworthiness in section 2.6.2, it follows that the problem of many hands occurs with respect to the responsibility-as-blameworthiness for the harm that will result from the failure to effectively mitigate climate change to an acceptable degree in the period 2000–2014.

Again the question may be asked whether this is a problem. The problem of many hands with respect to the responsibility-as-blameworthiness may result in failure to achieve the end of retribution (see Table 2.1). Future generations may blame the world population collectively, but no individuals can be blamed. This may be considered problematic for two reasons. First, if serious and avoidable harm is done, retribution is often considered desirable. However, blaming the world population as a whole seems rather meaningless given the very different causal and institutional roles played by various individuals. So for real retribution, individual responsibility seems important. Second, in as far as (potential) blame is considered an important

The Problem of Many Hands 89

motive for avoiding harm, lack of retribution also frustrates the aim of avoiding harm in the future.

2.7 CONCLUSIONS

We have characterised the problem of many hands (PMH) as a gap between individual and collective responsibility for a certain φ. In doing so, we have understood responsibility as having the same meaning on both the individual and collective level, leading to different varieties of the PMH, for example the PMH with respect to responsibility-as-blameworthiness.

In this chapter we have also investigated the conditions under which collectives can bear responsibility. To this end we have distinguished three types of collectives: organised groups, joint actions, and occasional collections of individuals. For each case, we gave an illustration of the PMH. We recognise that attributing responsibility in an individual case is always somewhat debatable and potentially controversial. Still, we think the examples we gave are convincing enough to see that the PMH might occur in all three kinds of collectives we have distinguished.

On a more general level, the examples suggest two more general lessons with respect to the PMH. First, we saw that the PMH does not (necessarily) imply a complete disconnect between individual and collective responsibility. In the examples, the individuals were still responsible for something, but they were not responsible for the φ for which the collective was responsible. As we have also seen, the PMH does not contradict the analysis of collective responsibility in terms of individual responsibility, as worded in what we called the reducability thesis (RT). The PMH only contradicts a strong version of the reducability thesis (SRT) that poses that if a collective is responsible for φ, each member of hat collective is also responsible for φ.

Second, the example suggests that the gap between individual and collective responsibility is brought about by the fact that the conditions for responsibility have a different meaning at the individual and collective level. Although there is a relation between the conditions at the individual and collective level, this relation is not a matter of simple aggregation. A collective might know things that none of the individuals in the collective knows, and might be free to do things that none of the individuals in the collective is free to do.

NOTES

1. Davis (2012: 14) makes a distinction between responsibility-as-simple-causation, responsibility-as-fault-causation, and responsibility-as-good-causation that might perhaps be helpful here.
2. Cf. what French calls the Corporate Internal Decision Structure (French 1984: Chapter 4).

90   *Ibo van de Poel*

3. We do not want to embrace methodological individualism here but only want to point out that our account is not at odds with it.

4. http://en.wikipedia.org/wiki/United_Airlines_Flight_93. Accessed 5 September 2012.

5. Based on (Morgenstern 1995; Kremer 2002) and the Online Ethics Center for Engineering and Science at Case Western University (http://temp.onlineethics. org/moral/lemessurier/index.html; accessed 17 December 2007).

6. There was in fact a third factor: people from LeMessurier's team defined the diagonal wind braces as trusses instead of columns so that no safety factor applied. The result was a smaller number of joints, which increased the structural deficiency. We leave this out because the building would also have been structurally deficient without this mistake; although the probability of failure would probably have been lower than once every sixteen years, it would still have been unacceptably high.

7. The building was designed with an electric damper that, if functioning, would reduce the probability of failure to once every 55 years. That damper might, however, fail, due to a power failure during a heavy storm.

8. It should be noted that Sinnott-Armstrong is not arguing that usual things are necessarily morally acceptable; rather, he thinks that they cannot qualify as cause. Sinnott-Amstrong's contrast between usual and unusual events is closely related to Mackie's notion of causal field (Mackie 1980: 35) and with the distinction between abnormal and normal conditions of Hart and Honoré (Hart and Honoré 1985: 33).

9. Again, this seems best understood as an argument about causality rather than about what is moral or immoral. Nevertheless, the argument clearly raises issues about moral obligations in a tragedy of the commons, a topic that will be discussed below.

10. This does not necessarily free individuals from moral responsibility, as Miller notes. He believes, nevertheless, that it frees some of the earlier emitters from their moral responsibility (Miller 2009: 132–133).

11. According to an even more recent Rasmussen Report, the percentage blaming planetary trends is up to 47% in December 2010. See: http://www. rasmussenreports.com/public_content/politics/current_events/environment_ energy/41_now_say_global_warming_is_caused_by_human_activity_more_ say_planetary_trends. Accessed 4 February 2011.

12. The first two of these obligation are probably best seen as responsibilities rather than duties because they do not necessarily require an action by the individual citizen to obtain the effect, although citizens do have supervisory duties to see to it that the effect is obtained and to take action if this is not the case.

13. Of course, this would then create individual moral obligations to coordinate efforts, but these seem to already be covered by the moral obligation stated in 2.

14. This statement refers to what we called responsibility 4 and 5 in section 2.6.3.

15. Here we are assuming that there is no effective collective agreement in place. Cf. our discussion in section 2.6.3.

16. Vanderheiden (2011) suggests that the wrong-doing consists in participation in a culture that permits or even encourages consumption patterns that directly contribute to global warming. Moreover, all citizens—even those who actively oppose current government policies—benefit from the consumption patterns, and hence, on his account, all citizens are therefore responsible although not necessarily to the same degree. Following David Miller (2004), Vanderheiden suggests that the only sincere opposition that would excuse a citizen from responsibility is to refuse the benefits of

The Problem of Many Hands 91

society's harmful practices. However, David Miller himself has suggested that his 2004 argument does not apply to the case of climate change because climate change is different in terms of knowledge and causality (cf. Miller 2009: 129–133).

REFERENCES

Arrow, K.J. 1950. "A difficulty in the concept of social welfare." *Journal of Political Economy* 58(4): 328–346.
Bovens, M. 1998. *The quest for responsibility. Accountability and citizenship in complex organisations*. Cambridge: Cambridge University Press.
Braham, M., and M. van Hees. 2012. "An anatomy of moral responsibility." *Mind* 121(483): 601–634.
Bratman, M. 1999. *Faces of intention : selected essays on intention and agency*. Cambridge, U.K. ; New York: Cambridge University Press.
Bucciarelli, L.L. 1994. *Designing engineers*. Cambridge, MA: MIT Press.
Caney, S. 2005. "Cosmopolitan justice, responsibility, and climate change." *Leiden Journal of International Law* 18: 747–775.
Copp, D. 2007. "The collective moral autonomy thesis." *Journal of Social Philosophy* 38(3): 369–388.
Davis, M. 2012. ""Ain't no one here but us social forces": Constructing the professional responsibility of engineers." *Science and Engineering Ethics* 18(1): 13–34.
Feinberg, J. 1968. "Collective responsibility." *Journal of Philosophy* 65(21): 674–688.
French, P.A. 1984. *Collective and corporate responsibility*. New York: Columbia University Press.
French, P.A. 1998. *Individual and collective responsibility*. 2nd ed. Rochester, VT.: Schenkman Books.
Gilbert, M. 1989. *On social facts*. London; New York: Routledge.
Harris, Ch.E., M.S. Pritchard, and M.J. Rabins. 2008. *Engineering ethics. Concepts and cases*. 4th ed. Belmont, CA: Wadsworth.
Hart, H.L.A., and T. Honoré. 1985. *Causation in the law*. 2nd ed. Oxford: Oxford University Press.
Held, V. 1970. "Can a random collection of individuals be responsible?" *Journal of Philosophy* 67(14): 471–481.
Hindriks, F. 2008. "The freedom of collective agents." *Journal of Political Philosophy* 16(2): 165–183.
Hindriks, F. 2009. "Corporate responsibility and judgement aggregation." *Economics and Philosophy* 25(2): 161–177.
Jamieson, D. 2010. "Climate change, responsibility, and justice." *Science and Engineering Ethics* 16(3): 431–445.
Johnson, B.L. 2003. "Ethical obligations in a tragedy of the commons." *Environmental Values* 12(3): 271–287.
Kremer, E. 2002. "(Re)examining the Citicorp Case: ethical paragon or chimera." *Practice* 6(2): 269–276.
Kutz, Ch. 2000. *Complicity: Ethics and law for a collective age*. Cambridge: Cambridge University Press.
List, Ch, and Ph. Pettit. 2002. "Aggregating sets of judgments: An impossibility result." *Economics and Philosophy* 18(1): 89–110
Mackie, J.L. 1980. *The cement of the universe. A study of causation*. Oxford: Oxford Univeristy Press.
Martin, M.W., and R. Schinzinger. 2005. *Ethics in engineering*. 4th ed. Boston: McGraw-Hill.

92 Ibo van de Poel

May, L. 1987. *The morality of groups: Collective responsibility, group-based harm, and corporate rights.* Notre Dame, IN: University of Notre Dame Press.

May, L. 1992. *Sharing responsibility.* Chicago: University of Chicago Press.

Miller, D. 2004. "Holding Nations Responsible." *Ethics* 114(2): 240–268.

Miller, D. 2009. "Global justice and climate change: How should responsibilities be distributed?" *The Tanner Lectures on Human Values* 28: 117–156.

Miller, S. 2007. "Against the collective moral autonomy thesis." *Journal of Social Philosophy* 38(3): 389–409.

Miller, S. 2010. *The moral foundations of social institutions: A philosophical study.* New York: Cambridge University Press.

Miller, S. 2011. "Collective responsibility, epistemic action and climate change." In *Moral responsibility*, edited by N.A. Vincent, I.R. van de Poel and J. Hoven, 219–245. Dordrecht: Springer.

Morgenstern, J. 1995. "The fifty-nine-story crisis." *The New Yorker* (May 29): 45–53.

Nihlen Fahlquist, J. 2009. "Moral responsibility for environmental problems— Individual or institutional?" *Journal of Agricultural and Environmental Ethics* 22(2): 109–124.

Nissenbaum, H. 1996. "Accountability in a computerized society." *Science and Engineering Ethics* 2(1): 25–42.

Pettit, Ph. 2007. "Responsibility incorporated." *Ethics* 117(2): 171–201.

Pritchard, M.S. 2001. "Responsible engineering: The importance of character and imagination." *Science and Engineering Ethics* 7(3): 309–402.

Searle, J.R. 1995. *The construction of social reality.* New York: Free Press.

Sen, A.K. 1970. *Collective choice and social welfare.* Edinburg: Oliver & Boyd.

Shue, H. 1993. "Subsistence emissions and luxury emissions." *Law & Policy* 15(1): 39–60.

Sinnott-Armstrong, W. 2005. "It's not my fault: Global warming and individual moral obligations." In *Perspectives on climate change science, economics, politics, ethics*, edited by W. Sinnott-Armstrong and R.B. Howarth, 285–307. Amsterdam: Elsevier/JAI.

Stern, N. 2006. *Stern review on the economics of climate change.* London: HM Treasury. (http://mudancasclimaticas.cptec.inpe.br/~rmclima/pdfs/destaques/sternreview_report_complete.pdf)

Thompson, D.F. 1980. "Moral responsibility and public officials: The problem of many hands." *American Political Science Review* 74(4): 905–916.

Tuomela, R., and K. Miller. 1988. "We-intentions." *Philosophical Studies* 53(3): 367–389.

United Nations. 1992. United Nations framework convention on climate change. (http://unfccc.int/resource/docs/convkp/conveng.pdf)

United Nations. 1998. Kyoto protocol to the United Nations framework convention on climate change. (http://unfccc.int/resource/docs/convkp/kpeng.pdf)

Vanderheiden, S. 2011. "Climate change and collective responsibility." In *Moral responsibility*, edited by N.A. Vincent, I.R. van de Poel, and J. Hoven, 201–218. Dordrecht: Springer Netherlands.

Wagenaar, W.A., and J. Groenewegen. 1987. "Accidents at sea: Multiple causes and impossible consequences." *International Journal of Man-Machine Studies* 27(5–6): 587–598.

Whitbeck, C. 1998. *Ethics in engineering practice and research.* Cambridge: Cambridge University Press.

3 A Formalisation of Moral Responsibility and the Problem of Many Hands

Tiago de Lima and Lambèr Royakkers

3.1 INTRODUCTION

Chapter 1 has listed several different meanings for the term 'responsibility'. For example, when we say that someone is responsible for a consequence φ, it may mean that one is 'accountable' for φ, or that one is 'blameworthy' for φ, or, that one has the 'obligation to see to it that' φ. As we have also seen, the application of these various meanings of responsibility depends on more basic concepts, such as moral agency, causality, wrong-doing, freedom, and knowledge. For instance, an individual i is accountable for φ if i is capable to act as a moral agent, behaves in a way that is not morally acceptable (i.e., does something wrong) and this behaviour causes φ. In addition, i is blameworthy for φ if i is accountable for φ, knows (or could know) that φ would be the case, and acts freely, i.e., i can chose to behave differently, and this different behaviour avoids φ.[1] Finally, i has the obligation to see to it that φ if i has the obligation that φ and i must ensure the occurrence of φ.

These different meanings of responsibility are classified in two categories. Accountability and blameworthiness are 'backward-looking responsibilities', i.e., responsibilities regarding the past, whereas 'obligation to see to it that' is a 'forward-looking responsibility', i.e., a responsibility regarding the future. Chapter 1 also argues that these three notions are related. Roughly, if an individual i has the obligation to see to it that φ but does not obtain φ, then i is accountable for $\neg\varphi$ and, if i does not provide a satisfactory account for $\neg\varphi$, then i is blameworthy for $\neg\varphi$.

In the present chapter, we propose a formalisation of the main ideas in Chapters 1 and 2. Using the basic concepts upon which the meanings of responsibility are defined, we construct a logic which enables to express sentences like 'individual i is accountable for φ', 'individual i is blameworthy for φ' and 'individual i has the obligation to see to it that φ'. Such effort contributes to the discussion about responsibility in at least two ways. First, it clarifies the definitions and also their differences and similarities. Second, it assesses the consistency of formalisation of responsibility, not only by showing that definitions are not inconsistent, but also by providing a formal demonstration of the relation between the three main meanings of responsibility argued for in Chapter 1. Moreover, the formal account can be used to derive new properties of the concepts, thus, giving new insights that can be used to advance the discussion. And finally, the formalism proposed here provides a framework wherein criteria for ascribing responsibilities can be stated and, if individuals are to be held responsible for outcomes, then, at least, justifications can be made clear.

Another aim in this chapter is to provide a formal tool that can help to detect the possible occurrence of the PMH. For that, we build up a logic for reasoning about collective and individual responsibility. This logic extends the Coalition Epistemic Dynamic Logic (CEDL). We add a notion of group knowledge, generalise the definitions of individual responsibility to groups of agents, and give a formal definition for the PMH. The PMH has primarily been studied in the context of organised agency. That is, the individuals involved are supposed to know their roles and be able to cooperate. Therefore, to address the PMH, we here focus the attention on situations where the set of individuals involved forms an 'organisation'. To that end, we extend CEDL again by adding organisational structures to its semantics. These structures define the power and coordination links between agents, which define how agents delegate tasks and communicate in the context of an organisation.

The rest of the chapter is organised as follows. In the next section we build up our logical framework. Then, in section 3.3, we propose a formalisation of the two kinds of responsibility discussed above: forward-looking and backward-looking responsibility. Section 3.4 presents the PMH in organisations, defines organisational structures and organisational actions, and presents an example of the application of the logic. After that, in section 3.5, we present some related work and compare them with the present approach. The last section draws conclusions and discusses possible future work.

3.2   THE FORMAL FRAMEWORK

In this section we present a logic that will be the basis of our formalisation of individual responsibility. This logic is a variation of the coalition epistemic dynamic logic (CEDL) presented in De Lima *et al.* (2010), which, in turn, is an extension of the well-known propositional dynamic logic (PDL) (Harel *et al.* 1984). PDL is a classical propositional logic augmented with modal operators '$[a]$'. A formula of the form $[a]\varphi$ means 'after every possible occurrence of event a, the consequence φ is true'. Thus, it permits expression of what consequences are caused by the occurrence of some given event a, where such events can be actions executed by one agent, actions executed by several agents, exogenous events or even programs. But because PDL does not have agents in its language, it does not enable expression of what consequences are caused by which agents of the scenario. To be able to express agent causality, CEDL extends it by actions that are 'enacted' by agents, in a similar way as done, e.g., by Royakkers (1998) and Wieringa and Meyer (1993) and also more recently by Herzig and Lorini (2010) and Lorini (2010). In CEDL, one can write formulae of the form $[(i, a)]\varphi$, meaning 'after every possible occurrence of event (i, a), the consequence φ is true', where the event (i, a) is the action a executed by agent i. Moreover, to be able to express agent knowledge, CEDL has modal operators K_i, in a similar way as done, e.g., by Grossi *et al.* (2007) and Herzig et al. (2000). In CEDL, one can also write formulae of the form $K_i\varphi$, meaning 'agent i knows that φ'.

The resultant formalism is a logic presenting some of the properties of PDL and epistemic logic (Fagin *et al.* 1995). In addition, because the actions of CEDL are enacted by agents, it is possible to define operators expressing agent abilities and agent obligations. It turns out that these operators are similar to the ones in coalition logic (Pauly 2001, 2001), alternating-time temporal logic (Alur 2002), and alternating-time temporal epistemic logic (Van der Hoek and Wooldridge 2003). The obligation operators are also similar to the ones in dynamic deontic logic (D'Altan *et al.* 1996, Meyer 1988, Meyer and Wieringa 1993). Therefore, CEDL constitutes a very expressive framework where one can express actions, knowledge, abilities, and obligations all at once.

The remainder of this section is organised as follows. The next section presents the models used to give semantics to CEDL. Then, section 3.2.2 presents CEDL language, its interpretation on the models and its complete axiomatisation. After that, section 3.2.4 defines operators enabling expression of agent abilities. And finally, section 3.2.5 defines operators enabling expression of agents obligations.

3.2.1 Models

The mathematical structures defined in this section aim at modelling environments inhabited by one or more entities called agents. These agents are able to execute actions in order to change the environment. These include epistemic actions, i.e., actions that change the knowledge of the environment of the agents, such as sensing actions, communication actions, etc., and also physical actions, i.e., actions that change the environment, such as toggling light switches, opening and closing doors, etc. The idea is to be able to describe scenarios where one may want to ascribe responsibilities to agents or simply want to verify whether agents are responsible or not for consequences. Then, ideally, these structures should be rich enough to express the important concepts that define the various conditions of responsibility discussed in Chapter 1, namely, moral agency, causality, wrong-doing, freedom, and knowledge. However, as the name suggests, these structures are meant to 'model' the reality and not to copy it. Hence, some simplifications are made. This means that the scenarios considered here include several underlying assumptions. Some of these assumptions are made because we consider them intuitive, thus, leading to a more correct framework. Some of them are made simply because we are not able to do otherwise. All along the presentation, and whenever we think it is necessary, we point out the assumptions made and their reasons. We believe that the simplifying assumptions are reasonable restrictions as a first approximation and do not form an insurmountable hindrance for our framework to be elaborated into a more realistic analysis of the real-world situations at which we aiming.

A model is defined for a given vocabulary, which consists of a triple of disjoint set $\langle P, N, A \rangle$ where:

- P is a countable (possibly infinite) set of propositional variables denoting propositional facts;
- N is a finite set of labels denoting agents; and
- A is a finite set of labels denoting the actions available for the agents.

We use Δ to denote the set of all joint actions available for the agents in N, which is defined as the set of all total functions δ with signature $N \to A$. In other words, $\Delta = \{\delta_1, \delta_2, \ldots\}$, where each δ_j is a set of pairs of the form $\{(i_1, a_1), (i_2, a_2), \ldots, (i_{|N|}, a_{|N|})\}$ (one pair for each agent in N) and where $i_m \in N$ and $a_m \in A$ for $1 \leq m \leq |N|$.

CEDL models are a specific kind of Kripke models, which consist of directed labelled graphs structures, where nodes represent possible worlds and relations between worlds represent (in our case) either *indistinguishability relations* or transitions. The indistinguishability relation for agent i represents the knowledge of i: the more worlds are indistinguishable for i, the less agent i knows about the scenario. The transition relation for some action δ represents the outcomes of δ: if w_1 is in the transition relation of δ with w_0 then it means that the occurrence of δ at w_0 leads to w_1. A graphical representation of such models is displayed in Figure 3.1.

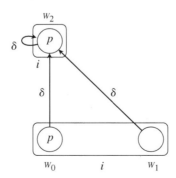

Figure 3.1 A graphic representation of a CEDL model. (Circles represent possible worlds, arrows represent transitions and rectangles enclose worlds that belong to the same indistinguishability relation.)

In such a structure, each possible world is labelled with a set of propositional variables from P, each indistinguishability relation is labelled with an agent from N, and each transition is labelled with a joint action from Δ. For example, consider the model in Figure 3.1. The propositional variable p is present in the label of w_0 and w_2 but it is not present in the label of w_1. This means that the propositional fact represented by p is true at w_0 and w_2, but it is false at w_1. Moreover, the indistinguishability relation between w_0 and w_1 is labelled with agent i, meaning that agent i cannot distinguish between these two worlds. Thus in our example, if w_0 (or w_1) is the actual world, then i considers it possible that either w_0 or w_1 is the actual world. This means that, if w_0 (or w_1) is the actual world, then i does not know whether the fact represented by p is true or false. And finally, the transition between w_0 and w_2 is labelled with joint action δ, meaning that the occurrence of δ at w_0 leads to w_2.

The formal definition is as follows. Let the vocabulary $\langle P, N, A \rangle$ be given, a CEDL model is a quadruple $\langle W, \mathcal{K}, \mathcal{T}, \mathcal{V} \rangle$, where:

- W is a non-empty set of possible worlds;
- $\mathcal{K}$ is a function with signature $N \to (W \times W)$, defining, for each agent $i \in N$, an equivalence relation between possible worlds, which represents the knowledge of agent i;
- $\mathcal{T}$ is a function with signature $\Delta \to (W \times W)$, defining, for each joint action $\delta \in \Delta$, a relation between possible worlds, which represents the transition associated to the joint action δ; and
- $\mathcal{V}$ is a function with signature $P \to 2^W$, defining, for each $p \in P$, the interpretation of the propositional variable p in the model.

To simplify notation, we sometimes write $\mathcal{K}_i$ instead of $\mathcal{K}(i)$, and also use $\mathcal{K}_i(w)$ to denote the set of worlds that i considers possible at w. That is, $\mathcal{K}_i(w)$ abbreviates the set $\{w' : (w, w') \in \mathcal{K}(i)\}$. Analogously, we sometimes write $\mathcal{T}_\delta$ instead of $\mathcal{T}(\delta)$, and also use $\mathcal{T}_\delta(w)$ to denote the set of possible outcomes of the occurrence of δ at w. That is $\mathcal{T}_\delta(w)$, abbreviates the set $\{w' : (w, w') \in \mathcal{T}(\delta)\}$.

Some assumptions are implicit in the definition of CEDL models. For instance, every relation K_i is an equivalence relation, i.e., they are all reflexive, transitive, and Euclidean. These are standard assumptions when modelling the knowledge of agents. Without entering into details, we just mention that they will enforce the following properties on our formalism:

- Truth: if agent i knows that φ is true, then φ is true;
- Positive introspection: if agent i knows that φ is true, then i knows that i knows that φ is true; and
- Negative introspection: if agent i does not know that φ is true, then i knows that i does not know that φ is true.

98 Tiago de Lima and Lambèr Royakkers

Negative introspection, for instance, rules out what is called ignorance, or unknown unknowns, which is a rather strong assumption to be made for human beings, but which does not seem to impair our analysis of the basic mechanisms at work in responsibility related issues and the problem of many hands.

Even with a small vocabulary, structures respecting the definition above can model many different scenarios. Some of them are interesting, but some may be considered strange, if not useless. For instance, the definition above does not forbid structures where, for some possible world $w \in W$ and for all $\delta \in \Delta$, we have $\mathcal{T}_\delta(w) = \varnothing$. This is considered a strange structure, because, in such possible world, no action is possible. In other words, in such a possible world, agents cannot act at all. We consider here that an action is every behaviour that takes time. This means that even 'doing nothing' is an action. In fact, this is a special kind of action that does not change anything, but that has an outcome and therefore has a non-empty transition leading to a possible world: one which has the same label as the possible world where such action is executed. We then arrive at the conclusion that there is always some action available for the agents in every possible world. Therefore, we impose the following constraint to CEDL models:

(C1) for all $w \in W$ there is $\delta \in \Delta$ such that $\mathcal{T}_\delta(w) \neq \varnothing$.

Constraint C1 is called 'activity'. It stipulates that, at all possible worlds of the model, there is at least one non-empty transition which is labelled by some joint action in Δ. In other words, at any moment, there is at least one executable action for each agent, which prevents those strange structures mentioned earlier from being CEDL models.

There is yet another constraint imposed to CEDL models:

(C2) for all $w \in W$, all $i \in N$, and all $\delta \in \Delta$,
we have $(\mathcal{T}_\delta \circ \mathcal{K}_i)(w) \subseteq (\mathcal{K}_i \circ \mathcal{T}_\delta)(w)$.

This constraint corresponds to 'no-forgetting' in Herzig *et al.* (2000) and 'perfect recall' in Fagin *et al.* (1995). It defines an interaction between accessibility relations and transitions. With this constraint, the knowledge of an agent either increases or stays the same, after the execution of any action. This means that agents never lose information, i.e., once an agent knows something, this agent will never forget it. This is obviously very restrictive but, at the same time, useful. For instance, it avoids to consider models where agents may keep losing information for whatever reason. Such possibility would make much more difficult (if not impossible) to derive some interesting properties of our formalism. We also note that, because each $\mathcal{K}_i$ is an equivalence relation, constraint C2 implies that action occurrences are perceived by all agents. The latter implies that the agents perceive the passage of time.

A Formalisation of Responsibility 99

For example, the structure in Figure 3.1 respects both C1 and C2. The first is respected because, for all possible worlds w, there is at least one transition from w to some possible world. The second is respected because the equivalent classes of the accessibility relation $\mathcal{K}_i$ does not increase its size when we follow a transition from one possible world to another.

3.2.2 Syntax and Semantics of CEDL

Let the vocabulary $\langle P, N, A \rangle$ be given, the language of CEDL is the smallest set $\mathcal{L}$ which satisfies the following conditions:

- $\top \in \mathcal{L}$;
- if $p \in P$ then $p \in \mathcal{L}$;
- if $\varphi \in \mathcal{L}$ then $\neg\varphi \in \mathcal{L}$;
- if $\varphi \in \mathcal{L}$ and $\psi \in \mathcal{L}$ then $\varphi \wedge \psi \in \mathcal{L}$;
- if $i \in N$ and $\varphi \in \mathcal{L}$ then $K_i\varphi \in \mathcal{L}$;
- if $\delta \in \Delta$, $G \subseteq N$ and $\varphi \in \mathcal{L}$ then $[\delta|_G]\varphi \in \mathcal{L}$,

where $\delta|_G$ is δ, but with its domain restricted to G, i.e., let δ be the joint action $\{(i_1, a_1), (i_2, a_2), \ldots, (i_{|N|}, a_{|N|})\}$, then $\delta|_G$ is the partial joint action formed by the set of pairs $\{(i_m, a_m): (i_m, a_m) \in \delta$ and $i_m \in G\}$.

In what follows, the common abbreviations for the operators $\vee$, $\rightarrow$ and $\leftrightarrow$ are also used, the symbol $\perp$ (contradiction) abbreviates $\neg\top$, and, to simplify notation, we sometimes write $[i_1: a_1, \ldots, i_n: a_n]\varphi$ instead of $[\{(i_1, a_1), \ldots, (i_n, a_n)\}]\varphi$. Moreover, as Δ, N and 2^N are finite sets, existential and universal quantification over these sets abbreviate disjunctions and conjunctions, respectively.

The meaning of formulae of the form $K_i\varphi$ is, as usual: 'agent i knows that φ'. The meaning of a partial joint action of the form $\{(i_1, a_1), (i_2, a_2), \ldots, (i_n, a_n)\}$ is: 'the agents in $\{i_1, \ldots, i_n\}$ execute their corresponding actions in $\{a_1, \ldots, a_n\}$ simultaneously (and we do not consider what the other agents do at the same time)'. And the meaning of formulae of the form $[\delta|_G]\varphi$ is: 'after every possible occurrence of $\delta|_G$, φ is true'. Furthermore, $\langle[\delta|_G]\rangle\varphi$ abbreviates $\neg[\delta|_G]\neg\varphi$.

To match their meanings, formulae from $\mathcal{L}$ are interpreted using 'pointed CEDL models'. The latter are pairs of the form $\langle M, w \rangle$, where $M = \langle W, \mathcal{K}, \mathcal{T}, \mathcal{V} \rangle$ is a CEDL model and $w \in W$. Then, the semantic interpretation of Boolean operators is the usual one. For formulae of the form $K_i\varphi$ we use the accessibility relation labelled with i: $K_i\varphi$ is true at the world w if and only if φ is true at all possible worlds w' accessible from w via the accessibility relation labelled with i, i.e., it is true if and only if φ is true at all worlds that the agent i considers possible at w. The interpretation of operators $[\delta|_G]$ is more complex. A formula of the form $[\delta|_G]\varphi$ is true at the world w if and only if φ is true at all possible worlds w' that are attained from w via some transition in $\mathcal{T}$ which is labelled with $\delta|_G \cup \delta'|_{N \setminus G}$. In other words, to verify whether $[\delta|_G]\varphi$ is true at some possible world w, we must verify whether φ

is true at all worlds w' belonging to $\mathcal{T}_{\delta'}(w)$ for all $\delta' \in \Delta$, provided that the restriction of δ' to G is equal to the restriction of δ to G, i.e., provided that $\delta'|_G = \delta|_G$. That is, we must verify whether φ is true at all G transitions from w no matter what the agents outside the group do.

Formally, the satisfaction relation $\models$, between pointed CEDL models and formulae from $\mathcal{L}$, is inductively defined as follows:

$M, w \models \top$
$M, w \models p$ iff $w \in V(p)$
$M, w \models \neg \varphi$ iff $M, w \not\models \varphi$
$M, w \models \varphi \wedge \psi$ iff $M, w \models \varphi$ and $M, w \models \psi$
$M, w \models K_i \varphi$ iff   for all $w' \in \mathcal{K}(i)(w)$ we have $M, w' \models \varphi$
$M, w \models [\delta|_G]\varphi$ iff   for all $\delta' \in \Delta$ and all $w' \in \mathcal{T}_{\delta|_G \cup \delta'|_{N\setminus G}}(w)$ we have $M, w' \models \varphi$

We note that $\delta|_G \cup \delta'|_{N\setminus G}$ is a set of pairs belonging to Δ. Thus, $\mathcal{T}_{\delta|_G \cup \delta'|_{N\setminus G}}$ is defined for all $w \in W$. As usual, a formula φ is valid (notation: $\models \varphi$) if and only if every pointed CEDL model $\langle M, w \rangle$ satisfies φ.

Example 1 (Light Bulb and Light Switch)

To better explain the definitions given so far, we now use a scenario that we call 'light bulb and light switch'. This scenario is inhabited by two agents: Alice (agent a) and Betty (agent b). They live in a strange house: its interior is illuminated by a light bulb, but the corresponding switch is located outside the house. In this scenario, Alice is inside the house and Betty is outside it, close to the switch. Thus, Alice can see whether the light bulb is on (p)

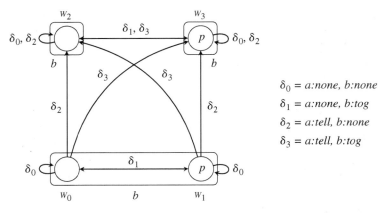

Figure 3.2 A CEDL model for the Light Bulb and Light Switch scenario. (The rectangles represent Betty's knowledge. To simplify the picture, Alice's knowledge is not represented. She has complete knowledge of the scenario, i.e., $\mathcal{K}_a(w) = \{w\}$ for all $w \in W$.)

or off (¬p) and tell (or rather shout) it to Betty (action tell*), but she cannot toggle the switch. Betty, on the other hand, can toggle the switch (action* tog*), but she cannot see whether the light is on or off. If she toggles the switch with the light on, it will turn off, and if she toggles it with the light off, it will turn on. Let the vocabulary be* $\langle P, N, A \rangle$*, where* $P = \{p\}$*,* $N = \{a, b\}$ *and* $A = \{none, tell, tog\}$*. A CEDL model for this scenario can be given by the structure in Figure 3.2.*

We assume that the light bulb is off, i.e., the actual world is w_0. We then use the definition of $\vDash$ to verify truth of some formulae in the pointed CEDL model $\langle M, w_0 \rangle$:

- $M, w_0 \vDash \neg p$.
  In words, the light is off. This is true because $w_0 \notin \mathcal{V}(p)$, i.e., p is not in the label of w_0.
- $M, w_0 \vDash K_a \neg p$.
  In words, Alice knows that the light is off. This is true because $M, w \vDash \neg p$ for all $w \in \mathcal{K}_a(w_0)$. (Recall that $\mathcal{K}_a(w) = \{w\}$.)
- $M, w_0 \vDash \neg K_b p \wedge \neg K_b \neg p$.
  Betty does not know whether the light is on or off. This is true because, there is a possible world that Betty considers possible (namely w_0) where the light is off and there is a possible world that Betty considers possible (namely w_1) where the light is on.
- $M, w_0 \vDash [a: none, b: tog]p$.
  After the parallel execution of Alice doing noting and Betty toggling the switch, the light is on. This is true because, first, $\delta_1 = a$: *none*, b: *tog*. Second, $N = \{a, b\}$, thus, for all $\delta' \in \Delta$, we have $\delta'|_{N \setminus \{a, b\}} = \delta'|_\emptyset = \emptyset$. Then, $\delta_1|_{\{a, b\}} \cup \delta' = \delta_1$, which means that $\mathcal{T}_{\delta_1|_{\{a, b\}} \cup \delta'|_{N \setminus \{a, b\}}}(w_0) = \mathcal{T}_{\delta 1}(w_0) = \{w_1\}$, for all $\delta' \in \Delta$, and finally, $M, w_1 \vDash p$.
- $M, w_0 \vDash [a: tell, b: tog]p$.
  After the parallel execution of Alice telling whether the light is on or off and Betty toggling the switch, the light is on. Similarly as before, we have that $\delta_3 = a$: *tell*, b: *tog* and $\mathcal{T}_{\delta_3|_{\{a, b\}} \cup \delta'|_{N \setminus \{a, b\}}}(w_0) = \mathcal{T}_{\delta_3}(w_0) = \{w_3\}$, for all $\delta' \in \Delta$, and also $M, w_3 \vDash p$.
- $M, w_0 \vDash [b: tog]p$.
  After Betty toggling the switch, the light is on. (Note that here we consider only the action executed by Betty.) This is true if and only if, for every action that Alice can execute at the same time as Betty, after its parallel execution with Betty's action *tog*, the light is on. We have just verified, in the two preceding items, that if Alice does nothing this is indeed the case, as well as if Alice tells Betty whether the light bulb is on or off. But these are the only two options Alice has. Therefore, the sentence 'after Betty toggling the switch, the light is on' is true. More formally, note that $\delta_1|_{\{b\}} = b$: *tog* and also $\delta_3|_{\{b\}} = b$: *tog*. Then, we just have to verify that $M, w_0 \vDash [\delta_1]p$ and also $M, w_0 \vDash [\delta_3]p$. But, this is what has been done in the two preceding items.

102 *Tiago de Lima and Lambèr Royakkers*

- $M, w_0 \vDash \neg[b: tog]\bot$.

  It is not the case that, after Betty toggling the switch, we have a contradiction. Because the formula $\bot$ is false in any possible world (by definition), then the latter sentence is equivalent to: 'it is not the case that the execution of Betty toggling the switch is not possible'. So, 'Betty is able to toggle the switch'. To show that it is true, we have to verify that $M, w_0 \vDash \neg[\delta_1]\bot$ or $M, w_0 \vDash \neg[\delta_3]\bot$. Both are the case, because $M, w \vDash \neg\bot$ for all $w \in W$ (by definition).

- $M, w_0 \vDash \neg[a: tell]K_b\neg p$.

  In words, it is not the case that after Alice telling whether the light bulb is on or off to Betty, she knows that the light is off. This is the case because the construction 'a:$tell$' does not pay attention to what Betty does at the same time. Then, it may be the case that, at the same time as Alice tells Betty that the light bulb is on, Betty toggles the switch. And, after such parallel execution, the light will actually be on. Therefore, it is not possible for Betty to know that this is off. (Note that it uses the assumption that agents cannot know false statements.) Indeed, we have that $M, w_0 \nvDash [a: tell, b: tog]K_b\neg p$. To show it, we first note that $\delta_3 = a$: $tell$, b: tog. Moreover, $\mathcal{T}_{\delta_3}(w_0) = \{w_3\}$. And also, $M, w_3 \vDash \neg K_b\neg p$. The latter is the case because $\mathcal{K}_b(w_3) = \{w_3\}$ and $w_3 \in (p)$.

Many other interesting (and more complex) formulae can be verified in this model. For instance, we leave it to the reader to verify that $M, w_0 \vDash [a: tell, b: none]K_b[b: tog](K_a p \wedge K_b p)$. In words, it means that if Betty does not know that the light is off after the parallel execution of Alice telling whether the light bulb is on or off to Betty and Betty doing nothing, Betty knows that after she toggles the switch, she and Alice know that the light is on. In other words, it means that if Betty does not know that the light is off and she waits for the announcement of Alice, then she knows that toggling the switch provides the two agents the knowledge that the light is on.

We now turn our attention to some important CEDL validities, displayed in Table 3.1.

Theorem 1

The principles in Table 3.1 are sound and complete with respect to the class of CEDL models.

The axiomatisation in Table 3.1 reveals one additional assumption that is implicit in CEDL models. This assumption corresponds to Axiom S, which is called *superadditivity*. It stipulates that if group G obtains outcome φ by acting as determined by the partial joint action δ and H obtains outcome ψ by acting as determined by the partial joint action δ', then the group of agents $G \cup H$ obtains outcome $\varphi \wedge \psi$ by acting as determined by the union

A Formalisation of Responsibility   103

Table 3.1   The axiomatisation of CEDL

(TAU)	All instances of the propositional tautologies	
(KK)	$K_i\varphi \wedge K_i(\varphi \to \psi)) \to K_i\varphi$	Deductive closure for knowledge
(T)	$K_i\varphi \to \varphi$	Truth
(4)	$K_i\varphi \to K_i K_i\varphi$	Positive introspection
(5)	$\neg K_i\varphi \to K_i\neg K_i\varphi$	Negative introspection
(KA)	$([\delta\,|_G]\,\varphi \wedge [\delta\,|_G](\varphi \to \psi)) \to [\delta\,|_G]\,\psi$	Deductive closure for action
(A)	$\exists_{\delta\in\Delta}\neg\,[\delta\,|_G]\bot$	Activity
(DA)	$\forall_{\delta'\in\Delta}[\delta\,|_G \cup \delta'\,|_{N\setminus G}]\varphi \to [\delta\,|_G]\varphi$	Deriving action
(S)	$([\delta\,|_G\,\varphi \wedge [\delta'\,|_H]\psi) \to [\delta\,|_G \cup \delta'\,|_H](\varphi \wedge \psi)$ (if $G \cap H = \emptyset$)	Superadditivity
(PR)	$K_i[\delta\,|_G]\varphi \to [\delta\,|_G]K_i\varphi$	Perfect recall
(MP)	From φ and $\varphi \to \psi$ infer ψ	Modus ponens
(NK)	From φ infer $K_i\varphi$	Necessitation for knowledge
(NA)	From φ infer $[\delta\,|_G]\varphi$	Necessitation for action

of their partial joint actions. In particular, this implies that the bigger the group, the more it can achieve. This seems to be an intuitive property.

3.2.3   Group Knowledge

To formalise collective responsibility (see Chapter 2, section 2.3.2), we have to provide a formalisation of *group knowledge*. Unfortunately, there is no consensus in the literature of what group knowledge means (see, e.g., the discussion in Goldman (2009)). Here, we choose to use the notion of *distributed knowledge*, found, e.g., in Fagin *et al.* (1995). In the language, we replace operators K_i by the more general K_G, which semantics is formally defined as follows. Let $G \neq \emptyset$:

$$M, w \vDash K_G\varphi \quad \text{iff} \quad M, w' \vDash \varphi \text{ for all } w' \in \bigcap_{i\in G} \mathcal{K}(i)(w)$$

Distributed knowledge among group G approximately describes the knowledge of someone who has complete knowledge of what each member of G knows. For example, assume that agent i knows that p is true but does not know whether q is true or false, whereas agent j knows that q is true but does not know whether p is true or false. Then, the group $\{i,j\}$ has distributed knowledge that $p \wedge q$ is true. This notion of knowledge is similar to the knowledge condition for collectives proposed in Chapter 2.

Proposition 2

The following schemata are valid in CEDL with distributed knowledge:

(KK')	$K_G\varphi \wedge K_G(\varphi \to \psi)) \to K_G\varphi$	Deductive closure for knowledge
(T')	$K_G\varphi \to \varphi$	Truth
(4')	$K_G\varphi \to K_G K_G\,\varphi$	Positive introspection
(5')	$\neg K_G\varphi \to K_G\neg K_G\,\varphi$	Negative introspection
(KS)	$(K_{G_1}\varphi \wedge K_{G_2}\psi) \to K_{G_1 \cup G_2}(\varphi \to \psi)$ (if $G_1 \cap G_2 = \emptyset$)	Knowledge superadditivity
(PR')	$K_G[\delta|_G]\varphi \to [\delta|_G]K_G\varphi$	Perfect recall

Note that with axioms KS and KK', one can derive both: $K_{G_1}\varphi \to K_{G_1 \cup G_2}$ (φ) and $(K_{G_1}\varphi \wedge K_{G_2}(\varphi \to \psi)) \to K_{G_1 \cup G_2}(\psi)$. However, whether these principles constitute a complete axiomatic system for CEDL with distributed knowledge, is left as an open question.

3.2.4 Ability and Knowing How Ability

Our aim in this section is to define operators to express agent ability. The first operator we define here expresses that 'by executing $\delta|_G$, the group of agents G ensures an outcome satisfying φ in the next step'. That is, formulae of the form $E_{\delta|_G}\varphi$ should mean that G can execute $\delta|_G$ (or, simply, $\delta|_G$ is executable) and that it necessarily leads to an outcome satisfying φ. It therefore amounts to the following abbreviation:

$$E_{\delta|\text{G}}\varphi := \neg[\delta|_G] \perp \wedge [\delta|_G]\varphi$$

Sometimes, we will need to express that some group of agents ensures an outcome φ by executing a sequence of actions. $\delta_1|_G; \dots ; \delta_n|_G$. This amounts to a similar abbreviation, which generalises the latter one:

$$E_{\delta_{1|G};\dots;\delta_{n|G}}\varphi := \neg[\delta_{1|G}] \dots [\delta_{n|G}] \perp \wedge [\delta_{1|G}] \dots [\delta_{n|G}]\varphi$$

The second operator defined here expresses that 'the group of agents G is able to ensure that φ is true in the next step'. That is, formulae of the form $\langle\langle G\rangle\rangle\varphi$ mean that G has an available action that G can execute and which ensures an outcome satisfying φ. Thus, the latter is given by:

$$\langle\langle G\rangle\rangle\varphi := \exists_{\delta\in\Delta}E_{\delta|_G}\varphi$$

We note that this is a well-formed formula, because Δ is finite, because A is finite.

A Formalisation of Responsibility   105

Example 2 (Light Bulb and Light Switch (revisited))

To exemplify operators $\langle\langle G \rangle\rangle$, we reuse the scenario of Example 1 and the model in Figure 3.2.

- $M, w_0 \vDash \langle\langle\{b\}\rangle\rangle\, p$.
  In words, Betty is able to ensure that the light is on in the next step. This is true because there is an action available for Betty such that she can execute and which ensures an outcome satisfying p. This action is *tog*. Let us see how it works formally. The claim is true if and only if $M, w_0 \vDash \exists_{\delta \in \Delta} E_{\delta|_G} p$, which is true if $M, w_0 \vDash E_{b:tog} p$. The latter is true if and only if $M, w_0 \vDash \neg[b: tog] \bot$ and $M, w_0 \vDash [b: tog]p$. Both are indeed the case, as we have already seen in Example 1.
- $M, w_0 \vDash \neg\langle\langle\{a\}\rangle\rangle K_b \neg p$.
  It is not the case that Alice is able to ensure that Betty knows that the light is off in one step. This is the case because there is no action available for Alice that ensures that Betty knows that the light is off in the next step. For instance, Betty can always toggle the switch, which leads to the situation where the light is on. Formally, the two options available for Alice do not lead, necessary, to a situation where the light is off. That is, we have that $M, w_0 \vDash \neg[a: tell]K_b \neg p$, as seen before, and also $M, w_0 \vDash \neg[a: none]K_b \neg p$.
- $M, w_0 \vDash \langle\langle\{a\}\rangle\rangle\langle\langle\{b\}\rangle\rangle K_b p$.
  Alice is able to ensure that after one step Betty is able to ensure after one more step that she knows that the light is on. In the first step, the action available for Alice that leads to that result is *tell*. The reader can verify that, if Alice executes *tell* and Betty does noting, then after that she knows that the light is off, and then she only has to toggle the switch to ensure that the light is on after one more step. On the other hand, if Alice executes *tell* and Betty toggles the switch, then after that she knows that the light is on, and then she only has to do nothing to ensure that the light is on after one more step. So, in any case, Betty will have an action that leads to a state where she knows that the light is on.
- $M, w_0 \vDash \langle\langle\{a,b\}\rangle\rangle p \wedge \langle\langle\{a,b\}\rangle\rangle\neg p$.
  Alice and Betty together are able to ensure that the light is on and they are able to ensure that the light is off. This is true because they may choose to execute, e.g., $a: none, b:tog$ to ensure that the light is on after one step. And also, they can choose to execute, e.g., $a: none, b:none$ to ensure that the light is off after one step. This shows that in this scenario, the agents are able to control the state of propositional variable p.
- $M, w_0 \vDash \neg\langle\langle\emptyset\rangle\rangle p \wedge \neg\langle\langle\emptyset\rangle\rangle\neg p$.
  'Both p and $\neg p$ are not unavoidable', which, in our example is 'the light can be on or off in the next step'. We note that this is a well-formed formula, because $\emptyset \subseteq N$ (see the last bullet of the well-formedness definition at the start of section 3.2.2). Thus, we can follow the definition of $\langle\langle\emptyset\rangle\rangle$, to verify that, for instance, the first conjunct $\neg\langle\langle\emptyset\rangle\rangle p$ is true at

106 *Tiago de Lima and Lambèr Royakkers*

w_0. To do so, it is enough to verify that for all $\delta \in \Delta$, the formula $[\delta|_\emptyset]p$ is false at w_0. The latter is the case if and only if for all $\delta \in \Delta$ there is $\delta' \in \Delta$ such that the formula $[\delta|_\emptyset \cup \delta'|_{\{a,b\}}]p$ is false at w_0. And the latter is indeed the case for, e.g., $\delta' = a$: *none*, b: *none*. To verify that the second conjunct is also true at w_0, we do the same reasoning but using $\delta' = a$: *none*, b: *tog*.

At this point, the reader may be wondering what interpretation should be given to $\langle\langle\emptyset\rangle\rangle$. Formulae of the form $\langle\langle\emptyset\rangle\rangle\varphi$ mean 'after the execution of any joint action, φ is true', which is equivalent to 'φ is true in the next step, regardless what the agents do' or even, 'it is necessary the case that φ true in the next step'.[2]

In the next proposition, we formulate three truths for CEDL and one sound rule of inference. We start with showing that no group can ensure the contradiction in the next step, which means that any group can always execute an action. Next we show that any group can always ensure the tautology in the next step. These two observations are of course nice features of the language. Then we show that superadditivity also holds for groups, and finally we prove that from a material implication between facts we may conclude to a material implication between the possibilities of a group to ensure those facts.

Proposition 3

The following schemata and rule of inference are valid in CEDL:

1. $\neg\langle\langle G\rangle\rangle \perp$
2. $\langle\langle G\rangle\rangle\top$
3. $(\langle\langle G\rangle\rangle\varphi \wedge \langle\langle H\rangle\rangle\psi) \to \langle\langle G \cup H\rangle\rangle(\varphi \wedge \psi)$ if $(G \cap H = \emptyset)$
4. From $\varphi \to \psi$ infer $\langle\langle G\rangle\rangle\varphi \to \langle\langle G\rangle\rangle\psi$

We remark that the formula $\langle\langle N\rangle\rangle\varphi \to \neg\langle\langle\emptyset\rangle\rangle\neg\varphi$ is valid. Indeed, we can derive it quite easily using Axioms S and A. This formula means that if the whole set of agents is able to ensure that φ is true after one step, then it is not the case that φ is necessarily false after one step. However, the converse is not the case. That is, $\neg\langle\langle\emptyset\rangle\rangle\neg\varphi \to \langle\langle N\rangle\rangle\varphi$ is not valid in CEDL. In words, just because φ is not necessarily false after one step, it does not mean that the whole set of agents are able to ensure it. It happens because we do not assume 'joint determinism' in CEDL, i.e., a joint action may have more than one possible outcome.[3]

Proposition 3.3 shows that the operators $\langle\langle G\rangle\rangle$ are similar to their CL and ATL homonyms. This means that these operators present well-known, and desired, properties of an operator supposed to model ability of agents. It is very important for our framework, because we will base our subsequent definitions in the intuition behind the concept of ability.

Nonetheless, this operator has a 'problem'. It has been argued several times (Agotnes and Van Ditmarsch 2008; Broersen *et al.* 2007, Jamroga and

A *Formalisation of Responsibility* 107

Agotnes 2007, and Jamroga and Van der Hoek 2004) that, when a logic of this kind is also able to express that agents' knowledge is incomplete, the operator just defined is not completely adequate. The same issue rises in our logic, and can be explained using the Light Bulb and Light Switch scenario again (Examples 1 and 2): let us recall that Betty is able to ensure that the light is on after one step. That is, $\langle\langle\{b\}\rangle\rangle p$ is true at w_0. In fact, this formula is true at w_1 too. The latter means that she knows it, i.e., $M, w_0 \vDash K_B\langle\langle\{b\}\rangle\rangle p$. Then, it may seem counterintuitive that Betty does not know that the action *tog* ensures p in w_0, i.e., $M, w_0 \vDash \neg K_b E_{b:\,tog}p$. However, the reader may verify that it is indeed the case. This means that although Betty knows that she is able to ensure that the light is on after one step, she does not know what she must do to ensure it! In game theory (Osborne and Rubinstein 1994) we say that an agent has a 'non-uniform strategy' for a given goal whenever:

> for every state that the agent cannot distinguish from the current state, there is a strategy whose execution leads to the goal;

and we say that an agent has a *uniform strategy* for a given goal whenever:

> there is a strategy such that for every state that the agent cannot distinguish from the current one, its execution leads to the goal.

In our example above, Betty has a *non-uniform strategy* for the outcome where the light is on. The formula $K_b\langle\langle\{b\}\rangle\rangle p$ expresses it. However, sometimes we would like to write a formula expressing that an agent has (or does not have) a uniform strategy for a given goal. In the language of coalition logic and ATL, the latter is not possible. But this is possible in CEDL. The formula $\exists_{\delta \in \Delta} K_i E_{\delta|i} p$ (which is false at w_0) expresses that Betty has a uniform strategy to obtain the goal p. In other words, it expresses that Betty knows how to ensure that the light is on after one step. Here, we call this a 'knowing how ability'. To be able to express it more succinctly, we define operators H_G, as follows:

$$H_G\varphi := \exists_{\delta \in \Delta} K_G E_{\delta|G}\varphi$$

The knowing how operator has some of the properties of the ability operator. For instance, we have the following.

Proposition 4

The following scheme and rule of inference are valid in CEDL:

1. $\neg H_G \bot$
2. $(H_{G_1}\varphi \wedge H_{G_2}\psi) \rightarrow H_{G_1 \cup G_2} (\varphi \wedge \psi)$ (if $G_1 \cap G_2 = \emptyset$)
3. From $\varphi \rightarrow \psi$ infer $H_G\varphi \rightarrow H_G\psi$

108   *Tiago de Lima and Lambèr Royakkers*

But not all properties are the same. For instance, $\langle\langle G\rangle\rangle\top$ is valid, whereas $H_G\top$ is not. Validity of the former means that there always some action available for G that is executable, because of Axiom A. The latter is not valid because agent G does not always know which action it is.

3.2.5   Obligations

In this section, we define an operator expressing agent obligations, as in deontic logic (see Meyer and Wieringa 1993). We do so by adapting the simple, yet effective, idea of Anderson and Moore (1957) to our framework, rewritten in D'Altan *et al.* (1996). The idea reads that 'φ is obligatory if and only if it is contingent, and failure to do what is required to make φ true would lead to the sanction.' For example, if it is obligatory for some agent i that the light is on, then in every possible world where it is false the agent i is sanctioned. The way the static and dynamic obligations are introduced in PDL in D'Altan *et al.* is based on ideas of Meyer (1988), which is important inspiration for our treatment of the subject.

From now on, we assume that the set of propositional variables of our language is $P \cup Vio$, where $Vio = \{vio_G | G \in 2^N \backslash \emptyset\}$. That is, for each agent, we introduce a new atomic formula vio_G, that has the special meaning: 'the group of agents G is in violation'. In addition, we require that our models now be quadruples of the form $\langle W, \mathcal{K}, \mathcal{T}, \mathcal{V}\rangle$, where $W, \mathcal{K}$ and $\mathcal{T}$ are defined as before but the domain of $\mathcal{V}$ is extended to the new set of propositional variables, i.e., $\mathcal{V}: (P \cup Vio) \to 2^W$.

In D'Altan *et al.* (1996), formulae of the form $O_G\varphi$ mean 'it is obligatory for G that φ is true'. The idea is that vio_G flags the states of the model that consists of a violation state for G. In other words, vio_G simply means 'G is in violation'. Thus, we define one obligation operator for each group of agents $G \in 2^N \backslash \emptyset$ with the following abbreviation:

$$O_G\varphi := \neg\varphi \to vio_G$$

Obligations satisfy some interesting properties.

Proposition 5

1. $\vDash O_G\top$
2. $\vDash O_G(\varphi \wedge \psi) \leftrightarrow (O_G\varphi \wedge O_G\psi)$
3. If $\vDash \varphi$ then $\vDash O_G\varphi$

We note that agents do not necessarily know their obligations, i.e., $O_G\varphi$ does not imply $K_G O_G\varphi$. Also, our approach permits models where violations are unavoidable. For instance, we have that $vio_G \to O_G\bot$ is valid, which also means that we do not impose Axiom D (i.e., $\neg O_G\bot$), which is present in some deontic systems. In our view it just means that dilemmas are possible

A Formalisation of Responsibility   109

(cf. Van Fraassen 1973). As in the classical Sartre's example, one can have the obligation to stay at home to look after an elderly mother and, at the same time, the obligation to join the resistance movement to fight the Nazis.

3.3   RESPONSIBILITY

With all the necessary ingredients at hand, we are now able to develop our formalisation of responsibility. First, we start with forward-looking responsibility for φ in section 3.3.1, which will be defined in terms of obligation as defined in the previous section. Next, in section 3.3.2, we will deal with the two kinds of backward-looking responsibilities, viz., accountability and blameworthiness. The first will be defined in terms of ensuring φ but not ensuring a violation state, and the latter will be based on knowingly causing φ, whereas avoiding φ is possible. The first notion is logical weaker than the second, and our definition will be closely related to the consequentialist route defining wrong-doing in Chapter 1. Section 3.3.3 establishes the relation between these two kinds of responsibility. Forward-looking responsibility for φ and ensuring $\neg\varphi$ implies accountability for $\neg\varphi$, and forward-looking responsibility for φ and knowingly causing $\neg\varphi$ implies blameworthiness for $\neg\varphi$.

For a thorough and readily understanding of the text to come, the reader should realise the following. Whereas the previous CEDL models were completely descriptive, the introduction of the vio_i for individuals makes the models fundamentally normative. Distribution of violation states of the various agents over the possible worlds in the model equals to the distribution of the obligations of these agents in the different worlds of the model. If, for instance, for some agent in none of the worlds, vio_i holds i has no obligations in the model. Intuitively, the violation states in the model vary with the agent's obligations. An agent therefore cannot accept nor reject obligations.

3.3.1   Forward-Looking Responsibility

In this section, we formalise one kind of forward-looking responsibility, namely, the 'obligation to see to it that'. The aim here is to augment our logic with operator R where formulae of the form $R_G^n(\varphi)$ are to be read as 'it is obligatory for G that i sees to it that φ is true after n steps'. But, before showing its definition, let us recall part of the informal discussion drawn in Chapter 1, where Goodin's ideas are used to define this meaning of responsibility. The argument advanced is the following quote from Goodin (1995: 83):

> The standard form of responsibility is that A *see to it that* φ. It is not enough that φ occurs. A must have 'seen to it' that φ occurs. 'Seeing to it that φ' requires, minimally: that A satisfy himself that there is some process (mechanism or activity) at work whereby φ will brought about; that A check from time to time to make sure that process is still at

110 *Tiago de Lima and Lambèr Royakkers*

work, and is performing as expected; and that A take steps as necessary to alter or replace process that no longer seem likely to bring about φ.

This is a complex definition. It is unlikely that we would be able to capture all its details in our framework. Nonetheless, we approximate it by the following inductive definition:

$$R_G^0(\varphi) := O_G\varphi$$

$$R_G^{n+1}(\varphi) := O_G H_G^{n+1} \varphi \wedge \langle\langle\emptyset\rangle\rangle R_G^n(\varphi) \text{ for } (n > 0)$$

where H_G^n stands for a sequence of n operators H_G, i.e., $H_G^0 \varphi := \varphi$ and $H_G^n \varphi := H_G H_G^{n-1} \varphi$. For example, $H_G^1 \varphi$ (which is the same as $H_G\varphi$) means 'Group G knows how to ensure that φ after one step', whereas $H_G^3 \varphi$ (which is the same as $H_G H_G H_G\varphi$) means 'Group G knows how to ensure that φ after three steps'.

The formula $R_G^0(\varphi)$ is equivalent to $O_G\varphi$. That is, $R_G^0(\varphi)$ is true at some world w if and only if, it is necessary the case that, $\neg\varphi$ implies a violation for G. But formulae $R_G^n(\varphi)$, for $n > 1$, are more than mere obligations that φ. They also capture the 'supervisory nature' of this kind of responsibility. For it is also necessary the case that, after $n - 1$ steps, $\neg H_G\varphi$ implies a violation for G. This means that, to avoid a violation, group G must find a way to be in the position to know how to ensure φ after one step. And analogously for $n - 2$, and so on until $n = 1$.

Note that this definition of forward-looking responsibility does not take indirect agency into account as is required in the definition given in Chapter 1, section 1.4: Here we define forward-looking responsibility as the case where the group must guarantee the outcome by itself. This is not appropriate for an organisational setting, where delegation actions and information actions are available. In section 3.4.4 we will redefine forward-looking responsibility when we introduce organisational structures.

Example 3 (Light Bulb and Light Switch with Violations)

Let us now see our operator R in action using a variation of Example 1. The only difference in this variation is that worlds w_0 and w_2 are violation states for Alice and also for Betty. Such scenario is depicted in Figure 3.3.

- $M, w_0 \models R_a^1 p$ and also $M, w_0 \models R_b^1 p$

  In words, it is obligatory for Alice to see to it that the light is on after one step, and the same obligation applies to Betty. We verify only Alice's case, because Betty's one is analogous. It is the case if and only if (1) $M, w_0 \models O_a H_a p$ and (2) $M, w_0 \models \langle\langle\emptyset\rangle\rangle R_a^0 p$. We have (1) because, $w_0 \models vio_a$. And we have (2) because, for every w' in the model, we have $M, w' \models \neg p \rightarrow vio_a$.

A Formalisation of Responsibility 111

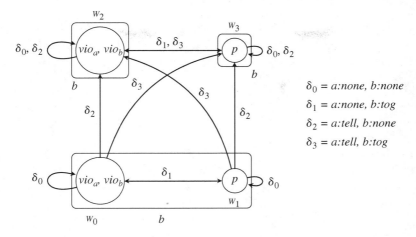

Figure 3.3 A CEDL model for the Light Bulb and Light Switch scenario where w_0 and w_2 are violation states. (As before, the rectangles represent Betty's knowledge. To simplify the picture, Alice's knowledge is not represented. She has complete knowledge of the scenario, i.e., $\mathcal{K}_a(w) = \{w\}$ for all $w \in W$.)

- $M, w_0 \models R_a^2 p$
  It is obligatory for Alice to see to it that the light is on after two steps. To show it, we have to show that (1) $M, w_0 \models O_a H_a H_a p$ and (2) $M, w_0 \models \langle\langle \emptyset \rangle\rangle R_a^1 p$. To show (1), we have to show that $\neg H_a H_a p \to vio_a$ is true at w_0. The reader can verify that this is indeed the case. To show (2), we have to show that for all $w \in W$ we have $M, w \models R_a^1 p$. It can be done in the same way as for w_0, which is done in the previous item.

We also note that $M, w_0 \models R_b^2 p$, and invite the reader to do the exercise of showing it.

It may worth to explain why we do not use the classical notion of 'seeing to it that' (henceforth stit) proposed in Belnap *et al.* (2001). Belnap *et al.*'s stit can be defined in our framework as follows. The sentence 'by executing $\delta|_{\{i\}}$, i sees to it that φ after one step' is expressed by the formula $\neg[\delta|_{\{i\}}]\bot \land [\delta|_{\{i\}}]\varphi \land \neg\langle\langle \emptyset \rangle\rangle\varphi$. Note that it amounts to our $E_{\delta|_{\{i\}}}\varphi$ plus the conjunct $\neg\langle\langle \emptyset \rangle\rangle\varphi$. This conjunct is there because, for Belnap *et al.*, it is not enough that φ is true after one step. It must be the agent i that influences the course of things to ensure that φ is true after one step. It can be argued that our operator E does not capture this latter meaning. For example, the formula $E_{\delta|G}$ is valid in CEDL, i.e., it is true at every world of every model. But this is not true at a given world because of the action executed by G. However, Belnap *et al.*'s stit is incompatible with the meaning of responsibility we are trying to formalise here. We show it using an informal example. Suppose that a teacher has the obligation to see to it that, after his class, the door of the classroom will be closed. Also suppose that the door of the classroom is connected to an automatic system that closes it exactly after his class finishes. Some minutes before finishing his class, the teacher has some options: (a) finish the class on time and then let the door be closed automatically by the system; (b) finish the class a bit earlier and then close the door himself; and (c) disable the automatic system and then close the door himself. It seems to us that in Belnap et al.'s terms, only (b) and (c) fulfil the teacher's obligation, whereas we think that all the three options fulfil the teacher's obligation. Recall that, as explained in Chapter 1, the obligation to see to it that φ does not require that φ is achieved by an action of the teacher. But it requires some supervision. Therefore, in our example, the obligation to see to it that the door will be closed implies that the agent supervises the process by himself. That is, if the teacher chooses (a), then the teacher must be sure that the system is working properly, or at least verify if the system closed the door after the class.

3.3.2 Backward-Looking Responsibility

In this section, we formalise two kinds of backward-looking responsibility, *accountability* and *blameworthiness*. The aim here is to augment the logic with two operators, $\mathcal{A}$ and $\mathcal{B}$. Formulae of the form $\mathcal{A}_{\delta|i}\varphi$ is to be read as 'after executing δ, agent i is accountable for φ' and formulae of the form $\mathcal{B}_{\delta|i}\varphi$ is to be read as 'after executing δ, agent i is blameworthy for φ'. Recall that the execution of δ also included 'do nothing' so that formulations used also capture responsibility for omissions and not only responsibility for actions. This has the advantage that the important notion of responsibility for omissions is also covered by our definitions. In the following section, accountability will be defined in terms of ensuring φ whereas not ending in a state of violation.

Accountability

Let us start by recalling the conditions for 'accountability' given in Chapter 1:

> ... an agent i is accountable for φ if i has the capacity to act responsibly (has moral agency), is somehow causally connected to the outcome φ (by an action or omission) and there is a reasonable suspicion that agent i did somehow something wrong.

The first condition for holding an agent accountable, 'moral agency', is a tacit assumption in our framework. In fact, our logical framework also assumes that all agents are rational and that they are perfect reasoners. This, for instance, means that agents can foresee all the logical consequences of the facts they know. Again, these assumptions may be seen as very restrictive ones, but, in a logical framework like ours, the relaxation of such

A *Formalisation of Responsibility* 113

assumptions would make it much more difficult (if not impossible) to derive some interesting properties.

The other two conditions for holding an agent accountable are causality and wrong-doing. We just make it precise that these two conditions must be related to each other, in the sense that the 'something wrong' did by the agent must be what is 'somehow causally connected to the outcome' for which the agent is accountable. So, first, we consider that agent i is causally connected to a given consequence φ whenever i ensures that φ is true and the action that ensures φ is wrong. And we consider that an action is wrong whenever it does not ensure a non-violation state. For the latter, it either means that a violation state is achieved by the execution of the action or, if the violation state is not achieved, it means that the agent did not take enough care in order to avoid it, what we also consider as a 'wrong-doing'. Putting everything together we have the following definition for accountability (which is already generalised to groups of agents):

$$\mathcal{A}_{\delta_1|_G; \dots ; \delta_n|_G} \varphi := E_{\delta_1|_G; \dots ; \delta_n|_G} \varphi \wedge \neg E_{\delta_1|_G; \dots ; \delta_n|_G} \neg vio_G$$

The latter definition stipulates that, after executing the sequence of actions $\delta_1, \dots, \delta_n$, group G is accountable for φ if and only if, by executing this sequence, G ensures that φ is true and also, by executing this sequence, G does not ensure a non-violation state.

Example 4 (Light Bulb and Light Switch with Violations (revisited))

To exemplify operator $\mathcal{A}$, we reuse the scenario of Example 3 and the model in Figure 3.2.

- $M, w_0 \models \neg \mathcal{A}_{\delta_{0|a}} \neg p.$
  Alice is not accountable for the fact that the light is off because her action (i.e., action *none*) does not ensure that the light is off. (Note that it is Betty that can toggle the switch and turn on the light.) It is true if and only if $M, w_0 \models \neg E_{\delta_{0|a}} \neg p \vee E_{\delta_{0|a}} \neg vio_a$. And it is true because the first disjunct is true. To see it, note that $M, w_0 \models \neg [\delta_{0|a}] \neg p.$
- $M, w_0 \models \mathcal{A}_{\delta_{0|b}} \neg p.$
  Betty meets the two conditions to be accountable for the fact that the light is off. First, she does ensure that the light is off by executing action *none* (because she could have decided to execute *tog*) and second, by her omission, she does not ensure a non-violation state. It is true if and only if $M, w_0 \models E_{\delta_{0|b}} \neg p \wedge \neg E_{\delta_{0|b}} \neg vio_b$. Note that both conjuncts are true in the model of Figure 3.2.
- $M, w_0 \models \neg \mathcal{A}_{\delta_{0|a}; \delta_{0|a}} \neg p.$
  This is similar in that for the first item, Alice is not accountable for the fact that the light is off, even after executing none twice. Again,

114 *Tiago de Lima and Lambèr Royakkers*

because she is not the one who can decide to toggle the switch. To show it, we use the same reasoning as for the first item again, but now twice.

We may say that, in this example, operator $\mathcal{A}$ works as expected. Note that Alice, who does not control the light switch, cannot be held accountable for the fact that the light is off. On the other hand, Betty, who does control the light switch, can be held accountable for the fact that the light is off. But, we will see in the next section that she cannot always be blamed for that, because she does not know the state of the light in the beginning.

Blameworthiness

The definition given in Chapter 1 for this meaning of responsibility is the following: agent i is blameworthy for consequence φ whenever i is accountable for φ and is not capable to give an acceptable account for it. Two accounts (excuses) are considered acceptable. The first one is ignorance: the agent i is excused (and thus is not blameworthy) for φ if i can show that she could not know that her behaviour would cause φ, or she could not know that her behaviour was wrong. The second is coercion. A possible interpretation of coercion is that the agent i is excused for φ if i can show that no behaviour that does not cause φ or that is not wrong is possible. For simplicity, we give the definition of blame in two steps (note the generalisation to groups of agents):

$$\mathcal{C}_{\delta|_G}\varphi := K_G E_{\delta|_G}\varphi \wedge \neg\langle\langle\emptyset\rangle\rangle\varphi$$
$$\mathcal{C}_{\delta_1|_G;\,\ldots\,;\delta_n|_G}\varphi := K_G E_{\delta_1|_G}\mathcal{C}_{\delta_2|_G;\,\ldots\,;\delta_n|_G}\varphi \wedge \neg\langle\langle\emptyset\rangle\rangle\mathcal{C}_{\delta_2|_G;\,\ldots\,;\delta_n|_G}\varphi \text{ (for } n>1\text{)}$$
$$\mathcal{B}_{\delta_1|_G;\,\ldots\,;\delta_n|_G}\varphi := \mathcal{C}_{\delta_1|_G;\,\ldots\,;\delta_n|_G}\varphi \wedge \neg\mathcal{C}_{\delta_1|_G;\,\ldots\,;\delta_n|_G}\neg vio_G \wedge R_G^n\neg\varphi$$

The illustration of the single-step case, so for one action, is:

$$\mathcal{B}_{\delta|_G}\varphi := \mathcal{C}_{\delta|_G}\varphi \wedge \neg\mathcal{C}_{\delta|_G}\neg vio_G \wedge R_G^1\neg\varphi$$

The definition of operator $\mathcal{B}$ uses operator $\mathcal{C}$. The latter operator means more than just 'ensure'. It could be seen as 'knowing causality'. That is, formula of the form $\mathcal{C}_{\delta|_G}\varphi$ mean 'by executing δ, group G knowingly causes φ'. The difference with ensuring φ is that the latter formula also means that the agent knows that the action ensures φ. Therefore, $\mathcal{C}_{\delta|_G}\varphi$ implies that the group G is not ignorant about the fact that the corresponding behaviour would cause φ, which means that this cannot be used as an account (excuse). In addition, the conjunct $\neg\langle\langle\emptyset\rangle\rangle$

φ means that a different behaviour, not necessarily leading to φ, was possible, also meaning that this cannot be used as an account (excuse). So, the definition of formula $\mathcal{B}_{\delta|_G}\varphi$ stipulates that, not only the group is accountable for φ, but the group cannot provide acceptable excuses for it, which, by the definition given initially, means that the group is blameworthy for φ.

Example 5 (Light Bulb and Light Switch with Violations (re-revisited))

To exemplify operator $\mathcal{B}$, we reuse the scenario of Example 3 and the model in Figure 3.3.

- $M, w_0 \vDash \neg\mathcal{B}_{\delta_{0|_a}}\neg p$.
  In words, Alice is not blameworthy for the fact that the light is off because her action none does not knowingly cause that fact. It is true if and only if $M, w_0 \vDash \neg\mathcal{C}_{\delta_{0|_a}}\neg p \vee \mathcal{C}_{\delta_{0|_a}}\neg vio_a \vee \neg R_a^1 p$. And it is true because the first disjunct is true. To see it, note that $M, w_0 \vDash \neg K_a E_{\delta_{0|_a}}\neg p$, because $M, w_0 \vDash \neg K_a[\delta_0|_a]\neg p$.

- $M, w_0 \vDash \neg\mathcal{B}_{\delta_{0|_b}}\neg p$.
  It is not the case that, after executing the action *none*, Betty is blameworthy for the fact that the light is off. It is true if and only if M, $w_0 \vDash \neg\mathcal{C}_{\delta_{0|_b}}\neg p \vee \mathcal{C}_{\delta_{0|_b}}\neg vio_b \vee R_b^1 p$. And it is true because the first disjunct is true. The reasoning is the same as for the item above. Note that $M, w_0 \vDash \neg K_b E_{\delta_{0|_b}}\neg p$, because $M, w_0 \vDash \neg K_b[\delta_0|_b]\neg p$. Recall from Example 4 that $M, w_0 \vDash \mathcal{A}_{\delta_{0|_b}}\neg p$, i.e., after executing action *none*, Betty is accountable for the fact that the light is off. But, we now see that, because she could not know the state of the light, she cannot be blamed for it.

- $M, w_0 \vDash \neg\mathcal{B}_{\delta_{0|_a};\delta_{0|_a}}\neg p$.
  It is not the case that, after executing action *none* twice, Alice is blameworthy for the fact that the light is off. To show it, we use the same reasoning as for the first item again, but now twice.

- $M, w_0 \vDash [\delta_{2|_a}]\mathcal{B}_{\delta_{0|_b}}\neg p$.
  After the execution of action *tell* by Alice and then the execution of action *none*, Betty is blameworthy for the fact that the light is off. It is true if and only if $M, w_2 \vDash \mathcal{B}_{\delta_{0|_b}}\neg p$. And it is true if and only if, $w_2 \vDash \mathcal{C}_{\delta_{0|_b}}\neg p \wedge \neg\mathcal{C}_{\delta_{0|_b}}\neg vio_b \wedge R_b^1 p$. Note that the latter is true, because, in w_2 Betty knows the status of the light switch, which means that she knows that executing *none* will lead to a violation. In addition, in w_2 Betty knows that there is another option that avoids the violation, namely the execution of *tog*. And finally, she is responsible for p after one step. The reasoning is the same as for the first item of Example 3.

3.3.3 The Relation between Forward-Looking and Backward-Looking Responsibilities

Given the definitions for operators R, $\mathcal{A}$ and $\mathcal{B}$ of the latter sections, we will explore whether the four conceptual relations between the different notions of responsibility established in Chapter 1 (section 1.6) are valid in CEDL. The four relations are formulated in terms of individuals, we will formalise these relations in terms of groups, which is even stronger.

1. The first relation was between responsibility-as-moral-obligation to see to something and accountability for something:
   If agent i had a forward-looking responsibility-as-obligation for φ and φ did not occur and 'not φ' is not caused by exceptional circumstances, then agent i is accountable for 'not φ'.

This can be formalised as follows:

$$(R_G^n(\varphi) \wedge E_{\delta_{1|G}; \ldots; \delta_{n|G}} \neg\varphi) \to \mathcal{A}_{\delta_{1|G}; \ldots; \delta_{n|G}} \neg\varphi$$

which is valid in CEDL.[4] This proposition says that: if it is obligatory for G to see to it that φ, and the sequence of actions $\delta_1; \ldots; \delta_n$ ensures $\neg\varphi$, then G is accountable for $\neg\varphi$.

2. The second relation was between accountability and blameworthiness:
   If agent i is accountable for φ and has no appropriate excuse why φ is the case then agent i is blameworthy for φ.

This can be formalised as follows:

$$(R_G^n(\varphi) \wedge C_{\delta_{1|G}; \ldots; \delta_{n|G}} \neg\varphi) \to \mathcal{B}_{\delta_{1|G}; \ldots; \delta_{n|G}} \neg\varphi$$

which is also valid in CEDL.[5] $R_G^n(\varphi)$ makes $\neg\varphi$ to count as a wrongdoing, and the sequence of actions $\delta_1; \ldots; \delta_n$ knowingly causes $\neg\varphi$ ($C_{\delta_{1|G}; \ldots; \delta_{n|G}} \neg\varphi$: 'accountable for $\neg\varphi$ without excuse'), then G is blamed for $\neg\varphi$.

3. The third relation was also between accountability and blameworthiness:
   If an agent i is blameworthy for φ and φ is the case, then agent i is also accountable for φ.

This can be formalised as follows:[6]

$$(\mathcal{B}_{\delta_{1|G}; \ldots; \delta_{n|G}} \varphi \wedge \langle \delta_1|G \rangle \ldots \langle \delta_n|G \rangle \varphi) \to \mathcal{A}_{\delta_{1|G}; \ldots; \delta_{n|G}} \varphi$$

This formula means 'if G is blamed for φ' then G is accountable for φ'. This is valid in CEDL.[7]

A Formalisation of Responsibility   117

4. Finally, we had that: If φ is not the case and i is not accountable for 'not φ', it follows that agent i did not have a forward-looking responsibility-as-obligation to see to it that φ was the case in the first place:

If agent i is not accountable for 'not φ' whereas φ is not the case and 'not φ' is not caused by exceptional circumstances then agent i had no forward-looking responsibility-as-obligation for φ.

This can be formalised as follows:

$$(\neg \mathcal{A}_{\delta_{1|G};\,\dots;\,\delta_{n|G}}\neg\varphi \wedge \langle\delta_1|_G\rangle \dots \langle\delta_n|_G\rangle\neg\varphi) \rightarrow \neg R_G^{\,n}(\varphi)$$

This formula is not valid in CEDL. It means 'if G is not accountable for $\neg\varphi$ then G is not obliged to see to it that φ'. This is not true because, with our definition, G cannot be considered accountable for $\neg\varphi$ when this is obtained due to actions of agents outside group G, even if G is obliged to see to it that φ. The formula would be valid, for example, if $G = N$, i.e., G is the entire group of agents:

$$(\neg \mathcal{A}_{\delta_{1|N};\,\dots;\,\delta_n N}\neg\varphi \wedge \langle\delta_1|_N\rangle \dots \langle\delta_n|_N\rangle\neg\varphi) \rightarrow \neg R_N^{\,n}(\varphi)$$

3.4   THE PROBLEM OF MANY HANDS

3.4.1   The PMH

As we have seen in Chapter 2, we can characterise the problem of many hands (PMH) in several ways. In this section we will deal with the PMH with respect to responsibility-as-blameworthiness (see Chapter 2, section 2.2). On the basis of this characterisation, we will show how we can model the problem of many hands in organisations, and show how organised groups of agents are more likely to avoid such problem. The PMH with respect to responsibility-as-blameworthiness arises in an organisation when the organisation is backward-looking responsible-as-blameworthy for some undesirable outcome but no member of the organisation can be held backward-looking responsible-as-blameworthy for this outcome. Let G be the set of members of a given organisation; it is formally given generally by:

$$PMH_{\delta_{1|G};\,\dots;\,\delta_{n|G}}\varphi := \mathcal{B}_{\delta_{1|G};\,\dots;\,\delta_{n|G}}\varphi \wedge \forall i \neg \mathcal{B}_{\delta_{1|i};\,\dots;\,\delta_{n|i}}(\varphi)$$

And for the single-step case:

$$PMH_{\delta_G}\varphi = \mathcal{B}_{\delta_G}(\varphi) \wedge \forall_i \neg \mathcal{B}_{\delta_i}(\varphi)$$

118   *Tiago de Lima and Lambèr Royakkers*

A formula of the form $PMH_{\delta_G}\varphi$ means that 'by performing δ_G, the PMH arises in group G with respect to the outcome φ'. If we follow the definitions of operator $\mathcal{B}$ we find out that we can paraphrase it as 'by performing δ_G, group G is backward-looking responsible for φ, but no agent i in G is backward-looking responsible for φ by performing δ_i'. Analysing the definitions of operator $\mathcal{B}$ a bit further, we realise that the PMH may arise from three different sources:

1. no forward-looking responsibility is ascribed to the individuals, or
2. the individuals that are forward-looking responsible for φ do not have the ability to bring it about (without the other individuals of the group), or
3. the individuals that are forward-looking responsible for φ do not have the necessary knowledge to bring about φ (without considering the knowledge of the other individuals of the group).

To address source 1, once a group is forward-looking responsible for outcome φ, we need to ascribe responsibility to at least one individual in that group. We call this individual the 'leader' of the group. Formally we have:

(A10) $R_G^n(\varphi) \to R_i^n(\varphi)$ if i is the leader of G.

and where the 'leader' i is a distinguished agent in the model (this is defined formally in the next section).

Now, to address source 2, we have to be sure that the forward-looking responsibility can be 'delegated' (directly or indirectly) to the individuals that have the ability to fulfil it. This will mean that the 'leader' should have the power to ascribe forward-looking responsibilities to other individuals of the group.

Similarly, to address source 3, we have to be sure that individuals can share information. In other words, that knowledge can be transmitted among individuals of the group. Therefore, a group that wants to avoid the PMH should organise itself in such a way that delegation actions and information actions are possible. In management theory, some ideas of how organisations can be built are given. Here, we use the ideas of Grossi *et al.* (2007), and define organisations as a kind of structure. Organisational structures are sets of relations between the roles in an organisation. A typical abstract example of such structures is the so-called *vertical differentiation* or *authority structure* of organisations, usually considered to be a hierarchy structure. These abstract types of structures are traditionally studied in the branch of sociology known as mathematical sociology (see Fararo 1997, Sorensen 1978).

Work on organisations (especially in multi-agent systems (MAS)[8]) presents organisational structure as something essentially mono-dimensional, although it often, but only implicitly, considers a multiplicity of structured aspects: authority, communication, delegation, responsibility, control, power, etc. The thesis we hold here, which is inspired by foundational work on social and organisation theory by Selznick (1948), Morgenstern (1951), and Giddens (1987), is that organisations do not exhibit one single structural dimension, but that they are instead multi-structured objects. In particular, we view organisational structure as hiding at least two relevant dimensions which we call: power and coordination.

These different structural dimensions are linked with as many specific activities that take place within any organised group of agents acting to pursue some goals. These activities, which we call *organisational activities*, consists in "managing the interdependencies between the activities" (Decker and Lesser 1995) of the group. In other words, they guarantee the group 'to act in an organised way'. We will analyse two of these activities: delegation and information, each of them related with one specific structural dimension. The *delegation activity*, concerning the flow of obligations within an organisation, is related with the structural dimension of *power*. The *information activity*, concerning instead the flow of knowledge within the group of agents, is related with the *coordination* dimension.

3.4.2 Organisational Structures

An organisational structure is a quadruple $\langle G, P, I, i \rangle$ where:

- G is a group of agents in N, representing the members of the organisation;
- P is a subset of $G \times G$, representing a power relation among the members of the organisation;
- I is a subset of $G \times G$, representing a coordination relation that results in an information flux relation among the members of the organisation;
- i is an agent in G, representing the 'leader' of the group,

and that satisfies the following semantic constraints:

(SC6) $j \in P^+(i)$ (for all $j \in G$)
(SC7) $P \subseteq I$

where P^+ is the transitive closure of P.

SC6 implies that every individual in the organisation can eventually be ascribed forward-looking responsibility for some outcome. SC7 guarantees that if an individual is ascribed forward-looking responsibility for some outcome, this individual can also be informed about it.

Let $\mathcal{O}$ be an organisational structure, the models of our logic are now tuples of the form $\langle \mathcal{O}, W, \mathcal{K}, \mathcal{T}, \mathcal{V} \rangle$. And its language is extended by the set

120 *Tiago de Lima and Lambèr Royakkers*

of atomic formulae $\{Power(i, j)|i, j \in G\} \cup \{Coord(i, j)|i, j \in G\}$. The satisfaction relation is the same as before plus:

$$M, w \vDash Power\,(i, j) \quad \text{iff} \quad (i, j) \in P$$
$$M, w \vDash Coord\,(i, j) \quad \text{iff} \quad (i, j) \in I$$

Note that from SC7 we immediately obtain:

(A11) $Power\,(i, j) \rightarrow Coord\,(i, j)$

Axiom (A11) expresses the desirable property: 'if agent i has power over agent j, then agent i can coordinate with agent j'.

3.4.3   Organisational Actions

Once organisational structures are in place, we can define organisational actions. The first kind of such actions consists of information actions. That is, we add the set of actions $\{$info$(G, \varphi): G \subseteq N$ and $\varphi \in \mathcal{L}\}$ to the set A of atomic actions of the language. For example, action $(i, $info$(G, \varphi))$ means 'agent i informs all members of G that φ'. We require that such actions satisfy the following two properties:

(A12) $\neg[(i, \text{info}(G, \varphi))] \neg \top \rightarrow K_i\varphi$
(A13) $Coord(i, j) \rightarrow [(i, \text{info}(G, \varphi))]K_j\varphi$ \qquad (for each $j \in G$)

Axiom A12 restricts the circumstances in which action info (G, φ) is executable. We impose that agents can inform only what they know will be true after the communication act. It follows that agents cannot lie.

Axiom A13 stipulates that informing actions are successful communication actions when the agents involved are appropriately related by a coordination link. This also means that the agents trust information that comes through the coordination link.

The second kind of organisational action consists of delegation actions. That is, we add the set of actions $\{$deleg$((G_1, n_1, \varphi_1), \dots, (G_m, n_m, \varphi_m))$: $G_1, \dots, G_m \subseteq N$, $n_1, \dots, n_m \in \mathbb{N}$ and $\varphi_1, \dots, \varphi_m \in \mathcal{L}\}$ to the set A of atomic actions of the language. In fact, this is a multiple-delegation action. Action $\{(i, $deleg$((G_1, n_1, \varphi_1), \dots, (G_m, n_m, \varphi_m)))\}$ means 'agent i ascribes forward-looking responsibility that φ_k after n_k steps to Gk, for each $1 < k < m$'. We require that such actions satisfy:

(A14) $Power\,(i, j) \rightarrow [(i, \text{deleg}((G_1, n_1, \varphi_1), \dots, (G_m, n_m, \varphi_m)))]$
$K_j R_{G_k}^{n_k}\varphi_k\}$
(for each $j \in G$ and each $1<k<m$)

A Formalisation of Responsibility   121

Axiom A14 stipulates that, when agent i delegates φ to G, it creates a forward-looking responsibility that φ for every agent in G, but only if agent i has the power to do so. Note that, in this definition of delegation, the actor of the delegation action keeps the responsibility. In addition, the agents in G also know their new responsibility. This is why power links must also be coordination links (see SC7).

Forward-looking Responsibility Redefined

As we already indicated, the definition of forward-looking responsibility in section 3.3.1 does not take into account indirect agency. Therefore, here we redefine forward-looking responsibility below corresponding to the definition given in Chapter 1. For the sake of readability it is given in two parts. In the first part we can see that the only difference from the definition of forward-looking responsibility is the presence of operator $\mathcal{R}$. The latter operator means *indirect responsibility*.

Definition 1

(We show only the first three; the others are analogous.)

$$R_G^0(\varphi) := O_G(\varphi \vee \mathcal{R}_G^0(\varphi))$$
$$R_G^1(\varphi) := O_G(H_G\varphi \vee \mathcal{R}_G^1(\varphi)) \wedge \langle\langle\emptyset\rangle\rangle R_G^0(\varphi)$$
$$R_G^2(\varphi) := O_G(H_G(H_G\varphi \vee \mathcal{R}_G^1(\varphi)) \vee \mathcal{R}_G^2(\varphi)) \wedge \langle\langle\emptyset\rangle\rangle R_G^1(\varphi)$$

Where $\mathcal{R}_G^n$ is defined as:

$$\mathcal{R}_G^0(\varphi) := \exists_{G_1'} K_G \left(Power(G, G_1') \wedge R_{G_1'}^0(\varphi_1) \right)) \wedge \ldots \wedge$$
$$\exists_{G_m'} K_G \left(Power(G, G_m') \wedge R_{G_m'}^0(\varphi_m) \right) \wedge K_G((\varphi_1 \wedge \ldots \wedge \varphi_m) \to \varphi)$$

$$\mathcal{R}_G^1(\varphi) := \exists_{G_1'} K_G \left(Power(G, G_1') \wedge H_{G_1'}\varphi_1 \wedge R_{G_1'}^1(\varphi_1) \right)) \wedge \ldots \wedge$$
$$\exists_{G_m'} K_G \left(Power(G, G_m') \wedge H_{G_m'}\varphi \wedge R_{G_m'}^1(\varphi_m) \right) \wedge$$
$$K_G((\varphi_1 \wedge \ldots \wedge \varphi_m) \to \varphi)$$

$$\mathcal{R}_G^2(\varphi) := \exists_{G_1'} K_G \left(Power(G, G_1') \wedge H_{G_1'}(H_{G_1'}\varphi_1 \vee \mathcal{R}_{G_1'}^1(\varphi_1)) \wedge R_{G_1'}^2(\varphi_1) \right)$$
$$\wedge \ldots \wedge \exists_{G_m'} K_G \left(Power(G, G_m') \wedge H_{G_m'}(H_{G_m'}\varphi_m \vee \mathcal{R}_{G_m'}^1(\varphi_m)) \right)$$
$$\wedge R_{G_m'}^2(\varphi_m)) \wedge K_G((\varphi_1 \wedge \ldots \wedge \varphi_m) \to \varphi)$$

where $Power(G, G') := \exists_{i \in G} \forall_{j \in G'} Power(i, j)$.

Informally, group G is forward-looking responsible for φ after n steps if and only if it is obligatory for G that it is able to bring about φ after n steps or that it is indirect forward-looking responsible for φ after n steps. The definition of indirect responsibility is the most complex part. Yet, it is intuitive. We consider that a group G is indirect responsible for φ if and only if there are groups $G_1', \ldots, G_m'$ under G's power that are able to bring about $\varphi_1, \ldots, \varphi_m$, or they are indirect responsible for $\varphi_1, \ldots, \varphi_m$, and such that

$(\varphi_1 \wedge \ldots \wedge \varphi_m) \to \varphi$. For example, if it is obligatory for G to see to it that the light is on in the next step, then either it is obligatory for G that G knows how to ensure that the light is on in the next step or it is obligatory for G that there is a group G' under the power of G for which it is obligatory to see to it that the light is on in the next step.

3.4.4 Avoiding the PMH: An Example

Consider an organisation with two bank accounts, 1 and 2. Alice (agent a) is the member of the organisation who manages the accounts. Betty (agent b) is the member who normally pays the bills for the organisation. And Carol (agent c) is the director of their department, but she has no access to the accounts.

Let $\langle M, w_0 \rangle$ be a pointed CEDL model, where M is depicted in Figure 3.4. It describes a situation where Betty will pay a bill after three steps using account 1. Alice knows that, but she does not know which account Betty will use. Alice also knows that none of the accounts has enough money to pay the bill, but she does know that both accounts together do. Group $G = \{a, b, c\}$ is ascribed the responsibility to have the bill paid and the balances non-negative after three steps, i.e., $M, w_0 \vDash R_G^3(bal(n) \geq 0)$.

Note that $M, w_2 \vDash C_{\delta^2|G} \neg(bal(n) \geq 0)$. That is, at w_2, if Alice places the money on account 2, Betty pays the bill from account 1 and Carol just waits, the group G knowingly causes a negative balance. This is true because $M, w_2 \vDash K_G E_{\delta^2|G} \neg(bal(n) \geq 0)$, $M, w_2 \vDash \neg C_{\delta^2|G} \neg vio_G$, i.e., it is not the case that G knows that δ^2 avoids a violation state. In addition, $M, w_2 \vDash R_G^1(bal(n) \geq 0)$, i.e., G is responsible for maintaining the balance of account n positive. Therefore, $M, w_2 \vDash \mathcal{B}_{\delta^2|G} \neg(bal(n) \geq 0)$. A similar reasoning will show that $M, w_0 \vDash \mathcal{B}_{\delta^7|G; \delta^5|G; \delta^2|G} \neg(bal(n) \geq 0)$.

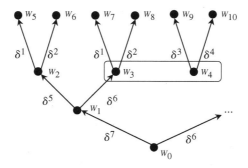

Figure 3.4 The CEDL model $M = \langle \mathcal{O}, W, \mathcal{K}, \mathcal{T}, \mathcal{V} \rangle$ for the example in section 3.4.5. (The dots represent possible worlds in W, the arrows represent transitions in $\mathcal{T}$, and the rectangle represents $\mathcal{K}(a)$. The joint actions and the valuation function $\mathcal{V}$ are detailed in Table 3. The organisation $\mathcal{O} = \langle G, P, I, c \rangle$, where $G = \{a, b, c\}$, $P = \{(c, a), (c, b)\}$, and $I = P \cup \{(b, a)\}$.)

A Formalisation of Responsibility 123

Table 3.2 The joint actions and valuation function $\mathcal{V}$ for the model M in Figure 3.4. (Action info abbreviates info$(a, [b: pay(2)]\neg \top)$ and action deleg abbreviates deleg$((a, 2, bal(n) \geq 0), (b, 1, H_a bal(n) \geq 0), (b, 2, paid))$. The bullets show where the atoms are true.)

	a	b	c
δ^1	tr(2, 1)	pay(1)	wait
δ^2	tr(1, 2)	pay(1)	wait
δ^3	tr(2, 1)	pay(2)	wait
δ^4	tr(1, 2)	pay(2)	wait
δ^5	wait	info	wait
δ^6	wait	wait	wait
δ^7	wait	wait	deleg

	vio_G	vio_a	vio_b	vio_c	bal$(n) \geq 0$
w_0					•
w_1					•
w_2					•
w_3			•		•
w_4					•
w_5					•
w_6	•	•	•	•	
w_7					•
w_8	•	•	•	•	
w_9	•	•	•	•	
w_{10}					•

Now, suppose for a moment that $P = \emptyset$, so that action deleg does not produce its normal effect of ascribing forward-looking responsibilities to Alice and Betty. That is, under this assumption, $\mathcal{V}(vio_a) = \mathcal{V}(vio_b) = \emptyset$. Then, we have $M, w_2 \vDash \neg\mathcal{B}_{\delta^2|_a}(bal(n) \geq 0)$, because there is no violation for Alice in the model. Therefore, $M, w_0 \vDash \neg\mathcal{B}_{\delta^7|_a;\delta^5|_a;\delta^2|_a}(bal(n) \geq 0)$. Similarly, there is no violation for Betty either, so $M, w_0 \vDash \neg\mathcal{B}_{\delta^7|_b;\delta^5|_b;\delta^2|_b}(bal(n) \geq 0)$. Because of Axiom A10, the violations for Carol are present in the model. However, we have $M, w_2 \vDash \neg\mathcal{B}_{\delta^2|_c}(bal(n) \geq 0)$. The reason for this is that at w_2 Carol cannot ensure a non-violation state no matter which action she decides to execute. Therefore, $M, w_0 \vDash \neg\mathcal{B}_{\delta^7|_c;\delta^5|_c;\delta^2|_c}(bal(n) \geq 0)$. This means that neither Alice, Betty, or Carol can be held backward-looking responsible for a violation state. Thus, $M, w_0 \vDash PMH_{\delta^7|_G;\delta^5|_G;\delta^2|_G}(\neg bal(n) \geq 0)$, i.e., by performing such actions, the PMH arises in group G with respect to outcome $\neg bal(n) \geq 0$.

Now, let us come back to the original configuration of P. In this case, after the execution of δ^7, Alice is forward-looking responsible for $bal(n) \geq 0$. Then, if δ^2 is executed at w_2, Alice is held backward-looking responsible, i.e., $M, w_2 \models \mathcal{B}_{\delta^2|_a}(\neg bal(n) \geq 0)$. That is, the PMH does not arise in the presence of the organisational structure proposed and the organisational actions info and deleg.

This example illustrates that we can avoid the PMH by introducing power relations to take delegation and indirect agency into account. The 'leader' of the group, Carol, has no action in her repertoire to ensure a non-violation state herself. It does not matter what she does, she will never be held backward-looking responsible. But with the introduction of the power relation she can be held responsible, because δ^6 does not ensure a non-violation state for Carol, whereas there is an action that does, namely, δ^7, because $M, w_2 \models K_c E_{\delta^7|_c} \mathcal{R}^2_{\{a,b\}} (bal(n) \geq 0)$.

Finally, it is also interesting to notice that the information action executed by Betty on w_1 is important to make Alice aware of which account she will use to pay the bill. We invite the reader to do the exercise of considering $I = \emptyset$. In this case, the action will not produce its effect and therefore, the PMH arises.[9]

3.5 CONCLUSION

Our formalisation of forward-looking and backward-looking responsibility is based on other, more basic, 'ingredients'. Here we use agents' actions, abilities, obligations, and knowledge. Earlier works on the formalisation of responsibility often do not deal with all of these ingredients (cf. Santos and Carmo (1996), and Dignum and Dignum (2012)). For instance, Santos and Carmo (1996) deal only with obligations and agents abilities. As we do here, they propose that responsibility should be paraphrased by 'obligation to ensure'. Their formalisation is done by using a logic wherein one can write formulae of the form $OE_i\varphi$, which stand for 'it is obligatory that i ensures φ'. The most interesting feature of this approach is the validity of the scheme $E_i E_j \varphi \to E_i \varphi$. It expresses that 'if agent i ensures that agent j ensures φ then i ensures φ'. This is a useful feature for modelling indirect agency that is not present in our framework. However, Santos and Carmo's logic is not appropriate to address our problem for two reasons: it does not permit to express agents' incomplete knowledge about the situation and also does not have actions in its object language. The fact that Alice has incomplete knowledge is crucial in the example presented in section 3.4.4, as well as the actions, because the problem is precisely that she needs to decide which action to execute.

In this chapter, we have presented a logic that extends PDL by epistemic formulae of the form $K_i\varphi$, expressing that agent i knows that φ (similarly to Grossi et al. (2007) and Herzig et al. (2000)), and also by enacted actions, i.e., formulae of the form $[\delta|_G]\varphi$, expressing that φ holds after the execution of δ by group G (similarly to Herzig and Lorini (2010), Lorini (2010), Royakkers (1998), and Wieringa and Meyer (1993)). It turns out that in our logic formulae of the form $\langle\langle G \rangle\rangle\varphi$, expressing that G has the ability to ensure φ, can be defined as simple abbreviations. Therefore, we can express operators with the same properties as the ones found in other logics of agency, such as coalition logic (Pauly 2001, 2002) and ATL (Alur 2002), but using a simpler semantics. In addition, our logic also enables us to give a solution to the problem of uniform strategies. With this tool in hand, we propose a formalisation of one notion of forward-looking responsibility, two notions of backward-looking responsibility, and also the relation between them. All these together enable us to model the PMH in organisations, and to show how organised groups of agents are more likely to avoid such problems.

Appendix

Proof of Theorem 1 (Sketch)

The proof is done by providing an equivalent alternative semantics for CEDL and then using the Correspondence Theorem (Blackburn et al. 2001, Sahlqvist 1975) with this alternative semantics.

First, for every CEDL model $M = \langle W, \mathcal{K}, \mathcal{T}, \mathcal{V} \rangle$ we build an alternative model $M^* = \langle W, \mathcal{K}, \mathcal{T}^*, \mathcal{V} \rangle$. That is, M^* is the same structure as M, but with a different transition function $\mathcal{T}^*$, which is defined as follows:

- $\mathcal{T}^*$ is a function from the set of all partial joint actions to $W \times W$, where $(w, w') \in \mathcal{T}^*(\delta_G)$ if and only if there is $\delta' \in \Delta$ such that $(w, w') \in \mathcal{T}^*(\delta|_G \cup \delta'|_{N \setminus G})$.

Alternative pointed models are tuples of the form $\langle M^*, w \rangle$, where M^* is as defined above and $w \in W$. The alternative satisfaction relation, $\vDash^*$, is the same as $\vDash$ for Boolean operators and for operators K_i plus:

$$M^*, w \vDash^* [\delta|_G]\varphi \text{ iff for all } w' \in \mathcal{T}^*_{\delta|G}(w) \text{ we have } M^*, w \vDash^* \varphi$$

Validity is defined as usual.

Second, let $\varphi \in \mathcal{L}$, we show by an induction on the structure of φ that $M, w \vDash \neg\varphi$ if and only if $M^*, w \vDash^* \varphi$.

Third, we show that alternative models satisfy the following constraints:

(C1') $\bigcup_{\delta \in \Delta} \mathcal{T}^*_{\delta|G}(w) \neq \emptyset$

(C2') $(\mathcal{T}^*_{\delta|G} \circ \mathcal{K}_i)(w) \subseteq (\mathcal{K}_i \circ \mathcal{T}^*_{\delta|G})(w)$

(C3') $\mathcal{T}^*_{\delta|G}(w) \subseteq \bigcup_{\delta' \in \Delta} \mathcal{T}^*_{\delta|G \cup \delta'|N \setminus G}(w)$

(C4') $\mathcal{T}^*_{\delta|G \cup H}(w) \subseteq \mathcal{T}^*_{\delta|G}(w) \cap \mathcal{T}^*_{\delta|H}(w)$

The first two are enforced by constraints C1 and C2 on CEDL models, respectively. The other two are enforced by the construction of $\mathcal{T}^*$.

Fourth, it is easy to see that all axioms in Table 1 are Sahlqvist's formulae (Blackburn et al. 2001, Sahlqvist 1975). Then, by using the substitution algorithm, we obtain that Axioms T, 4, and 5 correspond to reflexivity, transitivity, and Euclidicity of relations $\mathcal{K}_i$, respectively, and Axioms A, DA, S, and PR correspond to Constraints C1', C2', C3', and C4', respectively. Therefore, it follows from the Correspondence Theorem that the principles in Table 3.1 are sound and complete with respect to the class of alternative models. Because this semantics is equivalent to the semantics given earlier, then it is also sound and complete with respect to the class of CEDL models.

Proof of Theorem 2 (Sketch)

KK' to 5' are easy, and left for the reader. PR' is true because C2' is preserved for groups G by the definition of K_G. And KS is true because $\bigcap_{i \in G_1 \cup G_2} \mathcal{K}_i(w) \subseteq \bigcap_{i \in G_1} \mathcal{K}_i(w)$ for all $w \in W$.

Proof of Proposition 3

1. Suppose that $M, w \vDash \langle\langle G \rangle\rangle \perp$, for some arbitrary pointed model $\langle M, w \rangle$. Then, there is a δ such that $M, w \vDash \neg[\delta|_G] \perp \wedge [\delta|_G] \perp$, which is a contradiction.
2. From Axiom A, $\exists_{\delta \in \Delta} \neg[\delta|_G] \perp$ for all $G \subseteq N$. Because also $[\delta|_G]\top$, for all $\delta \in \Delta$ and all $G \subseteq N$, we have $\exists_{\delta \in \Delta}(\neg[\delta|G] \perp \wedge .[\delta|G]\top)$.
3. First, note that $\langle\langle G \rangle\rangle \varphi \wedge \langle\langle H \rangle\rangle \psi$ is equivalent to $\exists_{\delta \in \Delta}(\neg[\delta|_G] \perp \wedge .[\delta|_G]\varphi) \wedge \exists_{\delta' \in \Delta}(\neg[\delta'|_H] \perp \wedge .[\delta'|_H]\psi))$. Also note that (a) $\exists_{\delta \in \Delta} \neg[\delta|_G \cup \delta'|_H] \perp$ (by Axiom A), and also (b) $([\delta|_G]\varphi \wedge [\delta'|_H]\psi) \to [\delta|_G \cup \delta'|_H](\varphi \wedge \psi)$ (by Axiom S). Putting (a) and (b) together we have $(\langle\langle G \rangle\rangle \varphi \wedge \langle\langle H \rangle\rangle \psi) \to \langle\langle G \cup H \rangle\rangle(\varphi \wedge \psi)$.
4. From Axiom A, (a) $\exists_{\delta \in \Delta} \neg[\delta|_G] \perp$ for all G. And from $\varphi \to \psi$ we infer $[\delta|_G](\varphi \to \psi)$ (by Rule NA), and then (b) $[\delta|_G]\varphi \to [\delta|_G]\psi$ (by Axiom KA and Rule MP). Then, (a) and (b) together imply $\langle\langle G \rangle\rangle \varphi \to \langle\langle G \rangle\rangle \psi$.

NOTES

1. We are well aware that 'acting freely' may be interpreted differently, such as, e.g., absence of compulsion, which does not necessarily require alternative actions; or as availability of alternatives, which does not necessarily require the possibility to avoid the outcome, but may require the possibility to withdraw oneself from the causal chain; or even as having the possibility of avoiding an outcome at reasonable costs to the agent, which is even stronger than our interpretation. Our choice of being able to avoid outcome seems a reasonable middle way and fits our formal framework well.
2. This interpretation of $\langle\langle \emptyset \rangle\rangle$ is similar as given to its homonym in Coalition Logic (CL) and Alternating-time Temporal Logic (ATL) (Alur et al. 2002). In fact, for all $G \subseteq N$, the interpretation given to $\langle\langle G \rangle\rangle$ is similar to that in CL and ATL, but with some technical differences. Our $\langle\langle G \rangle\rangle$ is the fusion of ATL operators $\langle\langle G \rangle\rangle$ and X (which means 'next'). That is, our formulae of the form $\langle\langle G \rangle\rangle \varphi$ correspond to ATL formulae of the form $\langle\langle G \rangle\rangle X\varphi$. It turns out that our

128   *Tiago de Lima and Lambèr Royakkers*

   operator $\langle\langle G \rangle\rangle$ validates some of the axioms and inference rule of ATL operators $\langle\langle G \rangle\rangle X$ (as found, e.g., in Goranko and Van Drimmelen 2006).

3. It contrasts with ATL, where the formula $\neg\langle\langle\emptyset\rangle\rangle X\neg\varphi \rightarrow \langle\langle N \rangle\rangle X\varphi$ is valid. This is not the case here, though. This constitutes a difference from the logic proposed in De Lima *et al.* (2010). There, joint determinism is taken as an assumption.

4. Proof (sketch): By induction on n. In the induction step, $n = 1$. Note that $\mathcal{A}_{\delta_{1|G}}\neg\varphi$ abbreviates $E_{\delta_1 G}\neg\varphi \wedge \neg E_{\delta_{1|G}}\neg vio_G$. Thus, we just need to show that $R_G^1(\varphi) \wedge E_{\delta_1 G}\neg\varphi$ implies $\neg E_{\delta_{1|G}}\neg vio_G$. Indeed, because $R_G^1(\varphi)$ implies $\langle\langle\emptyset\rangle\rangle(\neg\varphi \rightarrow vio_G)$, which, together with $E_{\delta_1 G}\neg\varphi$ implies $E_{\delta_{1|G}} vio_G$. The induction step is similar.

5. Proof (sketch): By induction on n. In the induction step, $n = 1$. Note that $\mathcal{B}_{\delta_{1|G}}\neg\varphi$ abbreviates $\mathcal{C}_{\delta_{1|G}}\neg\varphi \wedge \neg \mathcal{C}_{\delta_{1|G}}\neg vio_G \wedge R_G^1 \varphi$. Thus, we just need to show that $R_G^1(\varphi) \wedge \mathcal{C}_{\delta_{1|G}}\neg\varphi$ implies $\neg \mathcal{C}_{\delta_{1|G}}\neg vio_G$. Indeed, because $R_G^1(\varphi)$ implies $\langle\langle\emptyset\rangle\rangle(\neg\varphi \rightarrow vio_G)$, which, together with $\mathcal{C}_{\delta_{1|G}}\neg\varphi$ implies $\mathcal{C}_{\delta_{1|G}} vio_G$. The induction step is similar.

6. Notice that we need $\langle\delta_1|_G\rangle \dots \langle\delta_n|_G\rangle\varphi$ in the formalisation instead of just φ, because it is the sequence of actions $\delta_1;\dots;\delta_n$ that leads to φ and that is the same sequence that makes G blameworthy and accountable.

7. Proof (sketch): Note that $\mathcal{B}_{\delta_{1|G};\dots;\delta_{n|G}}\varphi$ implies $E_{\delta_{1|G};\dots;\delta_{n|G}}\varphi \wedge \langle\langle\emptyset\rangle\rangle \dots \langle\langle\emptyset\rangle\rangle(\varphi \rightarrow vio_G)$. Thus, $\langle\delta_1|_G\rangle \dots \langle\delta_n|_G\rangle\varphi$ implies $\neg E_{\delta_{1|G};\dots;\delta_{n|G}}\neg vio_G$.

8. See Horling and Lesser (2004) for an exhaustive survey.

9. Note however, that under such assumption the model M must be changed. For instance, if action info does not produce any effect, worlds w_2 and w_3 should be similar.

REFERENCES

Ågotnes, T., and H. van Ditmarsch. 2008. "Coalitions and announcements." In *Proceedings of the seventh international joint conference on autonomous agents and multi-agent systems* (AAMAS 2008), edited by L. Padgham, D.C. Parkes, J. Müller, and S. Parsons, 673–680. Richland, SC: IFAAMAS.

Alur, R., T.A. Henzinger, and O. Kupferman. 2002. "Alternating-time temporal logic." *Journal of the ACM* 5(49): 672–713.

Anderson, A.R., and O.K. Moore. 1957. "The formal analysis of normative concepts." *The American Sociological Review* 22(1): 9–17.

Belnap, N., M. Perlo, and M. Xu. 2001. *Facing the future.* Oxford: Oxford University Press.

Blackburn, P., M. de Rijke, and Y. Venema. 2001. *Modal logic.* Cambridge: Cambridge University Press.

Broersen, J., A. Herzig, and N. Troquard. 2007. "A normal simulation of coalition logic and an epistemic extension." In *Proceedings of the 11th conference on theoretical aspects of rationality and knowledge* (TARK-2007, June 25–27), edited by D. Samet, 92–101. New York: ACM.

d'Altan, P., J.-J.Ch. Meyer, and R. Wieringa. 1996. "An integrated framework for ought-to-be and ought-to-do constraints." *Artificial Intelligence and Law* 4(2): 77–111.

Decker, K., and V. Lesser. 1995. "Designing a family of coordination algorithms." In *Proceedings of the first international conference on multi-agent systems (ICMAS-95)*, edited by V. Lesser, 73–80. Cambridge: The MIT Press.

De Lima, T., L. Royakkers, and F. Dignum. 2010. "A logic for reasoning about responsibility." *Journal of the IGPL* 18(1): 99–117, 2010. doi: 10.1093/jigpal/jzp073.

De Lima, T., L. Royakkers, and F. Dignum. 2010. "Modeling the problem of many hands in organisations." In *Proceedings of the 19th European conference on artificial intelligence* (ECAI 2010), edited by H. Coelho et al, 79–84. Amsterdam: IOS Press.

Dignum, V., and Dignum, F.P.M. 2012. "A logic of agent organisations." *Logic Journal of the IGPL* 20(1): 283–316.

Fagin, R., J. Halpern, Y. Moses, and M. Vardi. 1995. *Reasoning about knowledge*. Cambridge: The MIT Press.

Fararo, T.J. 1997. "*Reflections on mathematical sociology.*" Sociological Forum 12(1): 73–101.

Giddens, A. 1987. *Social theory and modern sociology*. Cambridge: Polity Press.

Goldman, A. 2009. "Social epistemology." In *Stanford encyclopedia of philosophy* (online), edited by E. Zalta. http://plato.stanford.edu/entries/epistemology-social/.

Goodin, R.E. 1995. *Utilitarianism as a public philosophy*. Cambridge: Cambridge University Press.

Goranko, V., and G. van Drimmelen. 2006. "Complete axiomatization and decidability of alternating-time temporal logic." *Theoretical Computer Science* 353 (1–3): 93–117.

Grossi, D., L. Royakkers, and F. Dignum. 2007. "Organisational structure and responsibility: An analysis in a dynamic logic of organised collective agency." *Artificial Intelligence and Law* 15(3): 223–249.

Harel, D., D. Kozen, and J. Tiuryn. 1984. "Dynamic logic." In *Handbook of philosophical logic, Volume II—Extensions of classical logic*, edited by D. Gabbay and F. Guenther, 497–604. Dordrecht: D. Reidel Publishing Company.

Herzig, A., J. Lang, D. Longin, and T. Polacsek. 2000. "A logic for planning under partial observability." In *Proceedings of AAAI'2000*, 768–773. Cambridge: AAAI Press/The MIT Press.

Herzig, A., and E. Lorini. (2010). "A dynamic logic of agency I: STIT, abilities and powers." *Journal of Logic, Language and Information*, 19(1): 89–121.

Horling, B., and V. Lesser. 2004. "A survey of multi-agent organisational paradigms." *The Knowledge Engineering Review* 19(4): 281–316.

Jamroga, W., and T. Ågotnes. 2007. "Constructive knowledge: What agents can achieve under incomplete information." *Journal of Applied Non-Classical Logics* 4(1): 423–475.

Jamroga, W., and W. Van der Hoek. 2004. "Agents that know how to play." *Fundamenta Informaticae*, 63(2–3): 185–219.

Lorini, E. 2010. "A Dynamic Logic of Agency II: Deterministic DLA , Coalition Logic, and Game Theory." *Journal of Logic, Language and Information* 19(3): 327–351.

Meyer, J.-J.Ch. 1988. "A different approach to deontic logic: Deontic logic viewed as a variant of dynamic logic." *Notre Dame Journal of Formal Logic*, 29(1), 109–136.

Meyer, J.-J.Ch., and R. Wieringa. (eds.) 1993. *Deontic logic in computer science*. Chichester: John Wiley and Sons.

Morgenstern, O. 1951. *Prolegomena to a theory of organisation*. U.S. Air Force, Project RAND, Research Memorandum. RM-734, ASTIA Document Number ATI 210734. Santa Monica, CA.

Osborne J., and A. Rubinstein. 1994. *A course in game theory*. Cambridge: MIT Press.

Pauly, M. 2002. "A modal logic for coalitional power in games." *Journal of Logic and Computation*, 12(1): 149–166.

Pauly, M. 2001. *Logic for social software*. (PhD thesis). ILLC, University of Amsterdam.

Royakkers, L.M.M. 1998. *Extending deontic logics for the formalisation of legal rules*. Dordrecht: Kluwer Academic Publishers.

130 *Tiago de Lima and Lambèr Royakkers*

Sahlqvist, H. 1975. "Completeness and correspondence in the first and second order semantics for modal logics." In *Proceedings of the third Scandinavian logic symposium*, edited by S. Kanger, 110–143. Amsterdam: North-Holland Publishing Company.

Santos, F., and J. Carmo. 1996. "Indirect action, influence and responsibility." In *Deontic logic, agency and normative Systems*, edited by M. A. Brown and J. Carmo, 194–215. Berlin: Springer.

Selznick, P. 1948. "Foundations of the theory of organisation." *American Sociological Review* 13(1): 25–35.

Sorensen, A.B. 1978. "Mathematical models in sociology." *Annual Review of Sociology* 4: 345–371.

Van der Hoek, W., and M. Wooldridge. 2003. "Cooperation, knowledge, and time: Alternating-time temporal epistemic logic and its applications." *Studia Logica*, 75(1): 125–157.

Van Fraassen, B. 1973. "Values and the heart's command." *The Journal of Philosophy* 70(1): 5–19.

Wieringa, R.J., and J.-J.Ch. Meyer. 1993. "Actors, actions, and initiative in normative system specification." *Annals of Mathematics and Artificial Intelligence* 7(1–4): 289–346.

4 Responsibility and the Problem of Many Hands in Networks

Sjoerd D. Zwart

4.1 INTRODUCTION

In this chapter we will apply the conceptual framework developed in the first part of the book to an example of an occasional collection of agents. It concerns the rise and fall of a manure processing factory in the Netherlands during the 1990s—the PROMEST case. We will investigate whether it features a problem of many hands regarding forward-, and backward-looking responsibility. To analyse this case we will also employ the dimensions of organisational power and coordination considered in Chapter 3. We will discuss the question of whether, and if so to what extent, these dimensions are helpful in learning how to avoid PMHs.

The outline of this chapter is as follows. First, in section 4.2 describe how to identify collections of agents possibly responsible for the inflicted harm by a joint action, something which is less trivial as appears on first sight. Then, in section 4.3, we describe the history of the PROMEST case and identify the actors involved in the related network. In section 4.4 we study whether the PROMEST case provides an example of a PMHs in terms of obligations or blame. In the fifth section we reintroduce the three organisational dimensions—power, coordination, and control—and apply them to the case at hand. While doing so, we draw lessons about how to decrease the likelihood of a PMH in more or less organised collections of actors.

4.2 NETWORKS AND HOW TO DELINEATE A POSSIBLY RESPONSIBLE COLLECTION

As no generally accepted definition of networks exists in the literature, we start with explaining how we will use the term. We take a network to be a finite set of agents, individuals, or organisations held together by social ties (e.g., Wasserman and Faust 1994). In principle, social networks can consist of many kinds of ties, such as friendship ties, exchange of material resources, exchange of information, or ties of authority, and analysts can focus on just those subsets of the social ties that serve their purpose.

132 *Sjoerd D. Zwart*

Networks do not cover isolated and unconnected agents. All agents in a network should have at least one social connection with some other actor. For instance, the relation 'both being carbon dioxide producers' relates me with some human being somewhere else in the world with whom I do not have any social tie. Although this relation establishes an indirect, causal connection, because together we causally contribute to global warming, it does not establish a social network between me and her. As this example shows, sometimes causal and social networks are unrelated. We consider the relational ties that hold a network together, like the agents, to be part of the social world and therefore social networks are part of (social) reality as well. We could have chosen our terms differently, but this way of formulation serves our purposes best. As part of reality, social networks develop over time as new relations come into being and old relations become obsolete.

As has been explained in Chapter 2, besides social networks, we distinguish between *collections, collectives*, and organisations. In the following a *collection of agents* is just a group of agents lumped together by causal connections to some harm; a *collective of actors* is a collection of agents that possibly qualifies for acquiring collective responsibility because of the ways the agents in the collection are tied together in the underlying social network.[1] The decisions of actor collectives have an impact on various stakeholders. We will call the actor-stakeholders, or *actors* for short, all those parties who affect or determine decisions or actions in a system or project; these are the active stakeholders. Additionally, we will call just *stakeholders* all those who are affected by the decisions made or actions taken by the actors. The latter are also referred to as passive stakeholders.[2] Passive stakeholders are only affected by the decisions of the other actors.

In our conception, social networks exist independently from some harm being done. These networks are an important part of social reality with or without the considered harm. Conversely, the collection of agents possibly responsible for some harm is a function of the harm occurred or envisaged. If the individuals of the possibly responsible collections are completely socially unrelated, identification of the responsible collection is relatively unproblematic. We just lump together all those individuals that are causally connected the harm. If, however, the agents causally connected to the harm are part of one or more underlying social networks, then the question of how to carve out these collections of the underlying stratum of the social networks is more complicated. This question is of the utmost importance for an adequate analysis of the problem of many hands.

The collection possibly held responsible for an occurred harm should be delineated relatively independent of the conditions for holding groups collectively responsible. If not, we run the risk of solving the PMH in a circular way. If the delineation of the group depends on the responsibility conditions, it creates the possibility of defining the relevant group in such a manner that one of the conditions for collective responsibility is not met and the PMH would never occur. How are we to establish independently the collection that qualifies for being a group responsible for some harm? The strongest criterion is the proximate causal one: the collection to be considered should at least cover the agents that together directly and causally brought about the harm. For example, in the CitiCorp example (Chapter 2) the contractor is a clear case of an agent that causally brought about a dangerous situation. How are we to fix the relevant collection around the agents that are proximate-cause related? At least two ways to proceed make sense.

First, we may just remain in the realms of the causal network and, in addition to considering the proximate-cause related agents, add more distal-cause related agents to the collection. Agents that did not directly cause the harm physically but had some more indirect influence should be included as well. To be sure, in real cases these more distal causes always play an important role—so much so that the Australian Transport Safety Bureau (ATSB) replaced their analyses in terms of 'causes' in its official accident reports with analyses in terms of 'contributory safety factors' (Walker 2009). In the CitiCorp case, a distal causal influence of the structural engineer LeMessurier was his unconventional design. Carrying out the design with welded joints was more difficult than with bolded joints. The problem with the causal connection approach is, of course, how to decide which causal ties are strong enough to include an agent as a member of the possibly responsible collection of agents.

A second way to proceed, therefore, would be to focus only on the proximate-causal agents and let the social networks decide about how to delineate the relevant collection. This way of proceeding, however, runs the risk of becoming circular at the moment analysts are going to advice how to change the collection structure to evade PMHs. Because if the social network had been different and the collection is fixed by means of the form of the underlying social network, the possibility arises to evade the PMH *by the definition* of the ties that hold the social network together. In that case, the same harm occurs, but the collection delineated by the social network cannot be held responsible. That would be an empty solution to the many hands problem and the analysis would not contribute to a decrease of societal harms being done by collections. We will therefore proceed by identifying the relevant collection along distal, causal lines between the (potential) harm and the agents involved. Clearly, we cannot give general rules which causal relations are strong enough for including an agent as part of the collection. The long history of accident reports for instance in the aviation industry, however, make us confident that in the context of a concrete harm it will be possible to set up a finite set of contributory (causal) factors which delineate the possibly responsible collection of agents.

One important issue about the proposed way to proceed concerns the observation that the many distal causes of some societal harm often progress along social ties of influence. In Chapter 3 we saw that supervision along hierarchical lines counts as causal (efficacy). One may therefore advance the objection then that focusing on the causal network does introduce parts of

134 *Sjoerd D. Zwart*

the social network again with the same danger of circular solutions of the PMH. The answer to this objection consists of two parts. First, although influences in a network often progress along social ties, it is only *causal* influences we focus on, not just any social tie. Second, a circular and therefore an empty solution of the PMH by a change in the underlying causal network is unlikely because of the following. Adapting this network would mean that either some agent formerly outside the collection has become responsible-blameworthy, which is impossible because its causal connection to the harm would have put it already in the collection at the start; or the causal network did change in such a way that the harm would not have occurred, which is a laudable and non-empty solution to the PMH. Moreover, it is impossible to solve a PMH by a change in the causality network that makes some agent leave the collection because this cannot make some other agent in the collection causally responsible who was not causally responsible before.

Finally, once the collection causally responsible has been identified along proximate and distal causal lines the question arises about the form of the social network that is underlying the collection of actors that is possibly responsible. To come to the relevant social ties, here, we will follow Chapter 3, which was inspired by the work of Grossi et al. (2007). After having studied the work on social and organisation theory (cf. Ebers 1999; Giddens 1987; Hammer and Champy 1994; Horling and Lesser 2004; Morgenstern 1951; Podolny and Page 1998; Spector 2007), Grossi and his co-authors came to the conclusion that organisations can be fruitfully analysed in terms of *power, coordination*, and *control*. We will take these social relations to be the most relevant for individual and collective moral responsibility attribution. Power concerns the *formal* relation of authority whereas coordination and control are behavioural interactions (cf. Wasserman and Faust 1994, Chapter 1). In accordance with Chapter 3, we will say that an actor has *power* over a second if that actor is able to impose actions on the second actor that serve the first actor's interest. Additionally, a network is *well-coordinated* if it facilitates the flow of knowledge and information among its actors. Finally, *control* in the network relates to actors monitoring each other's performances, which ultimately results in the ability to provide for backups in case of failure or violations of certain tasks.[3]

Interestingly, following the collection identification procedure just described, we naturally arrive at the three types of collectives distinguished in Chapter 2. Let some harm occur and let two or more actors be approximate or distal causes. If the underlying social network of these agents turns out to be relatively empty, i.e., there are no power coordination or control ties, we have identified an *occasional collection of agents* without a shared aim but which nevertheless collectively caused, or could have prevented, some harm (or achieved a good). The case of individual skaters moving around on a frozen lake when suddenly the ice gives way provides an example of harm being done by an occasional collection. At the opposite end of the scale, if a group turns out to have a strong hierarchical power structure, we have identified an *organised group* (sometimes even a 'corporate agent') that can chose collective aims by a collective decision procedure. In between the two extremes of no power ties and a strong power hierarchy, we may encounter in the social network a power distribution and coordination ties that help agents to come to acting 'on overlapping participatory intentions'. Of course these power distribution and coordination ties are contributing circumstances for the collection to be involved in their joint action. The procedure was only designed to find *possibly* responsible collections. To determine whether the collection with the power distribution and coordination ties just described is involved in a joint action we should verify a third necessary condition about how the actors used the power and coordination ties. We have to find out whether the members of the collective 'intentionally contributed to G's occurrence by doing particular parts and their conceptions of G sufficiently and actually overlap' (G is a state of affairs). If so, we have identified a *collection that is involved in a joint action.* Apparently, the underlying power, coordination ties, and control in a group bringing about some harm determine whether this group is an occasional collection or a corporate agent and are necessary conditions for a collective to be involved in a joint action.

Now that it is clear how we delineate possibly responsible groups, let us turn to the PROMEST case to find out how our framework fares in a real life example.

4.3 THE PROMEST CASE[4] AND ITS COLLECTION OF ACTORS

4.3.1 Introduction and Overview

Manure management on a regional scale started in the Netherlands in the 1970s. In 1969, the Christian agricultural board in Brabant (NCB) established one of the first regional manure banks in Tilburg. It was supposed to intermediate on a regional scale between farmers with a need and those with a surplus of manure. Many other regions followed the example in Tilburg, and the activities of some of those banks did even trespass the Dutch borders. A decade later, due to growing societal concerns about the environmental impact of intense agriculture, the Dutch agriculture sector was confronted with increasing opposition. This opposition required a reorientation in the world of agricultural interest organisations. Of all the problems surrounding the agricultural sector, the manure surplus problem attracted by far the most public attention. In the mid-1980s, this attention had assumed such dimensions that the ministers of agriculture and environment started to exert considerable pressure on the agricultural sector and, more specifically, on the farmers to take drastic measures to solve the surplus of manure problem. The establishment of the National Manure Bank and the PROMEST B.V. must be considered in the context of this hard unrelenting pressure.

136   *Sjoerd D. Zwart*

In the southern part of the Netherlands, where the manure problem was most pressing, the awareness of this problem came first. A steering committee called the *Stuurgroep Mestproblematiek Noord-Brabant*, established in 1984 by several agricultural organisations and public authorities, considered large-scale manure processing the best strategy for reducing the large manure surplus. The intended end products of processing were fertilizer granules, which would be sold to foreign farmers. The promising business of manure processing attracted many companies seeking to take advantage of the large amounts of money that became available. In 1986, PROMEST B.V. (henceforth PROMEST) was established, in which agricultural organisations, chemical companies, and financial companies cooperated to construct a large demonstration plant for the processing of 100,000 tons of manure annually. Construction of the plant started in 1987. Although the construction costs were high (23 million guilders, or 10 million euros) PROMEST expected to reduce costs through the construction of larger plants and lower investments costs in the following years. When construction started in 1987, preparations for an upgrade of the plant were already on their way.

PROMEST experienced many technical difficulties, some of which could only be solved by means of expensive remedies. Moreover, some doubted whether there was any market at all for the (unstable) granules leaving the factory (Bloemendaal 1995, 82). Due to ill-conceived design choices and technical problems, the overall plant performance was low. Nevertheless, the plan to upgrade the plant was carried through, and in 1992, contrary to recommendation of the plant's operational staff, an upgraded plant was opened. This led to a processing capacity of 600,000 tons of manure per year. The total investment costs increased to more than 100 million Dutch guilders (45 million euros), of which 40% were investment grants. Technical problems continued, just as the problems with the manure supply and the production of the granules (Bloemendaal 1995, 85). Attempts to secure the continuous supply of manure and to cover the exploitation costs were forbidden by EC regulations. Despite these regulations, the Ministry of Agriculture made the National Board (in Dutch: *Landbouwschap*) to reach an agreement with the regional boards about a Central Manure Exchange (*Mestcentrale*) in 1994. The farmers became obliged to deliver their manure to this central exchange to safeguard sufficient manure supply for PROMEST. Eventually, the plant, which had never operated at full capacity, was shut down in 1994, less than two years after the upgrade. An important cause of the premature bankruptcy was the insufficient supply of manure, which was due to the high price producers had to pay for delivering their manure to the factory. The farmers had cheaper ways of getting rid of their manure and were not willing to pay more to PROMEST. Because of the relatively small amount of available raw material, PROMEST had to sell their end product for prices that could not compete with the prices of other products on the market.

To analyse this case in terms of responsibility and the PMH, we should first identify the harm being done. To do so we consider the hierarchy of goals related to the PROMEST case. On the most general level, all parties had a substantial stake in the continuation or even extension of the livestock in the Netherlands. This was most directly the case for the individual farmers and the agricultural boards, but it was also part of the bread and butter of the other parties mentioned. For various reasons, this general goal required the achievement of a subordinated goal, viz. to get rid of the surplus of the Dutch manure in the most effective, economic, politically acceptable, and ecologically sound way. This goal was most urgent for the Ministry of Agriculture and the agricultural boards, but the other parties involved had a stake in this issue as well. Finally, on the most concrete level, as the PROMEST consortium had a considerable contribution to make to the intermediate goal, all parties involved were also implied to a larger or lesser extent when it came to a steady and large enough supply of manure to the PROMEST plant. To keep our case study as concise as possible we will focus on the failure of achieving this third, most concrete goal of the collection. We will concentrate therefore on the question of responsibility distribution within the network for the failure of not establishing a steady and large enough manure supply for the PROMEST plant.

Besides the PROMEST consortium, the parties causally connected to the failure of manure supply are the regional agricultural organisations (on the national level united in the Agricultural Board); the Ministry of Agriculture and other public authorities; the National Manure Bank; the individual farmers; and the General Inspection Service (In Dutch: *Algemene Inspectie Dienst*, AID). We consider the European Community as setting the constraints for the problem that had to be solved.

4.3.2   The Agents

In this section, we describe the individual agents of the PROMEST case and address the question whether they were actors in the collection or just stakeholders only undergoing the outcomes of the activities within the collection.

PROMEST Consortium
In the 1980s, at the time of serious political pressure to solve the manure surplus problem, two regional agricultural organisations from the south of the country (NCB and LLTB) took the initiative to construct the PROMEST plant. In 1986, they established the first manure processing company (Bloemendaal 1995, 81). In the consortium, also, two financial and several technical companies cooperated, such as chemical processing companies, machinery suppliers in the cattle feeding industry, and suppliers of drying and separation machinery. Whereas research institutes, such as the Agricultural-Economic Institute (in Dutch: *Landbouw-Economisch Instituut*, LEI) showed that the manure processing would lead to an exploitation shortage

138 *Sjoerd D. Zwart*

of 30–40 Dutch guilders (15 euros) per ton of manure at minimum, most companies were overly optimistic about the costs. Some even predicted to be able to gain a net profit from the processing. Together the partners in this consortium established the private company PROMEST B.V. (equivalent to the English Ltd legal form).

We consider the PROMEST consortium to be an actor in the manure supply issue. On first sight one might think they were passively undergoing the decisions of the individual farmers about where to buy the rights to bring their manure. In fact, however, PROMEST's decisions about the price the farmers had to pay for providing the plant with their manure causally influenced the final shortage of the manure supply. This price was too high. Moreover, all decisions PROMEST made about their technology and their marketing determined the price of their end product and therefore of the minimum price they could pay for the raw material. For these reasons, the PROMEST consortium was at least one of the distal causes of the shortage of manure supply and it is therefore an actor in the collection of agents possibly responsible for that shortage.

Regional and National Agricultural Organisations

On the national level, the agricultural organisations cooperated in the Agricultural Board (in Dutch: *Landbouwschap*), which was established in 1954. In the Agricultural Board, organised farmers and agricultural workers successfully cooperated and succeeded in obtaining a representational monopoly, excluding others from negotiating with the Ministry of Agriculture on behalf of the farmers. In the 1980s, due to the growing environmental concerns, especially regarding the problems related to the manure surplus, the Agricultural Board was confronted with political opposition to the expanding livestock. In 1984, an interim bill on the limitation of expansion of pig and poultry farming was passed through Parliament without consultation of the Board. This led to the first 'tangible' crack in the close relationship between the Agricultural Board and the Ministry of Agriculture.

The agricultural organisations from the northern and southern regions pursued different interests within the National Board because the manure problem was not equally urgent in all parts of the country. Because the manure problem was most pressing in the southern part of the country, the regional organisations from this part urged for solutions based on solidarity, whereas the regional organisations in the northern part of the country were more in favour of a 'polluter pays' approach to the manure problem. The Board came with the initiative to let the life-stock farmers in the south and east of the country pay levies on the production of manure to the National Board, as they were the cause of the manure surplus. In 1994, the regional boards, who were in favour of installing the Central Manure Exchange (*Mestcentrale*), advised the farmers to adjourn the levy payment as the National Board did postpone payments to PROMEST.[5] Discussions within the Agricultural Board made the Board appear less univocal and, as a result, less powerful towards the policy makers. Partly due to the changing position of the Agricultural Board within the policy regime—and also because of the internal disagreements—the agricultural organisations lost their credibility to the individual farmers, and consequently their support, which ultimately led to the request to dissolve the Board in 1995 (Krajenbrink 2005, 409; Wisserhof 2000, 186).

At the time, the National Agricultural Board had substantial power, and could and did make decisions affecting the supply of manure. It was therefore at least a distal cause of the shortage of manure supply. Interestingly, the regional agricultural boards NCB and LLTB even accused the National Board of being the main cause of the possible bankruptcy of PROMEST (*Reformatorisch Dagblad*, 19 November 1994) because at the end, it refused to provide PROMEST with the necessary liquidity.

As initiators of the PROMEST plant, the two regional agricultural organisations, NCB and LLTB, were one of the proximate causes of its existence. Regarding the steady and large enough manure supply, the regional boards, as intermediates between individual farmers and the National agricultural board, were at least important distal causes of the shortage of manure. In 1994, e.g., they advised farmers not to pay the levies imposed by the National Board. Considering the way the regional boards were united in the National Board, one may wonder whether their causal influence was important enough to be called actors. After all, even though these regional, agricultural organisations represented the majority of the life-stock farmers in the southern Netherlands, one may doubt whether their decisions could guarantee a satisfactory manure supply. To assess the important causal influence of the regional boards, one needs only to consider the role of the northern boards in the demise of the National Board and the refusal to show solidarity with the farmers of the south of the country. These two issues were important distal and perhaps even proximate causes as to why the manure supply faltered. The national and regional boards were important actors in PROMEST collection.

Ministry of Agriculture

Until the early 1980s, the agricultural policy was established by the 'green front': the institutionalised exchange between the Ministry of Agriculture, the Board of Agriculture, and members of the Parliamentary Committee on Agriculture. Due to the growing opposition from the public, a change in the agricultural policy was required. In the course of the 1980s, the gradual decline of this green front resulted in a shift from consensus building with the agricultural organisations to top-down decision making and interference. Instead of the technocratic ideal of optimisation of the livestock production per animal per acre and the promotion of unlimited growth, the Ministry of Agriculture was forced to consider limits to growth. Due to public and political pressure and legislation by the European Community, agriculture in general and the intense livestock farming in particular became subject of political debate. Manure processing was seen as one of the dominant solutions to

140   *Sjoerd D. Zwart*

deal with environmental problems and the government provided support for large centralised plants. In general, the Ministry of Agriculture and the agricultural industry were against a high degree of government intervention in the manure market and supported free market solutions. This was one of the causes of the restricted discretionary powers of the National Manure Bank, which we will discuss below (Frouws 1994, 114–117).

Clearly the Ministry of Agriculture is one of the actors in the PROMEST manure supply issue. Although EU regulations restricted its possibilities, the Ministry could have made various decisions about how to secure a large and steady stream of manure in the direction of PROMEST. The Ministry of Agriculture, therefore, is an important actor in the manure supply issue.

National Manure Bank

In 1986, the Agricultural Board established the *National Manure Bank* besides and above the regional manure banks mentioned in section 4.3.1. It started as a foundation and was supposed to mediate between manure buying, selling, and processing on a national scale. Moreover, it was also supposed to be instrumental in the bookkeeping of the manure on a national scale. The Bank was financed with general levies, as opposed to the surplus levies, so the farmers in the areas without a manure surplus had to pay as well. Due to opposite regional interests, the agricultural organisations disagreed on the discretionary power on inspection, disciplinary law, and administration of the levies that should be given to the National Manure Bank. During the discussion on the interim bill in 1986, the oppositions within the Agricultural Board could not be bridged. The most controversial point was whether the National Bank should be entrusted with a so-called buying duty. In the end, this task was indeed imposed on the National Manure Bank and in 1988 sufficient storage capacity was arranged. The result was a National Manure Bank with only limited power, which made it impossible for the Bank to organise and manage the manure supply (Frouws 1994, 115–117). Despite its limited discretionary power, the National Manure Bank was one of the main parties selling, buying, processing, and bookkeeping manure on a national scale, and was for that reason at least one of the distal causes for the insufficient manure supply.

Individual Farmers

Although the cooperation of the individual farmers was essential, in the sense that the farmers had to supply the manure, they were not actively involved in the design and decision process of the PROMEST plant. Hence, there was no alignment between the design choices made by the technology companies and the agricultural organisations, on the one hand, and the preferences and practices of the farmers on the other. Partly due to the failure of the agricultural organisations to promote the farmers' interests in the manure legislation, and partly due to the internal disagreements within the Board, the farmers no longer felt represented by the agricultural organisations from the late 1980s onwards. They lacked a sense of urgency concerning the manure surplus. Accordingly, they made short-term economic choices. Processing manure proved to be twice as expensive as distributing the manure unprocessed. Hence, most farmers chose to distribute the manure instead of supplying it to PROMEST.

The proximate cause of the shortage of manure supply at the PROMEST factory was the farmers not delivering this precious raw material. For that reason the farmers were important actors in the PROMEST manure supply issue. Obviously, an individual farmer would not have been able to provide the enormous amounts of manure needed, but collectively the farmers could bring about a sufficient manure supply. To be precise, every individual farmer was causally related to the insufficiency of manure supply and was therefore an agent in PROMEST case network, but it was only as a group that they formed the proximate cause for this insufficiency.

AID

The General Inspection Service (Algemene Inspectiedienst, AID) is the controlling body of the Ministry of Agriculture. Its core task is to control and maintain regulations with regard to the agricultural sector. From the start of enforcement of the manure legislation onwards, the role of the AID remained unclearly articulated. In the late 1980s, the AID warned that it was not equipped with sufficient capacity to fulfil the controlling duty with respect to the manure legislation. Supported by the Ministry of Justice and the consultancy firm Oranjewoud—which investigated the 'maintenance of manure legislation'—the AID complained that the manure legislation was not controllable, and that there were too many opportunities for fraud. Consequently, in the policy report of the AID in 1993, it was officially stated that "due to the limited controllability . . . the commitment to the manure legislation will be reduced" (Bloemendaal 1995, 69). Also, in relation to the National Manure Bank, the task of the AID was ill-defined, and as a result, the bookkeeping of the manure flow became problematic. At first sight, because the AID was the controlling body of the Ministry, one might be tempted to consider the AID an actor in the network. Yet, as soon as one recalls that network control was defined as the ability to provide for a backup in case of failure or violations, one realises that the AID was not in control in this latter sense. For that reason, we consider the AID to be just a stakeholder in the PROMEST case. They only had the obligation to see it to that the bookkeeping of the manure was executed by the rules and played no causal role in the shortage of manure at the gates of PROMEST.

Research Institutes

Although several research institutes dominated the biogas niche in the late 1970s and early 1980s, their role in the PROMEST case was limited. Some research institutes participated in a national research program on manure processing in 1988 and 1989 and performed research on parts of the plants. Their role in technological development, however, was restricted, and their

142 *Sjoerd D. Zwart*

warnings for too-optimistic expectations about the economics of manure processing were discarded (Raven 2005, 77). As the causal connections between the research institutes and the insufficiency of the manure supply were almost absent, we consider them to be only stakeholders in the PROMEST case. If the harm considered was the bankruptcy of PROMEST, perhaps the causal links would have been somewhat stronger and perhaps they would have qualified as actors.

European Community (now European Union)
Finally, we will discuss the role of the European Community. Established in the 1960s the EC Common Agricultural Policy (CAP) was aimed at creating a situation of self-sufficiency within Europe, such as to reduce the risk of food shortage in the member states. However, by subsidising production of basic farm products, almost permanent surpluses were created. In the 1980s, due to the combination of growing environmental concern and excessive expenditures by the EC, the agricultural policy gradually changed to the broader aim of sustainable agriculture, including a focus on food quality and safety, animal welfare, and preservation of the environment. In 1984 quota on the production of dairy were introduced and in 1988 an upper limit to the expenditures by the EC was set. In the 1980s, the large agricultural countries of the United States, New Zealand, and Australia urged the EC to reduce its price support and export subsidies. The 1992 reform of the CAP included an adjustment to the needs for a more free agricultural market, as a result of which the support by national governments became limited (Krajenbrink 2005, 311). It was with regard to the latter that the EC became involved in the network: it forbade the structural subsidy of the exploitation costs of the plant because that would hamper fair competition between member states. We do not consider the causal connection between the EU and the insufficiency of the manure supply strong enough to make them actors in the PROMEST network. The European Communion only set the preconditions and constraints within which a solution to the PROMEST manure supply problem had to be found. None of its possible actions was or could have been directly interfered with the specificities of the manure supply at PROMEST. The EU actions could not have directed at the well-being of one specific manure plant. Setting the constraints may be determinative, but it is not one of the events that directly lead to the harm. Moreover, the subsidy restrictions were well-known before PROMEST was set up. Taking these arguments into account, we conclude that the EU is at most a stakeholder in the PROMEST network.

4.3.3 What Kind of Group?

To apply our conceptual framework to the PROMEST case, we have to address the question of whether the agents described above form an organised group, a collective involved in a joint action, or an occasional collection. Before doing so, we should observe one important approximation in our analysis of the PROMEST case. We suppose the PROMEST network to be *static* during the period of construction and operation of the plant (1986–1994), i.e., we assume that the actors and stakeholder roles within the network remained more or less the same within the given time span. Evidently, this is an approximation because, for instance, the Ministry of Agriculture in the 1980s shows a shift from a client ministry, solely oriented towards the agricultural interest, to a ministry of general administration (Frouws 1994; Wisserhof 2000, 176–177), and a change in a node in a network is a change in the network itself. Moreover, in the time frame considered, the social relations between farmers and the agricultural boards changed as well. These shifts, however, do not seem to impinge on the core of our network analysis and the way the network has reacted to the failure of manure supply.

What kind of the group is formed by the collection of actors identified above? As the actors did not have a collective decision procedure in place to form collective aims, the collection certainly did not qualify as an organised group, or 'corporate agent', which can form collective aims using a collective decision procedure. The collection identified, however, could have engaged in a joint action guaranteeing a sufficient supply of manure. Then, the collection would have been a clear case of a collective involved in a joint action. The joint action would have been characterised by the participatory intentions of the actors in the collection that ultimately lead to sufficient manure supply. The farmer actors, however, refrained from bringing their manure to PROMEST as they had opposite stakes, and refraining to provide PROMEST with sufficient manure is not a collective action because it is not characterised by a collective aim. Within the tri-partition of collections as taxonomy, the collection identified above is most appropriately characterised as an *occasional collection of individuals lacking the collective aim to provide PROMEST with sufficient manure*. They collectively caused the harm of the manure shortage, and collectively could (as physical modality) have prevented this harm. In fact, the PROMEST group lies somewhere in between a collective involved in a joint action and an occasional collective. The shared benefit of getting rid of the manure surplus in a durable and sustainable way ties the agents together and does not leave the PROMEST group as just occasional. Overcoming their individual stakes, most agents in the collection could have (at least as a technical modality) taken up a joint action to prevent the occurred harm. The first thing the PROMEST case therefore teaches us is that the three kinds of collections distinguished are three ideal types, rather than a partition.

The previous paragraph leads to the question of whether the PROMEST collection meets the *capacity condition* regarding the insufficient supply of manure. The question reads whether in the specific context it is reasonable to expect from the PROMEST collection to undertake a joint action or organise itself in such a way that the plant is provided with a sufficient supply of manure (φ). We think for various reasons this question should be answered positively. First, considerable investments were already made and the PROMEST collection is the only one that can efficaciously bring about φ.

144 *Sjoerd D. Zwart*

Second, establishing φ helps to solve, in a sustainable and durable way, the Dutch manure surplus problem, which important actors in the collection have helped creating. Third, it adequately responds to the mounting political pressure and threats to do something about the problem. And finally, the agricultural sector is of enormous economic importance, and the collection has an important stake in this sector and in bringing about φ. Establishing φ is closely related to the bread and butter of all actors in the collection.

Finally, let us address the question whether also the agents in the PROMEST collective, most of which are groups of individuals, fulfil the *capacity condition*. In accordance with Chapter 2, for organised groups (or 'corporate agents') and collectives involved in a joint action we assume that the capacity condition for collective responsibility is met because they have collective aims. The latter holds for: the PROMEST consortium; the regional and national agricultural organisations; the Ministry of Agriculture; national manure bank; the AID; the research institutes; and the European Community. All these actors and stakeholders are engaged in joint actions, and therefore meet the capacity condition for groups. This leaves us with the farmers, about whom we think we may reasonably assume that almost all meet the capacity condition individually. But to find out whether the farmers also meet the capacity condition as a group we should answer the question of whether it is reasonable to expect from the (occasional) collection of farmers that they undertook a joint action or organised itself in such a way that φ was jointly prevented. The farmers successfully organised themselves regionally and nationally in various ways. These ways of organisation did not, however, succeed in preventing not-φ, despite serious attempts of some regional boards to do so. The failure to present not-φ does not prove the impossibility for the farmers to organise themselves to establish φ, but it illustrates the difficulty in doing so. To our minds, the differences between the stakes of the individual farmers across the country were so enormous that it is unreasonable to expect that they could organise themselves nationally to prevent not-φ from happening. The occasional group of all individual Dutch farmers therefore does not meet the capacity criterion and cannot be held forward or backward responsible for φ.

4.4 PROMEST AND THE PROBLEMS OF MANY HANDS

In the foregoing we carved out the occasional collection of PROMEST BV, the Ministry, the boards, the bank, and the farmers, as being possibly responsible for the harm of insufficient manure supply, and we saw that the collection, the agents, and stakeholders all met the capacity condition, which will be left out of the consideration in the present section. Here we will address the question of in what sense, if any, the PROMEST case provides an example of a PMH regarding responsibility-as-obligation, and regarding responsibility-as-blameworthiness. Let us start with considering the question of whether the PROMEST case provides a PMH_O.

4.4.1 PROMEST: A PMH Regarding Obligations?

The responsibility-as-obligation in the PROMEST case concerns an adequate manure supply (let us call the latter φ). Chapter 1 gives the conditions under which an actor or a collective is forward-looking responsible. Beside the capacity condition, which is met by the collection and its agents, it mentions the causality and the normative condition. Let us discuss these two conditions regarding the collection and its elements.

The PROMEST Collection
According to Chapter 2, for forward-looking responsibility, the *causal condition* focuses on causal efficacy, which relates to what actions a collective can undertake and what outcomes it can achieve or avoid. With regard to the PROMEST collection, the causality condition states that under sufficient cooperation, the collection had enough causal efficacy to achieve φ. We think that the PROMEST collection meets this condition and that it could have provided the plant with a steady and large enough amount of manure. Thus, the PROMEST collection fulfils the condition of causal efficacy for forward-looking responsibility.

This brings us to the *normative* condition. In our case, the normative condition claims that φ is acceptable—even desirable—and the PROMEST is the collection that should bring φ about. For responsibility-as-obligation, the normative condition refers to moral obligations, which may be grounded along consequentialist, deontological, and virtue ethics lines. As for the consequentialist route, φ is desirable and should be accomplished by the PROMEST collection, because φ establishes considerable happiness among large numbers agents. Also, this collection is the only one that can bring about φ as a consequence of its actions, which answers the quest for the distribution principle in a trivial way. Although the collection did not voluntarily assume forward-looking responsibility, deontologically, the PROMEST collection had the obligation to bring about φ, because φ repaired to considerable extent damage that was due to action of the collection. The virtue ethics argument is somewhat harder to set up. One might argue, for instance, that if one would accept the idea of groups being more or less virtuous, the collection had established φ, provided it was virtuous. Although the argument along the virtue lines is perhaps less convincing than the consequentialist and deontological arguments, all three routes clearly point in the direction that the PROMEST collection had a rather strong moral obligation to establish φ. The collection was obligation-responsible for φ. What about the agents in the collection?

The Individual Actors
Now that we have seen that the PROMEST collection is morally forward looking responsible, we should consider the question of whether at least one of its actors can reasonably be held forward-looking responsible for φ. To do so, we first look at the causality condition, which is the same for the

146 *Sjoerd D. Zwart*

consequentialist, deontological, and virtue ethics route. Regarding forward-looking responsibility, this condition requires a causal efficacy of the agents, such that either the agent can bring about φ itself or via other agents. The descriptions of section 4.3 show that none of the agents meets this causality condition, except perhaps for the farmers and the Ministry. As the only possible proximate causes of φ the farmers as a group could establish φ. Also, the Ministry fulfils the causality condition, as it could have used its supervisory power to force the farmers to establish φ.[6]

To find out whether the PROMEST case instantiates a PMH regarding forward-looking responsibility we have to find out whether the two remaining candidates that meet the causal efficiency condition also satisfy the normative condition, as the other individual agents cannot be held individually responsible for φ. Following Chapter 2 we will discuss the normative condition not only along deontologist, but also along consequentialist and virtue ethic lines. Let us start with the farmers.

Individual Farmers

With regard to the individual farmers it suffices to observe that for obvious reasons none of them meets the causality condition. None of them was individually able to see to it that φ. Thus, none of the individual farmers was individually obligation-responsible for φ. As a collective, however, the farmers *were* able to bring about φ. They used, however, cheaper ways to get rid of their manure. Also, collectively they did not see to it that φ. Their situation resembles that of the individual car users in the global warming case (cf. Chapter 2, section 2.6). None of the individual car users can stop global warming, whereas all the car users together could—at least in theory. In the same sense, none of the farmers could individually establish φ, whereas, technically speaking, the group of all farmers could. Parallel to the global warming case, therefore, we may ask if the individual farmers do not have the responsibility-as-obligation to see to it that *collective agreements* are achieved, which would bring about φ. Indeed we think the individual farmers have this obligation and that many of them took it seriously. The many discussions within and between the local and national agricultural boards make the case in point. Note that these discussions show that the farmers took their responsibility to come to collective agreements, which would effectively bring about φ. These discussions do not mean, however, that, just as the individual car users in the global warming case, the individual farmers had the responsibility-as-obligation to bring about φ.

If the farmers are not forward-looking responsible for φ, what was the responsibility of the bodies in which they organised themselves, such as the local and the National agricultural boards? For them, φ was clearly not morally objectionable; it was even virtuous for them to bring it about. Moreover, due to the discretional power of the National Board and the enormous influence of the local boards on the farmers, their causal influence in the network was considerably larger than that of PROMEST and the national manure bank. Most interestingly, the two local boards in the south of the Netherlands even held the National Board responsible for the bankruptcy of PROMEST because it did not accept their proposals for the manure bank and stopped providing money for PROMEST. Interestingly, we observed that some local agricultural boards, mainly in the south, promised to see to it that φ, they voluntarily assumed the obligation-responsibility on the basis of initiative and judgment. Does this make them responsible-as-obligation for φ? Not exactly, because these local boards did not have the causal efficacy to make φ happen. This is because local boards in the north opposed the solidarity point of view propagated in the south, and individual farmers were free to sell their manure elsewhere. Although these southern boards had a good position in the network to bring about φ, they were not forward looking responsible for φ due to lack of power in the network.

As the National Board had more power, perhaps they were obligation-responsible for φ. Strictly speaking it was not, because they failed the causality condition, and on top of that they also represented the local boards in the north of the country that opposed the solidarity solution of the southern boards. Within the deontological route, we conclude that the National Board did not assume the obligation-responsibility for φ. This is not to say that the National Board did not try to make φ happen. It did acknowledge the desirability of an efficient PROMEST and it took some obligation-responsibility acquired along the consequentialist route. It imposed levies, put money in PROMEST, and facilitated the discussions between the northern southern boards. It had some responsibility toward the southern boards, but also toward the Ministry, to remain united and not to keep investing money in a business without a future. In sum, the agricultural boards were better placed in the network than PROMEST BV or the manure bank. They had more influence, and some local board even assumed responsibility. But, finally, the causal power of the boards in the network was limited to such an extent that they cannot reasonably be held obligation-responsible for φ.

Ministry of Agriculture

Let us now consider the position of the Ministry of Agriculture. Despite being caught between international and national political powers, the Ministry was the most causal efficacious agent in the collection; it was in the best position to bring about φ.

In addition, it may be argued along deontological lines that the Ministry had created expectations with respect to bringing about φ as they subsidised part of the construction costs. One may even claim that the Ministry almost assumed the obligation-responsibility. Indeed, subsidising PROMEST seems to underwrite the willingness to help to keep PROMEST on its feet. Despite its best position in the network and its subsidies and its positive stakes in the project, we doubt the Ministry can really be hold forward-looking responsible for φ.

Although the Ministry did create some expectations, it never explicitly promised to see to it that φ. More importantly, however, they had not only

148 *Sjoerd D. Zwart*

to deal with the stakes of the manure-producing farmers, but also with those of other important stakeholders. The Ministry thought that imposing φ by force would inflict so much collateral damage that it had to abandon the idea.

We will illustrate this idea of collateral damage. One way to impose φ was installing a Central Manure Exchange body with a delivery duty for all farmers. In December1994, the National Board installed an exchange body with a much weaker duty, and already this weakened version met with fierce opposition. For instance, the manure traders and the "contractors, who were hired to transport manure feared for their income, if the central processing exchange succeeded in keeping the process costs low. The large livestock farmers feared that delivery of manure to the central exchange would be more expensive than direct delivery to crop farmers."[7] Because the agricultural sector was fundamentally divided about how to solve the problem of manure surplus, and because of broader political reasons, the Ministry tended to prefer free market solution to centrally orchestrated ones. Interestingly, the Ministry of Agriculture changed its PROMEST attitude through time. At the start, it had high expectations of PROMEST's manure processing and considered it the best way to attack the manure problem. At the beginning of 1995, however, these expectations were tempered and it was said that PROMEST could make only a limited contribution to solving the manure problem.[8] Although we may reproach the Ministry for changing its attitude toward the PROMEST project through time, we think the collateral damage argument is strong enough to deny it the forward-looking responsibility for φ.

The upshot of section 4.4.1 is therefore that although the PROMEST collection can be reasonably held forward-looking responsible for φ; this cannot be claimed for any of its actors. PROMEST, the National manure bank, the local and national boards and the individual farmers were not enough causally efficacious, and the Ministry had to cope too much with opposite stakes to only look at φ and bring it about unconditionally. Thus, as the collection, and none of its actors, had the responsibility for φ as-moral-obligation, the PROMEST case provides an example of a PMH regarding forward-looking responsibility.

4.4.2 PROMEST: Who Is to Blame?

In the present section we will address the question of which agent is *backward-looking* responsible and morally blameworthy for the failure to bring about sufficient manure supply at the PROMEST plant (not-φ), and we will investigate whether a PMH regarding blameworthiness occurred. We will proceed along the following lines. First, we will find out whether the collection or agent is *causally* responsible for not-φ, i.e., whether the actions of the collection or agent were a link in the causal chain that lead up to not-φ. Doing so, we will use a liberal causality notion, which also covers omissions and supervisory power. Second, we will find out whether the collection or agent did something (morally) *wrong*, and we will see that both consequentialist and deontological arguments will play a role in such an assessment. In the deontic route, the wrong-doing conjecture consists in the suspicion of a breach or transgression of a duty which relates to an agent's actions. According to the consequentialist route, the wrong-doing conjecture consists in the suspicion of not fulfilling one's responsibility-as-obligation, i.e., not discharging of one's supervisory duties to see to it that φ, where in our case φ is the prevention of harm being done. As a third step, when the collection or agent is considered to be accountable, we will see whether it can be *excused* because it was coerced or did not know about φ; if not, it will be blameworthy for φ. Finally all the outcomes of the responsibility-as-blameworthiness considerations will answer the question of whether the PROMEST case is an instance of a PMH regarding blameworthiness.

The PROMEST Collection
We start with the question whether the PROMEST collection was a link in the causal chain leading up to not-φ. Clearly, the failure of the collection to come to a joint action played a decisive causal role in the failure to bring about φ. If it had not been for the activities of the PROMEST collection, there would not have been the question of sufficient manure for the PROMEST plant. In this sense, the collection actually caused not-φ. The collection not only played this decisive role, it was also causally efficacious with respect to not-φ. We think we may claim that if the supervisory duties in the collective to see to it that φ had been sufficiently exercised under normal circumstances, φ would have been achieved.

Regarding the wrongdoing condition along the consequentialist route, the collection clearly did bring about bad consequences. It suffices to show that the lack of manure supply was one of the reasons of PROMEST went bankrupt, which caused a loss of 45 million euro of investments, beside much individual and organisational frustration. In addition, in this concrete case, a more deontological argument points in the same direction of the collection's wrongdoing. In the previous section we saw that the PROMEST collection could be reasonably held forward-looking responsible for establishing φ. And in Chapter 1 we saw that an agent is basically accountable for a state-of-affairs not-φ if that agent was forward-looking responsible for φ but did not see to it that φ. Despite the fact that the collection had the causal power to bring about φ, it did not occur. The occurrence of not-φ as a bad consequence and the failure to prevent not-φ (even though it was capable of establishing φ) both indicate wrong-doing of the PROMEST collective, and that it is accountable for not-φ.

To establish the moral blameworthiness of the PROMEST collection we have to consider the question of whether the collection meets the knowledge and freedom conditions. Regarding the knowledge condition for collections, we proposed in Chapter 2 that the knowledge of the collection is

150 *Sjoerd D. Zwart*

the knowledge that would become known if all group members shared their knowledge effectively with all other members. How does the PROMEST collection fare with this condition? We think the PROMEST collection straightforwardly satisfied the knowledge condition. Not only did PROMEST share explicitly the information that the manure supply was not large and steady enough, but all the actors involved were well acquainted with this fact.

One may object that not all relevant information was shared by PROMEST. Indeed, during the few years of operation, rumours rose on fraudulent bookkeeping by PROMEST, concerning both the manure supplied by the farmers and the amount of manure actually processed. The different controlling bodies disagreed on who had to assess the bookkeeping of PROMEST (Bloemendaal 1995, 87–88). The Manure Bank asked the AID to submit the bookkeeping to closer scrutiny, but the latter refused the responsibility for inspection and returned it to the Manure Bank. After all, the AID lacked the required information because PROMEST was exempted from its obligation to publish the exact selling numbers of their products. This exemption was, however, never officially approved, and the Ministry of Agriculture even denied it had ever been granted. We should therefore accept the statement that the authorities lacked information on the exact turnover of the PROMEST plant. Despite this, the actors in the collection knew—or at least could reasonably know—that not-φ was the case. Indeed, all actors in the collection knew that the manure supply to PROMEST was insufficient to entertain a healthy business. The suggested bookkeeping irregularities do not account for not-φ. We may conclude, therefore, that the PROMEST collection satisfied the knowledge condition.

How did the collection fare with the freedom condition? In Chapter 2 we opted for a terminology according to which a collection acts freely if at least some of its actors participate freely and intentionally in the joint action. Moreover, we assumed that a collection can freely perform all those actions (or prevent or attain all those outcomes) that would be available to the collection and its subsets provided its actors cooperate fully and optimally coordinated their actions.

Did the PROMEST collection act freely in the above sense when it did not prevent not-φ? We observe that in the PROMEST case, none of the actors in the collection was coerced to let not-φ happening. The last statement does imply freedom of the collection, only on penalty of committing the fallacy of composition. But besides the freedom of the individual actors, we do not see any indication of coercion of the PROMEST collection. Of course, the national and international legislation did set the boundaries for possible solutions, but these boundaries did not force not-φ in any way. We conclude, therefore, that the PROMEST collection satisfies the freedom condition because it was not coerced in any way.

All in all we should conclude, therefore, that the collection was accountable for not-φ, it was well-informed about not-φ, and was not coerced to establish not-φ in any way. Because all processes were standard, predictable and there was no force majeure, we think we may reasonably blame the collection for not-φ, despite initiatives of individual agents trying to bring about φ.

The PROMEST Actors

Now that we established the blameworthiness of the PROMEST collection, it is interesting to see whether this collective blameworthiness reduces to that of one of the actors in the collection. Consequently, we will discuss the possible blameworthiness of the actors.

PROMEST

With regard to PROMEST, it should be acknowledged, we think, that it is not accountable for not-φ because it did not meet the causal efficaciousness condition. It cannot be maintained that if PROMEST had properly fulfilled its supervisory duties to see to it that 'φ', under normal circumstances, not-φ would not have occurred. It was too dependent on others in the network for the establishment of φ. Consequently, PROMEST is not accountable, and therefore not blameworthy, for not-φ. PROMEST calls, however, the suspicion of wrongdoing on itself regarding other φs. This is the case where PROMEST started a new 45 million euro enterprise with borrowed private money based on a technology that had not proven its mettle yet. They tried to set up a lucrative business taking advantage of serious environmental and societal concerns (perhaps this made the farmers also abhorrent to the idea delivering their raw material to the PROMEST plant and to pay substantially for that) whereas the processing costs were known to be too high. Moreover, to be successful, they had to arouse high and unrealistic expectations about the application of the partially unknown technology about which various specialists in the field raised critical voices such as for example engineering firms and Wageningen University. At the end, PROMEST had difficulties to secure a niche in the market, their product was too expensive, and the farmers had to pay too much to deliver their manure to PROMEST. Although PROMEST is not blameworthy for not-φ, it seems to be at least accountable for some factors φ' that substantially contributed to not-φ.

The Farmers

As we saw above, the farmers individually lacked the causal power to establish φ or to prevent not-φ. For that reason, individually their contribution in the causal chain leading up to not- φ is so limited that they cannot be held accountable for not-φ in the same sense car user cannot be hold accountable for global warming. Did the behaviour of the farmers in the collection not give rise to the suspicion of any wrongdoing? The consequentialist nor the deontological route point in this direction, because individually they did not cause not- φ, and they did not share the aim or even the participatory intentions to establish not-φ. In accordance with the global warming case in

152   *Sjoerd D. Zwart*

Chapter 2, we may assign the farmers the duty to urge their representative bodies to come to an agreement about how to cope with φ. For all we know, however, they did so, but these bodies failed to come to a national agreement on the issue. Of course, the northern farmers could have displayed somewhat more solidarity, and the southern farmers could have been more aware that their activities were primarily the cause of the manure problem. In our opinion, however, these considerations fail to make them individually accountable for not-φ, nor for the failure of the PROMEST enterprise, and because they are not accountable, they cannot be blamed for not-φ.

The Regional Boards

The regional boards had a much better position in the collection to prevent the occurrence of not-φ. But still as individual regional boards they did not have enough power in the network to cause φ to happen. So it cannot be said that if the regional boards had properly fulfilled their supervisory duties to see to it that 'not φ', under normal circumstances, φ would not have occurred. Neither did they bring about the bad consequence φ. The suspicion of wrongdoing may be considered to arise parallel to that of the individual farmers. The regional boards did not cause not-φ, and neither did they share the aim or even the participatory intentions to establish not-φ. Somewhat more solidarity of the Northern boards and somewhat more self-reflection of those of the south could have been instrumental to come to a practical solution. The wrongdoing suspicion is swiftly tempered, however, if one realises that the board had to defend the stakes of their members. None of the boards, especially those of the north, liked the idea of bankers and factory owners getting rich on the expense of their hard work. We think the most serious suspicion of wrong-doing regarding φ of the regional boards lies with the two southern boards (NCB and LLTB) that started the PROMEST concern. This suspicion lies in the fact that they not only they started the PROMEST enterprise and were very enthusiastic about an engineering fix of the manure problem that had not proven its mettle and various specialist were cautious about, but also they promoted the expansion of the enterprise to a national scale without consent of the other boards involved. Considering this new scale they should have orchestrated their engineering solution as a much more concerted effort among all regional boards, and not just starting as a duo and trying to convince the colleague boards later. Again, the suspicion of wrongdoing just described does not directly concern the specific φ, but the more general way in which PROMEST initiative has turned into a disaster. Thus, again the regional boards are not accountable, let alone blameworthy, for not-φ.

The National Board

The National agricultural board had an even better position in the collection than the regional boards to establish φ. They could pose levies on the surplus production of manure, and to some extent they could fall back on the power of the Ministry if their discretional power fell short for the plans they intended to carry out. The National Board undeniably has tried to achieve φ. They established the Central manure exchange with the task to manage the national manure streams and to facilitate establishing φ. Perhaps this central exchange unit had insufficient discretional power, which was hotly debated among the regional boards within the National Board. The board fulfilled its supervisory duty, although this did not result in the desired effect. Because the circumstances were not extraordinary, we think we may conclude that the National Board did not meet the causality condition because they really took up the challenge to bring about φ. The conduct of the National Board, therefore, does not arouse the suspicion of wrongdoing with regard to not preventing not-φ. It did try to get an agreement between all the local boards and the other stakeholders, but the various stakes turned out to be incompatible to such an extent that the agreement was impossible. The National Board and the related Central Manure Exchange did not *cause* not-φ, nor did they share the aim or participatory intentions of not-φ, and are therefore not accountable for it. A fortiori they are not blameworthy for not-φ.

The Ministry

Being the most powerful actor in the collection, the Ministry of Agriculture was the best equipped in the network to prevent the occurrence of not-φ. They had the possibility to implement agricultural laws, which should be approved by the parliament of course, but the Ministry could take initiatives to establish φ. If the Ministry had properly fulfilled its supervisory duties to see to it that 'φ', under normal circumstances, indeed not-φ would not have occurred. The Ministry was the most direct causally efficient in the collection. Moreover, by subsidising one third of the construction costs, they raised expectations about their willingness to sustain the enterprise. In addition, at the start the Ministry seemed to believe in PROMEST's technical fix of the manure problem, a belief that was tempered in the course of time. Apparently, the Ministry did not check the viability of the PROMEST technical fix sufficiently at the start of the project. Although the Ministry did not voluntarily assume the responsibility-as-obligation for establishing φ and we do not hold the Ministry forward-looking responsible for establishing φ, its powerful position in the collection, its subsidies for the building costs, and its stakes in solving the problem of the manure surplus in the Netherland at least may arouse the suspicion of wrongdoing with regard to φ. We think it may reasonably be argued that if there is some actor in the collection accountable for not preventing not-φ, despite its other obligations, that actor should be the Ministry. For that reason, the only possible candidate for being blameworthy for not- φ is the Ministry of Agriculture.

For the Ministry to be blameworthy for not-φ, it should satisfy the knowledge and the freedom criterion. As we have observed above, all parties involved in the PROMEST case were explicitly acquainted with the fact

154 Sjoerd D. Zwart

of the insufficient manure supply at the gates of the PROMEST plant. The Ministry was no exception, and it therefore satisfies the knowledge condition as well. The only issue that remains to be assessed therefore is the question as to what extent the Ministry acted freely. Although formally, the Ministry acted freely in the sense it had large discretional power; we should recognise, however, that as an overarching agricultural organisation, the Ministry had to take into account the stakes of *all* agricultural stakeholders. And taking these other stakes into account, we should acknowledge that enforcing φ did not at all guarantee the best consequences for all. From the perspective of all stakeholders in Dutch agriculture business, the Ministry was not free to enforce φ on the PROMEST-collection.

On the whole, we think the Ministry can be held accountable for not having prevented the occurrence of not-φ; it is being excused, however, and not blameworthy for not-φ because it did not have the moral freedom to enforce φ unilaterally in the agricultural network.

In sum, most actors in the collection, except for the National Board, raise the suspicion of at least some wrong-doing regarding some state of affairs leading to not-φ. It seems to be a general feature of PMHs, that the various actors can be held accountable for different states of affairs φ', φ'', etc. that are only indirectly related to the state of affairs φ under investigation. In the PROMEST case, none of the actors is directly accountable for not-φ, perhaps with one exception. Considering its powerful place in the network, its stimulating subsidies at the start, and its substantial stake in the manure surplus problem, the Ministry of agriculture could be considered to arouse suspicion of wrongdoing for not executing its power to prevent not-φ from happening. The conclusion of the present section then reads that because the collection is blameworthy for not-φ but none of its actors is, the PROMEST case present also a problem of many hands regarding responsibility as blameworthiness.

The overall conclusion of section 4.4 reads therefore that on a strict reading the PROMEST case poses PMHs regarding obligation and blameworthiness. Only under a less stringent reading we may hold the Ministry accountable for the insufficient manure supply but even then the Ministry cannot be blamed for not-φ because of its other obligations.

4.5 ORGANISATIONAL DIMENSIONS

In this section, we will apply the organisational dimensions power, coordination, and control to the PROMEST case to find out how changes along these three dimensions may affect the likelihood of a problem of many hands. The reader may recall that two actors are connected by a *power* relation if one is able to make the second actor to perform actions that serve the first actor's interest. Other activities related to the power dimension are, for instance, lobbying and delegating tasks. Besides the extreme case in which one can coerce others to perform actions against their will, the power relation is also relevant in more lenient cases of responsibility attributions because hierarchies contribute to responsibility distributions within groups. Next, we saw that *coordination* is related to the flow of knowledge within a network. Typical activities within this dimension are informing and disseminating knowledge. Social networks consist of links along which information is sent and knowledge is shared. As sharing information is easier than changing power relations, however, we consider power or formal relations to be more constitutive of social networks than coordination. Although power relations may change over time, it requires much more time and effort than just exchanging some information by e-mail. Moreover, to some extent, coordination depends on power relations because powerful actors can impose information ties. Finally, we will call a network *well-controlled* if actors are monitoring each other's performances which will result in an increased number of fall-back options and strategies when certain developments do not turn out as anticipated and deviant behaviour is recognised. These fall-back options and strategies may be delegating the task to some other agent or providing means to facilitate or enforce the original actor to achieve the desired end.[9]

The three organisational dimensions are not independent. First, let us note that in networks with strongly centralised power, the most powerful actor can establish coordination by installing appropriate lines of information flow. Moreover, it can stimulate control in the network by appointing agents responsible for monitoring and communicating unforeseen problems. Second, long lines of power transfer ask for better coordination in the network to keep all the actors well-informed, which underlines another dependency between power and coordination. We will return to the issue of long power lines in the next sections. Third, improved control will go hand in hand with increased information exchange in the network; thus, improving control implies improving coordination.

To illustrate the relevance of the power, coordination, and control relations for the PMH, consider again the CitiCorp case as discussed in Chapter 2. If the contractor had not asked for approval at LeMessurier firm, which had power over the contractor in this construction task, he was clearly the only one to blame for the construction failure. The contractor, however, *did* ask for permission to substitute welded joints with bolded ones; he received the permission of the approver, and the information was disseminated. This permission changes the situation considerably. The moment the architectural firm consented to the change, LeMessurier's firm and the contractor became jointly responsible. Moreover, the moment LeMessurier became aware of the fact that the joint technology employed was inadequate, he took appropriate action.

The LeMessurier case nicely illustrates the control dimension within the network. It shows the relative difference between the formal power relations and the behavioural coordination and control relations. No one in

156   *Sjoerd D. Zwart*

the network did something wrong to the extent that he or she would be eradicated from the network. The harm did not change the power relations; but a change in the coordination, the approver asking LeMessurier would have prevented the harm; moreover, probably, the control that was present in the network prevented much more serious harm. In the next section we will apply the organisational dimensions to the PROMEST case. Using the three organisational dimensions, we will come to lessons to be learned that will help to decrease the likelihood of a PMH.

4.5.1   Organisational Dimensions in the PROMEST Case

In section 4.3.3 we observed that the PROMEST collection stands midway between an occasional collection and a collective involved in a joint action. All parties involved had a positive stake in the issue how to get rid of the surplus of the Dutch manure in the most effective, economic, politically correct, and ecologically sound way. For this reason, the organisations and individuals in the PROMEST network are to some extent involved in a joint action, but only partially. Because as far as the joint action is concerned, with sufficient manure supply for PROMEST, φ, we do not think the members of the collection 'intentionally contributed to φ's occurrence by doing particular parts and their conceptions of φ sufficiently and actually overlap'. To what extent, then, could the organisational power, coordination, and control dimensions have influenced and approved the stream of manure direction the PROMEST consortium? To consider this question, let us first have a look at the power relations in the network.

Power Relations
The power relations between the Ministry of Agriculture and the Agricultural Board were grounded in the representational function of the Board. From the late 1980s, the agricultural field became more diverse. Because the manure surplus was not equally urgent in all parts of the country, the different regional agricultural organisations had different interests and diverging agendas. As such, the legitimacy of the representation weakened, and so did the influence of the Board in the development of the manure policy and the support by the farmers decreased as well. Proper representation and support for negotiated decisions requires some minimal sense of homogeneity within the group.

The powerful position of the National Board was initially due to its strong relation with the Ministry of Agriculture. The establishment and implementation of the manure policy came from the close collaboration between the Agricultural Board and the Ministry of Agriculture, which were interdependent. Although the Ministry of Agriculture was the most powerful actor in the network, for some actions it had to ask permission from the EC. The Ministry proposed a system of obligatory levies to subsidise the PROMEST plant, but this so-called exploitation levy was not allowed by

EC rules (Raven 2005: 76). The Ministry of Agricultural actively lobbied for permission to impose this exploitation levy permanently, and the EC rejected their requests several times.[10] As power is defined as the ability to impose actions on other actors to pursue one's own objectives, the rejection of the exploitation levy should be interpreted in two ways. The Ministry was unsuccessful in challenging the power of the EC, and the EC was successful in maintaining its power over the Dutch Ministry of Agriculture. The Ministry did not have the power to pursue its objective to impose permanent exploitation levies.

Focusing on the power relations, we readily descry the generation of a problem of many hands. Power was transferred from the Ministry via the Agricultural Board to the National Manure Bank and to the farmers, subsequently, without adequate control activities. Along this line of power transfer we see two developments. The obvious observation is a diminishing of power such that the final actors lack the power to bring about the desirable state of affairs. Moreover, the longer the line of power delegation becomes, the larger the risk that the aims at the bottom of the line do not cover those at the top; the problem changes along the line of actors. Whereas for the Ministry and the Board the problem was the surplus of manure, for the Bank the main problem was effective distribution. As soon as the Ministry or Board bestowed the task regarding the manure on the Bank, the problem was outsourced and was sufficiently taken care of in the eyes of the Ministry; for the receiving end of the line, the manure Bank, the problem was conceived differently. Consequently no one owned the problem as it was originally conceived.

Finally, regarding the relation between possible PMHs and power relations in the network we should note the following. In the PROMEST case, the power distribution in the network allowed for local initiatives with implications for the entire network but did not always allow for successful mending operations by the initiators when serious problems occurred. Due to the political pressure by the authorities and private interests, regional boards were able to start the PROMEST initiative, having considerable repercussions in the entire Dutch farming industry. These boards, however, lacked the power to guarantee sufficient manure at the gates of PROMEST. Decentralised collections with actors having the power to undertake initiatives with ramifications for the entire network but lacking the power to solve ensuing problems are more likely to create PMHs than more hierarchical networks.

Coordination Relations

It should be observed that in the case at hand the problem of the insufficiency of the manure supply did not seem to be due to an inadequate information flow. In general, the actors in the network were well aware of the problem. The difficulty was the choice of the appropriate solution, not a lack of information. Besides the generally acknowledged insufficiency of manure supply, we descry two other coordination issues in the case at hand.

158 Sjoerd D. Zwart

The first relates to the inertia and lack of information about the implementation of the manure policy. It was this inertia which strengthened the farmers' wait-and-see attitude. As long as manure legislation was uncertain, the farmers were unwilling and even unable to enter into long-term contractual obligations, such as supply contracts. Undoubtedly, the uncertainty about long-term manure policy has contributed to the insufficient manure problem. The second coordination issue relates to the uncertainty about the roles of, and the relation between, the intermediary organisations, such as the National Manure Bank and the AID, throughout the period of the PROMEST affair. Although the Bank was in fact established to solve the mediating problems of manure supply, it seemed to have helped to create its own problems, such as lack of clarity, regarding their monitoring tasks. Especially in the present case, these intermediary organisations could have played a contributory role in distributing responsibilities. Adequate monitoring would have helped to establish trust and collaboration in the network. The Bank has failed to fulfil this function.

The general lesson to be learned, therefore, is that the less information is shared about the final goal of the network, the less the participants are willing and able to engage in collective action. Indeterminacy about the collective goals cultivates individualism, and actors will retreat on their own islands. This in turn diminishes the possibility to turn a collection of actors into a collective that acts on participatory intentions or into an organised group that can adopt a collective aim and can undertake a shared action to avoid collateral damage.

To illustrate one of the mediating problems just mentioned, we may consider the allegations about fraudulent manure bookkeeping at PROMEST. Regarding these allegations, the Manure Bank and the AID were asked to subject PROMEST's bookkeeping to a closer inspection. Both governmental bodies lacked, however, the required information to carry out the inspection, because PROMEST was allegedly exempted from its obligation to prove the selling of the processed products. The exemption was, however, never officially approved, and the Ministry of Agriculture even denied that it had ever been granted. How can the farmers, in such a situation of uncertainty and lack of information and trust, be expected to pay extra money for delivering the raw material at the gates of an enterprise that is supposed to make profits for its stakeholders?

Control

The PROMEST network was a collection of actors, in which power was decentralised, and its fall-back options regarding insufficient manure supply failed miserably. The various actors in the network had their own stakes and were looking forward to see whether these stakes were in danger and, if so, acted accordingly. No actor in the network assumed the overall monitoring task, i.e., the task to put fall-back options into place that will help to overcome possible future problems in the process of making the industrial processing of manure.

Responsibility in Networks 159

As the PROMEST case developed, the difficulty of insufficient manure supply did emerge, and various actors recognised this problem. PROMEST observed the lack of manure but seemed to accept that they could not do anything about it. It was their problem, but they did not accept responsibility. The same held for the agricultural boards from the south. The manure supply problem did threaten their interests, but again they were not powerful enough to turn the tide. The Ministry took initiatives to solve the manure problem. As mentioned, they lobbied in Brussels for an exploitation levy for PROMEST and they installed the Central Manure Exchange to manage the manure streams, which had to provide PROMEST with sufficient manure. Neither of the two actions solved the problem.

Because the most powerful actor in the network was unable to cope with the difficulty when it occurred, we think that the network could only have been able to deal with the problem successfully if serious fall back options had been set up long before the problem occurred. When the problems did occur, the developments had too much inertia to be stopped in time. When the PROMEST plant was built, no actor in the network had put into place necessary fall-back options—or did take the hazard seriously.[11] Apparently, when various actors collaborate for their own private agenda, they are unlikely to look forward to discern possible problems and install fall-back option to evade them. Oftentimes, they are even not able to do so without other actors. One of the lessons to be drawn from the PROMEST episode is therefore that the danger of unforeseen or unanticipated problem increases with the extent to which actors in the collective try to achieve their own private agendas, rather than to collaborate in accomplishing the aim of the collective.

From another perspective the manure supply problem may also be framed in terms of *problem ownership*. The reactions of the different actors in the network illustrate two concepts of 'problem ownership', viz., (1) threatening of your stakes, (2) moral responsibility to solve the problem. In sense (1) many actors in the PROMEST network acknowledged lack of manure at the PROMEST factory as their problem, but in sense (2) almost none accepted responsibility, and therefore the PROMEST case displays PMHs. We will return to the question of problem ownership in the next section.

4.5.2 Lessons to Be Learned

This section is dedicated to lessons to be learned from the PROMEST case with regard to PMHs. These lessons concern the relation between the organisational dimensions power, coordination, and control, and the occurrence of PMHs. Let us discuss how the application of these dimensions in the previous section helps to find maxims about how to avoid PMHs.

First Lesson: About the Degree of Organisation

We define the degree of organisation of a group of agents in terms of the organisational dimensions power, coordination, and control amply

160   Sjoerd D. Zwart

explained above. The most important observation related to power in the PROMEST network was the following. Pursuing to a considerable content their own agenda, the southern agricultural associations with help of the Ministry could start building an industrial manure processing plant on such a large scale that it had ramifications for the entire national agricultural sector. Many problems due to these building initiatives were, however, too large for these associations to cope with and the asymmetry between the power to initiate and the power to repair forms an important part of the PROMEST problem. More generally, the lesson reads: in decentralised collections with actors having the power to undertake initiatives with ramifications for the entire network but lacking the power to solve ensuing problems are more likely to create PMHs than more organised networks. If we generalise this lesson we come to the next proposition:

> *(org) The more organised a group in terms of power, coordination and control the smaller the likelihood of a PMH.*

This proposition is backed up by the work of Raymond Boudon who distinguishes between (1) *interdependence systems* like markets or queuing lines where power relations, functions and roles play a minimal role and the underlying actor relation is one of competition and (2) *functional systems* like universities where the actors work together having different roles. In Boudon's words, "[f]unctional systems are defined as systems of interaction whose main category is roles". Systems of interdependence, on the other hand, are "those systems of interaction where individual actions can be analyzed without reference to the category of roles" (Boudon 1981: 255). Boudon associates unorganised systems with interdependence systems and organised systems with functional ones, and claims that the introduction of organisation is often due to the wish to evade collateral damage. "The transition from an unorganized system to an organized system is often due to the manifest will of social agents to eliminate undesirable emergent effects" (Boudon 1981: 257). Thus increase of organisation in a collection of actors contributes to more possibilities to "eliminate undesirable emergent effects", and therefore to a smaller likelihood of collateral harm. The reason for diminishing the likelihood of collateral harm is closely related an increase in possibilities of task delegation and possibilities of enforcing information transfer. In our terminology, generally, occasional collections are more likely to inflict non-intended harm or collateral damage than organised groups with the same performance.

Note that the first lesson is couched in terms of the extent of *organisation* of the collection and not of centralised *power* alone. Increase of only central power does not suffice. To avoid PMHs, the increase of power should at least be accompanied by an increase of coordination and, especially, control. "[T]he process of organization inevitably implies the introduction of norms and constraints which restrict the margin of individual autonomy and, therefore, include certain categories of actions in roles" (Boudon 1981: 257).

Increase in central power alone does not suffice to decrease the likelihood of a PMH for two reasons. First, central power may require long lines of power transfer from the most powerful to the least one and in practice the responsibility of harm being done often evaporates along these long and complicated hierarchical lines, a phenomenon frequently observed in countries where all the power comes to centralised governments. Moreover, PROMEST case showed that passing on the responsibility for some state of affairs downwards along a line of power runs the risk of changing the interpretation of what should be done, eclipsing the aims of higher level actors for the actors at the lower ends.

Second, increase of centralised power may even counterproductive in preventing PMHs. If the actors in a collection recognise that together they are contributing to some change in the world without being directed by a power hierarchy redundancy in the system or the performed action becomes often built decentralised or locally. The actors who recognise the possible harm take the precautions they can to prevent problems. These precautions come close to the mutual control within the collective. Organised groups with a strong hierarchy tend to take measures centrally to prevent harm. Actors in these groups tend or sometimes are ordered not to bother about problems of unintended harm. Sometimes decentralised measures of precaution are more effective than centralised, and in such cases strong centralised power does not decrease the likelihood of PMHs. It remains to be seen whether regarding precautions, decentralisation of power is always the most effective option.

Second Lesson: About Task Distribution

The second lesson to be learned from the PROMEST case is that every problem should be clearly and justly distributed among the actors. Every individual problem should be attributed to one specific actor, if possible, and shared responsibility should be kept to a minimum. Although sufficient manure supply was connected to the interest of PROMEST and of the local agricultural board in the south, they did not have enough power to make it happen. Moreover, it was not entirely clear who was given the task of guaranteeing sufficient manure supply. One might object that the national Manure Bank was allotted the task of managing the manure streams in the Netherlands. But even if that were the case, something that might be challenged on good grounds, the appointment of the responsibility would not have been just because the organisation did not receive enough discretional power to fulfil such a task.

The role played by the intermediating organisations in the PROMEST case suggests that if these crucial intermediaries fail to carry out their tasks due to unclear or unjust responsibility attribution, the network organisation as a whole weakens. That intermediary organisations play a crucial role within networks is confirmed in the literature on innovation management,

162 *Sjoerd D. Zwart*

where it is shown that intermediaries can both enable connectedness in a network but also create institutional inertia (cf. Howells 2006). The second lesson from the PROMEST case therefore reads:

> *(appoint) Definite responsibilities should be explicitly appointed as much as possible to the individual actors in the collection, and these responsibilities should be justly appointed such that the individual actor should be well equipped to exercise their responsibilities.*

The latter condition of just appointment is vital for avoiding PMHs. In other words, the second lesson reads that we should avoid as much as possible diffuse responsibilities attribution to subgroups of agents.

A clear cut distribution of the individual tasks (or obligation-responsibilities) may also be expressed in terms of clear 'problem ownership'. Here, we mean with 'problem owner' the actor that is appointed to see to it that some state of affairs does not occur and not the actor whose stakes are threatened. Lack of ownership on the first reading may cause major performance problems due to the fact that no single actor is responsible for the whole process (Hammer and Champy 1994). Difficulties within the chain of tasks relating the different actors greatly complicate the identification of the actor responsible for the ultimate outcome. This holds the more if the harm is an outcome of a joint action. If all issues are justly appointed to actors in the network, PMHs are much less likely to occur, because all recognised responsibilities are traceable to actors in the collection. In this sense the remedy comes down to saying 'prevent PMHs to occur' and is almost circular. The non-circular advice for collective actions is to avoid as much as possible opaque and shared problem ownership in terms of responsibility appointments to groups of network actors.

It should be realised, however, that the responsibility attributions referred to can only concern those problems in a joint undertaking that are generally acknowledged. Many PMHs are due to issues not generally foreseen and recognised as problems. We may distinguish two different situations. First, it may be that some or even all actors in the collection are well-aware of the issue, but do not consider it worthwhile to discuss it with the other actors. The authors encountered such a situation when applying the network approach to new developments in the waste water technology. It turned out that the researcher and the users of the newly developed technology both did dismiss responsibility of the so-called 'secondary emissions'. These were emissions that were not yet regulated at the time, but which were likely to be regulated in the near future (Zwart et al. 2006, section 4.3.4). Beside practical difficulties, such as time and money, collections of actors can, in principle, anticipate issues of this first sort. Second, problems may develop that none of the actors in the collection thought off. How to come by future problems, which are not considered by any actor in the collection, is even more difficult than those of the first sort. The openness of acting in dynamic circumstances always carries with it the possibility of totally unforeseen problems. Actors engaged in collaborative action should always recognise this possibility and should therefore accept the forward-looking responsibility of being on their guard for spotting and identifying possible problems of collateral damage. In collective action, the lesson of the present section also emphatically applies to this obligation-responsibility.

Third Lesson: Control

In section 4.5.1, we saw that in the developments of collaborative action some problems became insurmountable when they occurred, even for the most powerful in the collective. Moreover, we observed that PROMEST collection lacked, what in the social psychology of group processes has been called, (group) cohesiveness—or at least one of its main components: *task cohesion* (Forsyth 2009: 120; Carron and Brawley 2000: 94) many actors collaborated in the collection to pursue their own agendas and to achieve their own aims, which frequently did not match with the overall aims of the collective. The PROMEST collection was indeed more of a collection of agents than a collective with one goal. To a considerable extent, the incompatibility of the different stakes made this collection liable for the development of non-anticipated difficulties. An important lesson to be drawn from the PROMEST episode, we think, is therefore that the danger of unforeseen or unanticipated problems increases with the degree of cohesiveness:

> (cohesive) *The likelihood for a collection to encounter unanticipated difficulties in achieving their aims is inversely proportional to its degree of cohesiveness.*

The cohesiveness in a collective is related to the control its members mutually exercise to find out how colleague actors are fulfilling their job as part of accomplishing their group tasks. In the foregoing, we operationalised this control dimension with the extent to which the collective has backup options available in case of unforeseen failure or difficulties. The next lesson to be learned regarding PMHs is:

> (control) *Increasing control within a collection decreases the likelihood that this collection will get involved in PMHs.*

Increase of control can be achieved in two different ways; first, by increasing mutual interest, and second, by clearer and more distinctive distribution of responsibility-as-obligation. According to (appoint) the latter contributes to fewer PMHs in a direct way, and the former helps to increase the cohesiveness in the collection, which according (cohesive) decreases unanticipated difficulties, which decreases the likelihood of PMHs as well. As control is a forward-looking affair it is most directly connected to PMHs with regard to obligations, but its scope is larger than that. In the first chapter, we saw

164   *Sjoerd D. Zwart*

that if an actor failed to take her responsibility-as-obligation to seeing to it that not-φ and φ did happen nevertheless, this actor might be accountable or blameworthy for the occurrence of φ. Thus (control) also decreases the likelihood of the PHM_A and PHM_B.

We would like to end this section with a word of caution and a promising look ahead. The aim was to come with lessons drawn from the PROMEST case to decrease the likelihood of PMHs. On close inspection, this is an empirical means-end question about social reality: What to do to avoid PMHs? From this perspective, our lessons should be interpreted as explorative hypothesis based on only one, perhaps atypical, case study about the extreme, complex realities of social groups and their dynamics. Nevertheless, we think the case study has convincingly showed the relevance of conceptual and empirical investigations into the relations between individual and group responsibilities for PMHs. We would therefore warmheartedly welcome empirical research into group behaviour and dynamics by sociologists and psychologists into the question of how these responsibilities relate and how PHMs can be avoided most effectively.

4.6   CONCLUSIONS

This chapter had three objectives: The first was to find out how our conceptual framework of the first two chapters would fare in practice. The answer to that question reads that the framework is flexible enough and makes sufficient distinctions to adequately cope with an empirical case like the PROMEST one. The second aim was to find out whether the PROMEST case did in fact exhibit PMHs, and indeed it did. We discerned a PMH regarding obligations, as well as blameworthiness. The third objective was to find out to what extent the power, coordination, and control dimensions are helpful in analysing the PMHs observed and what lessons are to be learned for diminishing the likelihood of PMHs to occur. Using these dimensions we concluded that to decrease the likelihood of PMHs we should (org) increase the group's organisation (appoint), increase just and explicit responsibilities attributions in the collection, and (control) increase group control.

NOTES

1. In our terminology, organisations and hierarchies are also networks.
2. For more on stakeholder analysis in the agricultural contexts, see Grimble and Wellard (1997).
3. Nb. this is different from the control or freedom condition—second excusing condition—in Chapter 1.
4. Our case description is inspired by an elaboration of Sections 3 and 4 of Doorn et al. (2011).
5. *Reformatorisch Dagblad*, 19 November 1994.

Responsibility in Networks   165

6. Interestingly, a PMH may occur one level lower, as in the Ministry not everybody agreed about the question of to what extend the manure problem should be left to the free market, which was the main argument for not forcing the farmers to bring their manure to PROMEST.
7. *Trouw*, 8 December 1994.
8. *Trouw*, 23 August 1995.
9. Control should not be confused with brute coercion or with clinical cost-benefit calculations. It is rather connected to subtle group pressures, outlooks, commitments, and observing deviancies, which will not remain without consequences. In our setting, we relate control with taking precautionary actions.
10. The Ministry managed to receive permission to install exploitation levies, temporarily, in 1993 and 1994.
11. We will leave the question of whether the PROMEST network or one of its actors is responsible—blameworthy, accountable, or forward-looking—for the absence of the fallback options, and whether this absence poses also a PMH for another occasion.

REFERENCES

Bloemendaal, F. 1995. *Het mestmoeras*. The Hague: Sdu Uitgevers.
Boudon, R. 1981. *The logic of social action: An introduction to sociological analysis*. Boston: Routledge and Kegan Paul.
Carron, A.V., and L.R. Brawley. 2000. "Cohesion conceptual and measurement issues." *Small Group Research*, 31(1), 89–106.
Doorn, N., R.P.J.M. Raven, and L.M.M. Royakkers. 2011. "Distribution of responsibility in socio-technical networks: the Promest case." *Technology Analysis & Strategic Management* 23(4), 453–471.
Ebers, M. ed. 1999. *The formation of inter-organizational networks*. Oxford University Press.
Forsyth, D.R. 2009. *Group Dynamics* (5th edition.). Australia; Belmont, CA: Cengage Learning.
Frouws, J. 1994. *Mest en macht: Een politiek-sociologische studie naar belangenbehartiging en beeldvorming inzake de mestproblematiek in Nederland vanaf 1970/Manure and power: A political-sociological study of interest articulation and policy formation concerning the manure problem in Netherlands since 1970*. Doctoral thesis: Agricultural University of Wageningen.
Giddens, A. 1987. *Social theory and modern sociology*. Oxford: Polity Press.
Grimble, R., and K. Wellard. 1997. "Stakeholder methodologies in natural resource management: a review of principles, contexts, experiences and opportunities." *Agricultural Systems* 55(2), 173–193.
Grossi, D., L.M.M. Royakkers, and F. Dignum. 2007. "Organizational structure and responsibility: An analysis in a dynamic logic of organizational collective agency." *Artificial Intelligence and Law* 15(3): 223–249.
Hammer, M. and J. Champy. 1994. *Reengineering in the corporation; a manifesto for business revolution*. New York: Harper Business.
Horling, B. and V. Lesser. 2004. "A survey of multi-agent organizational paradigms." *The Knowledge Engineering Review* 19(4): 281–316.
Howells, J. 2006. "Intermediation and the role of intermediaries in innovation." *Research Policy* 35(5): 715–728.
Krajenbrink, E.J. 2005. *Het landbouwschap: 'zelfgedragen verantwoordelijkheid' in de land- en tuinbouw, 1945–2001*. Groningen.
Morgenstern, O. 1951. *Prolegomena to a theory of organizations*. Manuscript.

166 *Sjoerd D. Zwart*

Podolny, J.M., and K.L. Page. 1998. "Network forms of organizations." *Annual Review of Sociology* 24(1): 57–76.

Raven, R.P.J.M. 2005. *Strategic niche management for biomass: A comparative study on the experimental introduction of bioenergy technologies in the Netherlands and Denmark.* Doctoral thesis: Eindhoven Technical University.

Spector, B. 2007. *Implementing organizational change: Theory and practice.* Upper Saddle River, N.J Pearson Prentice Hall.

Walker, M.B., 2009. "Causation: What is it and does it really matter?" *ISASI Forum* 42(2): 4–8.

Wasserman, S., and K. Faust. 1994. *Social network analysis in the social and behavioral sciences. Social network analysis: Methods and applications.* Cambridge University Press:. 1–27.

Wisserhof, J. 2000. "Agricultural policy making in the Netherlands: Beyond corporatist policy arrangements?" In *Political modernisation and the environment: The renewal of environmental policy arrangements*, edited by J. Tatenhove, B. Arts and P. Leroy, 175–197. Dordrecht: Kluwer.

Zwart, S.D., I.R. van De Poel, H. van Mil, and M. Brumsen. 2006. "A network approach for distinguishing ethical issues in research and development." *Science and Engineering Ethics* 12(4): 663–684.

5 A Procedural Approach to Distributing Responsibility

Neelke Doorn

5.1 INTRODUCTION

In this chapter, we will look at a procedure for the fair distribution of responsibility-as-obligation as a way to overcome the problem of many hands with respect to responsibility-as-obligation. In Chapter 1, we have seen that there are three routes towards acquiring responsibility-as-obligation: the consequentialist, the deontological, and the virtue-ethics route. The last of these routes is based on responsibility-as-virtue, which will be discussed in the next chapter. In both the consequentialist and the deontological route, the fair distribution of responsibility-as-obligation is an important issue.

In the consequentialist route, responsibility is distributed on basis of the desirability of a certain state-of-affairs φ and a distribution principle. However, in a pluralist society there will often be moral disagreement about what the right distribution principle is. In this chapter we will look at a procedural solution to this problem, in particular we will propose a fair procedure for distributing responsibility. In the deontological route, responsibility-as-obligation is acquired on basis of promises or commitments. Often such promises and commitments will not be made in isolation but will depend on what promises and commitments other actors are willing or expected to make. An important consideration here, again, will be whether the actors perceive the resulting distribution of responsibility as fair, and people may have different rationales for when a distribution of responsibility is to be deemed fair.

Fairness of a responsibility distribution may be achieved by adopting a distribution principle that is fair and then allocating responsibility according to that principle. However, as indicated above, in a pluralist society there will likely be considerable moral disagreement about what distribution principle is fair. Insights from political philosophy show that fairness could also be achieved in a more procedural way. According to a procedural approach to fairness, a responsibility distribution can be rendered fair if it is established in a fair way, i.e., if it is the result of a fair procedure. Such a procedural approach is especially promising because empirical research has shown that despite the fact that people have different rationales for distributing responsibility, they may nevertheless agree on how responsibility

168 *Neelke Doorn*

should be distributed in an actual case (Doorn 2010b, 2010c). This suggests that agreement on principles or rationales for distributing responsibility is *not* required in order to come to an actual distribution of responsibility-as-obligation that is deemed fair by all parties involved.

In this chapter, we develop an approach that is based on procedural political theory. The underlying thought is that people do not have to agree on a substantive distribution principle, which tells when a person is responsible, as long as they agree on the *procedure* for distributing the responsibilities (and given that they have a shared understanding of what responsibility means. The latter is important to prevent people from talking at cross-purposes). If such a procedure, or its outcome, is accepted by all people involved as representing the 'fair terms of cooperation', this might help reconcile the pluralist responsibility conceptions and, ultimately, alleviate the problem of many hands. In order to test the applicability of political theory to responsibility distributions, the model of procedural justice is applied to a real case. The guiding question is whether a procedural approach contributes to reconciling the pluralist responsibility conceptions.

The outline of this chapter is as follows. Following this introduction, we sketch a procedural approach to justice based on Rawls' political liberalism in section 5.2. After explaining the approach, we describe in section 5.3 two procedural norms that are derived from policy and innovation theory. Subsequently, in section 5.4 we apply the approach to an empirical case in order to see whether the method contributes to reconciling the pluralist responsibility conceptions. In the final section conclusions are given, together with recommendations for further research.

5.2 A PROCEDURAL APPROACH TO JUSTICE: RAWLS' POLITICAL LIBERALISM

In a pluralist society, people have different views on what responsibility amounts to and under what conditions one is responsible. Whereas some people defend a virtue ethical approach to responsibility, others take a deontological or consequentialist stance (see, e.g., Nihlén Fahlquist 2006; Williams 2008; Goodin 1995 for a discussion of some of these approaches). Responsibility conceptions can differ in at least two ways. First, people may have a different understanding of what responsibility actually *means* (for example, giving an account of something, to compensate for potential loss, to have a task to do something, to take care of something; cf. Chapter 1). Second, people may have different conceptions on when a person *is* responsible. In this chapter, we focus on the second type of diversity: diversity in opinions on when a person is responsible.

In order to do justice to this pluralism of responsibility conceptions, there is a need for a distributing procedure that leads to a workable agreement but that, at the same time, leaves room for different responsibility conceptions without favouring any one in particular. Simply distributing on the basis of majority rule is potentially unfair to groups representing minority views.

In networks, these different perspectives on responsibility may all be represented by the different actors constituting the network. Moreover, if we recognise the political ideal of pluralism, these different perspectives are all *legitimate* (although sometimes with qualifications) and they can therefore not be reduced to one single perspective.[1] This pluralism in responsibility conceptions leads to the problem of how to distribute responsibilities. Because networks often lack strict hierarchical relations, decision-making is done on the basis of mutual negotiations rather than top-down decision-making. It remains therefore open how responsibilities should be distributed. Even if people would agree what an engineer's responsibility involves (e.g., the task to prevent certain risks stemming from a technology), it is not obvious how this responsibility should be distributed among the engineers constituting the research team. Should it be done in as early a stage of technology development by the team member doing fundamental research or by the team members commercially exploiting the technology? The answer to this question is partly dependent on the responsibility conception one endorses. The pluralist thesis implies that the diverse and competing visions of responsibility cannot be reduced to one overarching conception. Hence, people should somehow find a consensus concerning how responsibilities are to be distributed. However, what counts as a *justified* consensus remains open; not any consensus will do. Even in the absence of a strict hierarchy, power relations may still be present. Critics of consensus policy often warn that the promotion of consensus is coercive, notwithstanding its democratic aims (Young 2000; Mouffe 2000). The promotion of consensus runs the risk of negotiating the interests of the most powerful. If one actor defends a virtue ethical approach to responsibility but agrees to distribute responsibility according to tasks in order to gain something else in return, it is questionable whether the agreement counts as a *justified* consensus. In order to assess which kind of consensus can be considered justified (where justified is understood as 'doing justice to pluralism without favouring one view over the other'), we need a framework that incorporates both the ideal of consensus and that of pluralism.

In political theory, the idea of procedural justice has emerged as a way to provide such a framework. The term procedural justice refers to the way procedures (e.g., decision-making procedures) are structured so that their outcomes can be considered fair. The term is especially relevant in pluralist societies where people often cannot agree on substantive views on what justice amounts to. An example of procedural justice is the principle that those who are affected by a certain decision be afforded the opportunity to participate in the decision-making.

In recent decades, different solutions have been proposed to find a workable middle ground between the ideals of consensus and pluralism, all balancing substantive views on justice with procedural requirements. A highly developed and differentiated procedural political theory is Rawls' political

170   Neelke Doorn

liberalism.[2] Rawls attempts to propose the formal conditions under which the decision-making can be deemed fair. His theory is particularly attractive because it provides both an elaborated *justificatory* framework and a *constructive* framework for encouraging reflection (Doorn 2010a).

Central in Rawls' theory are the concepts of overlapping consensus and wide reflective equilibrium (WRE). Rawls' aim was to develop a criterion of justice that would be agreed upon by all under conditions that are fair to all (Rawls 2001: 15). Although Rawls at first wanted to develop a substantive theory of justice for a relatively homogeneous well-ordered society, he revised this idea of a well-ordered society in his later work. Recognising the permanent plurality of incompatible and irreconcilable moral frameworks within a democratic society, he introduced the concept of overlapping consensus. People are able to live together despite conflicting moral values and ideals as long as they share a moral commitment to the society's basic structure.

One of the leading ideas of the reflective equilibrium approach is the desirability to make one's considered moral judgments cohere with one's moral principles and one's background theories on morality. Considered judgments are well-considered and deeply rooted opinions that unambiguously approve or disapprove actions in a concrete situation. Working back and forth between the considered judgments, moral principles and background theories, every agent should strive for equilibrium between these three elements of morality.

5.2.1   Narrow and Wide Reflective Equilibrium

Inspired by his student Norman Daniels, Rawls distinguished between narrow and wide reflective equilibrium (Daniels 1979; Rawls 2001). In the case of a narrow reflective equilibrium, one tries to solve a moral problem by achieving coherence between considered judgments and moral principles. In the case of a narrow reflective equilibrium one thus leaves general normative and descriptive background theories out of the equation. Such theories possibly undermine the outcome because, due to their level of generality, they are also related to considered judgments about situations that are otherwise disconnected from the moral problem under consideration (Daniels 1979: 258).

From an external point of view, a narrow equilibrium may be characterised as Kantian, utilitarian, or may be based on virtues, but the person that achieves the equilibrium does not consider such general ethical theories. Regarding another moral problem the same person may arrive at an equilibrium, in which the principles may contradict those of the previous equilibrium; also, other people may come to a different narrow reflective equilibrium on the same issue.

A reflective equilibrium is called wide if it comprises considered judgments, applied principles, and general philosophical and background theories, and makes them cohere. Because of its broader basis, such a wide reflective equilibrium is considered more stable in time, and more viable

A Procedural Approach 171

regarding other moral problems than a narrow equilibrium, which runs the risk of being too one-sided or subjective.

In a sense, the method of the narrow reflective equilibrium is a descriptive, rather than a justificatory method. It is suitable for 'anthropological' research into the morals of the actors in a network. A wide reflective equilibrium, however, clearly contributes to the justification of moral judgments as well as to the development of moral theories because it balances moral background theories with moral judgments and principles.

The reflective equilibrium approach can be used for an ethical assessment of a network where moral questions are at stake. Take for instance an R&D network in which a new artefact is developed that might put human safety at risk. To come to a considered judgment about this risk, we would ask the actors in the network whether they have thought about the risk, and if so, how they argue about this risk from their viewpoint. The various answers of the actors might be viewed to be in narrow reflective equilibrium and this first inventory might be viewed as an 'anthropological study'. If the actors in the network have different moral viewpoints, probably the actors will disagree about how to solve the ethical issue.

If, however, the actors opt for a wide reflective equilibrium, they may reach a consensus, because their background theories become subject of debate. By taking into consideration different relevant background theories the actors will achieve new equilibriums in which some may revise their initial considered judgments. This scenario is more plausible if the actors have the same background theories from the start. In that situation, one might expect a certain convergence to the same wide reflective equilibrium. A crucial question is thus whether the actors in a network share the same background theories. The sparse empirical evidence that is available suggests that this is often not the case (Grin and van der Graaf 1996a); also the empirical material we present in this chapter suggests divergence rather than convergence at the level of background theories in a network.

Divergence of background theories in networks casts doubts on the possibility of achieving a shared wide reflective equilibrium. It is unlikely that the actors will achieve a consensus for the same reasons: If actors have dissimilar background theories, they will probably have different reasons underpinning their considered judgments. In such situations a so-called overlapping consensus might still be achievable.

5.2.2 From Reflective Equilibrium to Overlapping Consensus

In *A Theory of Justice*, Rawls (1999 [1971]) justified 'justice as fairness', his moral rationale for organising the modern welfare state, in terms of a shared wide reflective equilibrium.[3] This means that in wide reflective equilibrium, everyone is committed to 'justice as fairness' for the same reasons. In *Political Liberalism*, Rawls (1993) has proposed a more modest view on how to justify 'justice as fairness' (see also Rawls 2001). He there defends the view

172 *Neelke Doorn*

that people with different worldviews might achieve different wide reflective equilibriums. Nevertheless, he still claims that people are likely to share a common 'module' in their various wide reflective equilibriums, which contains the same elements as 'justice as fairness'. At first sight, this might seem an unrealistic claim: if people have different worldviews, why would we expect an overlapping consensus? Although different worldviews do not exclude overlapping opinions on concrete cases, they do not make such overlap likely to occur. According to Rawls, an overlapping consensus with respect to 'justice as fairness' is nevertheless likely to occur, because people with different worldviews are likely to share at least some beliefs about reasonable pluralism. These beliefs include, among others, beliefs about the existence of a boundary between the public and non-public; even if people with different worldviews might disagree about where exactly to draw this boundary. They also include the belief that the state should not force people to hold certain non-public values. These beliefs about reasonable pluralism, according to Rawls, allow for a *pro tanto* justification of 'justice as fairness', i.e., a justification that draws only on judgments, principles, values, and background theories relevant for the public domain. The ideas about reasonable pluralism protect the module 'justice as fairness' from a person's non-public values. Rawls assumes that the political conception for which the *pro tanto* justification holds is by and large complete. That is, the political values specified by it can be suitably "ordered, or balanced, so that those values alone give a reasonable answer . . . to all, or nearly all" (Rawls 1995: 142–143) relevant questions.

This manoeuvre is also interesting for morality in networks. It allows for a distinction between private and public reasons regarding justification. Even if actors have different background theories, they might develop an overlapping consensus by restricting themselves to considerations and background theories in the public domain. Such an overlapping consensus is justified if all actors can give their, possibly different, *pro tanto* justification of it.

5.3 PROCEDURAL NORMS FOR NETWORKS

The reflective equilibrium approach as developed by Rawls and Daniels is usually seen as a method for justification of moral judgments. Rawls, for example, introduced the notion of 'overlapping consensus' as part of the attempt to justify 'justice as fairness' as the organising principle for the welfare state. Nevertheless, Rawls makes also the factual claim that such an overlapping consensus is attainable, and is even likely to occur in the real world (Rawls 1995: 144). The wide reflective equilibrium approach can therefore also be interpreted as a constructive method for achieving an overlapping consensus. Along such lines, we argued in the previous sections that actors in a network can achieve an overlapping consensus in actual practice by striving for a reflective equilibrium and accepting or making certain public/non-public distinctions.

In this section, we further pursue this idea. In particular, we will argue that two sets of procedural norms that have been discussed in the literature (e.g., Grin and van der Graaf 1996a; Grin and van der Graaf 1996b; Schot and Rip 1997; Sclove 1995; Wynne 1995) are instrumental in achieving a justified overlapping consensus in networks. These two sets of norms are (1) first and second order reflective learning, and (2) openness and inclusiveness.

5.3.1 First and Second Order Reflective Learning

Most scholarly literature on learning goes back to the work of Fischer (1980, 1995) and Schön (1983). Fischer conceptualises his 'levels of argumentation' (he does not refer to learning or reflection explicitly) within the context of policy making. Schön refers to the professions of engineering, architecture, management, psychotherapy, and town planning to show how professionals meet challenges by engaging in a process of 'reflection-in-action'. A distinction is generally made between two levels of learning or reflection: lower-order versus higher-order discourse (Fischer 1980) or reflection (Grin and van der Graaf 1996b; Schön 1983), and single-loop versus double-loop learning (Argyris and Schön 1978; Sabatier and Jenkins-Smith 1993) or adaptive versus generative learning (Senge 1990). Although the contexts and the exact definitions differ, the distinction between the two types of learning in all cases is more or less similar. In the lower-order category, the learning process is a kind of technical or instrumental learning. It is reactive, short-term focused, within a context of fixed objectives (as applied to policy), a context of fixing new problems within the same problem definition and procedures (as applied to organisation), or a context of technological design optimisation (Brown et al. 2003; Hoogma et al. 2005). In the higher-order category of learning, the objectives, problem definitions, and procedures are not tested but questioned and explored (Hoogma et al. 2005). It therefore involves the redefinition of policy goals and changes in norms and values (Brown et al. 2003). This higher-order learning is also more long-term focused. In the remainder of the text, we will use the term 'reflective learning' to refer to these higher-order learning processes.

The effect of learning can be conceived as a threefold shift (Brown et al. 2003): (1) a shift in framing of the problem; (2) a shift in principle approaches to solving the problem and in weighing of choices between alternatives; and (3) a shift in the relationships among actors in a network as well as the broader sphere. It is especially this third shift together with the object of higher order reflective learning (appreciative systems and overarching theories) which makes higher order reflective learning such an important phenomenon in the context of responsibility distributions. In the discussion

174 *Neelke Doorn*

of procedural justice, it was explained how the wide reflective equilibrium approach can be used to decide on issues in a context of reasonable pluralism (i.e., in a situation with diverse and competing interests). Reasonableness requires that people recognise the legitimacy of other actors in the network with other moral views. Lower-order learning occurs when people become aware of their position in the network and the possible differences in actor roles, agendas, perceptions, values, and interests among the actors. The awareness of these differences enhances the instrumental rationality of the actors in the sense that they realise that the other actors enable or constrain the achievement of certain goals (Van de Poel and Zwart 2010: 181). In case of reflective learning, actors are not only aware of these differences but they also recognise the *legitimacy* of these other views. Reflective learning therefore includes reflection on the desirable properties of the network as a whole. Additionally, it might help distinguishing between private and public values, that is, between arguments that are and that are not legitimate and important for an actor fulfilling a specific role in the network. Reflective learning might thus contribute to achieving an overlapping consensus concerning a fair distribution of responsibilities among actors within a network displaying a large variety of value systems and background theories (Van de Poel and Zwart 2010: 181).

According to Grin and Van der Graaf, higher order reflective learning is much rarer than lower order learning. They hypothesise that higher order reflection is the most likely to occur between actors from different kinds of communities, such as policy coalitions, managers, or engineers, because these actors are not antagonistic and are interested in different parts of reality. Higher order learning is less likely between actors from the same community, especially if these actors have different ideological views, as is the case with policy coalitions (Grin and van der Graaf 1996a, 94).

5.3.2 Openness and Inclusiveness

Besides first and second order reflective learning, a second set of procedural norms relates to issues of openness and inclusiveness (cf. Sclove 1995). Inclusiveness means that all actors and all relevant considerations are included in a network. As a first order approximation we propose to call an actor relevant if it is a stakeholder, that is, if it is has a reasonable stake in the development of an issue at stake in the network. We add the notion of reasonable stake because we do not want to call each actor that claims to have a stake a stakeholder. As test for reasonableness of stakes, we propose Rawls' criterion whether it can stand the test of public reason, that is, whether the stake can be argued on the basis of public reasons and is not only based on private reasons. We propose to call a consideration relevant if it is a reasonable consideration of a stakeholder, with 'reasonable' similarly defined as in the case of stakes.[4]

A Procedural Approach   175

Openness and inclusiveness are related to the attitudes of the actors in the network but are also, at least partly, considered to be characteristics of the network. The criterion of openness calls for an open discourse, which means that it is not only important that all relevant actors are included, but that they have equal opportunities for participating in and contributing to the decision-making process as well. If a group of actors with different fields and levels of expertise are engaged in a conversation, it is important that the vocabulary used by the experts is understandable to all. The criterion of openness also requires that people feel free to bring in unwelcome arguments. If some actors are discouraged to do so and remain silent, the overlapping consensus that is arrived at cannot be justified as being fair. Whereas reflective learning enables the creation of an overlapping consensus, openness and inclusiveness are instrumental to achieving a *justified* consensus. Together, openness and inclusiveness determine when an overlapping consensus can be considered fair. They prevent unjustified shortcuts to a wide reflective equilibrium or overlapping consensus. The latter could be the case when people with unwelcome arguments are excluded from the network.

The reader might suspect, by introducing the notion of a 'justified' consensus, we want to smuggle in our own substantial notion on what good reasons are for achieving a consensus. That is, however, not the case. The point is that not any overlapping consensus will do; at least two restrictions apply. One is that for each actor the consensus should be justifiable within his or her own wide reflective equilibrium, even if the justification is sometimes limited to a *pro tanto* justification. In this respect, an overlapping consensus differs from a mere compromise, which actors are willing to accept because they think they have made a good deal, but which they cannot justify in terms of a wide reflective equilibrium. The second restriction is that the consensus covers all relevant actors and considerations. Of course, the question which actors and considerations are relevant and should be involved in the network is a moral question. One cannot escape this question, however, by simply striving for a consensus without specifying who and what is to be incorporated in achieving this consensus. We assume that this second criterion is met if the network is open and inclusive.

The criterion of openness and inclusiveness thus provides procedural legitimacy to the overlapping consensus that is achieved in the network. In addition, the requirement that each actor should be able to justify the resulting overlapping consensus in an actor-specific wide reflective equilibrium adds some substantial bite to this procedural criterion. A substantive criterion for justification on the level of the network as a whole is, however, not presumed. This would bring us back to the idea of a shared wide reflective equilibrium and we argued before that that is usually unattainable in a network (see section 5.2.1).

5.3.3 The Relation between Reflective Learning and Inclusiveness and Openness

As the two procedural norms we have considered stem from different sources, one might wonder how these two sets of norms are related. It is worth noting that the role of the two sets of norms in achieving a justified overlapping consensus is fundamentally different. As we have argued, reflective learning is desirable because it is instrumental in achieving a consensus in the network; this instrumentality is empirically testable. Conversely, a network needs to be open and inclusive for an overlapping consensus to be justified. The desirability of this requirement cannot be verified empirically, although it can be empirically assessed whether a network is open and inclusive. Another constraint that needs to be met for an overlapping consensus to be justified is that each actor should be able to justify the consensus in terms of her own wide reflective equilibrium. Rawls also formulated this latter requirement to distinguish an overlapping consensus from a mere compromise.

Although we introduced openness and inclusiveness as procedural criteria for the justification of an overlapping consensus, it is worth noting that they may also be instrumental for reflective learning. In an open network, new and original perspectives on the issue at stake are welcomed and are likely to facilitate and trigger first and second order learning. Openness and inclusiveness may, conversely, also hinder reflective learning. For first order learning, some convergence and closure are prerequisites. Some agreement, for instance, about the central problem definition is necessary to cooperate productively together. Such agreement might conflict with the requirement of openness, which means that the existing problem definition is open for discussion.

It has been argued that for networks engaged in a common project, such as the one we will discuss in section 5.4, the development of a monitoring system based on Ambient Intelligence technology, a certain shielding off from the environment is needed for the project to succeed (Law and Callon 1988). If outsiders continuously interfere in the network, it becomes virtually impossible to achieve something. The inclusion of too many new actors in a network hinders also second order reflective learning. Argyris et al. (1985) have suggested that actors will not engage in second order learning if they are in threatening situations. Including new actors in a network may sometimes be threatening for the actors involved as it might lead to strong disagreements and strongly diverging problem definitions.

Thus, whereas openness and inclusiveness sometimes encourage reflective learning, in other circumstances they hinder it. Consequently, some authors have maintained that openness and inclusiveness are only valuable insofar as they lead to reflective learning (Schot and Rip 1997). We have argued, however, that openness and inclusiveness are worth striving for independent from their effect on reflective learning because they are necessary for achieving an overlapping consensus that is justified.

With these two procedural norms, we will now analyse whether they are indeed beneficial to achieving a distribution of responsibility that is considered fair by all parties involved.

5.4 CASE STUDY

5.4.1 Case Description

In this section, we briefly discuss a case study covering the development of a prototype application for in-house monitoring of patients, based on Ambient Intelligence (AmI) technology.[5] This project was studied as part of an ethical parallel study (see Van de Poel and Doorn (2013) for a description of this kind of ethical research). The aim of ethical parallel research is to carry out ethical investigations parallel to, and in close cooperation with, a specific technological R&D project. The R&D project described here was carried out by a consortium of 12 Small and Medium Enterprises, several universities, two independent industrial research institutes and a scientific research centre in rehabilitation technology.[6] In the project, a use case was developed to serve as an example of what can be done with this technology and to focus on the work of the demonstration activities of the project. The use case describes a situation of in-house monitoring of the daily activities of a patient with Chronic Obstructive Pulmonary Disease (COPD), a chronic lung disease. In the project, end users, including both patients and health care professionals, were consulted to clarify their wishes and demands with respect to the monitoring application to be created. After a first experimental set-up of the application, explorative experiments with real users were carried out to determine its functional and technical requirements in more detail. Afterwards the experimental application were evaluated both in terms of the technical specifications and in terms of the objectives set to improve quality of life of the patients.

In the original research proposal, the technical researchers identified the social acceptance of the currently developed technology as a crucial element of the success of the project.[7] The main focus of the author's ethical investigations was therefore on the necessary conditions for getting the technology socially accepted. On the basis of a series of interviews with 13 representatives of the different institutional partners involved in the project, a list of 'moral issues' was identified (see Table 5.1).

The interviewees were asked to think of 'moral issue' in as broad a way as possible: anything related to risks and moral values (e.g., social acceptance, human well-being, privacy, society, and sustainability) was considered relevant.[8] According to the technical researchers, these issues should be addressed in order to gain social acceptance. Subsequently, a workshop was organised in which the issues were discussed in more detail. This workshop was organised in a *Group Decision Room* (GDR; an electronic

178 *Neelke Doorn*

Table 5.1 Moral issues related to social acceptance

Moral issues

Making sure that the application does not interfere with everyday life (invisibility of technology)

Setting the requirements of the security of this applications (how secure is secure enough?)

Striking the right balance between user friendliness, reliability and functionality

Making sure that end users (patients, their family & friends, clinicians) are able and willing to use the application

Starting a broad societal discussion about the desirability of these kinds of (monitoring) applications

Addressing questions related to data storage and data access (legal aspects)

Inventorying/monitoring potential risks of the present application

Identify how technological choices affect the social acceptance

---

brainstorming facility which allows for anonymous discussion and voting). This facility was chosen to fulfil the criterion of power free discussion and equal voice for all, which is central to the procedural approach. The aim of the workshop was to trace the different rationales for distributing the responsibility for addressing the moral issues. At the start of the workshop responsibility was defined as 'the task to see to it that X', where X could refer to any of the moral issues. Responsibility was thus understood as responsibility-as-obligation. In the remainder of this chapter, we use the term 'moral task' for the responsibility to address particular moral issues.

The workshop was structured along the lines of the wide reflective equilibrium approach to encourage reflection on the different layers of morality (considered judgments, principles, and moral background theories) in the hope that this would facilitate learning processes as well. Table 5.2 shows a summary of the empirical findings (see Doorn 2010c, 2012) for a detailed presentation of the results). The eight rows correspond to the eight workshop participants. The moral background theories of each participant (Column 2 in Table 5.2) were traced on the basis of the Ethical Position Questionnaire, a psychometric scale to measure ethical ideologies (Forsyth 1980; Forsyth et al. 1988).[9] The participants were asked to distribute the 'moral tasks' over the different project activities. It was also possible to say that something was beyond the scope of the project ('outside project').[10] This distribution was made twice by the participants with a discussion in between in order to assess whether the participants converged to a common opinion in the course of the workshop. In addition, the different participants' rationales for distributing responsibilities were traced on the basis of a discussion about conditions for responsibility (Column 3). The rationales are described in terms of recurring arguments that were used by the participants to make their case. Column 4 shows the activity that was

A Procedural Approach   179

Table 5.2   Summary of empirical findings of the workshop

Actor	EPQ typology	Type of argumentation	Project activity primarily responsible
1	Absolutist/ Situationist	Fairness (workload); Workplace relations	Clinical Experimentation
2	Subjectivist	Goal-directed; Efficacy	Project Management
3	Situationist	User perspective; Societal; Efficacy ("getting things done")	Clinical Experimentation
4	Absolutist/ Situationist	Societal; User perspective; Fairness (workload)	Project Management/ Outside project
5	Absolutist	Fairness (workload)	Research on Software
6	Absolutist/ Exceptionist	Fairness (workload); User perspective	Clinical Experimentation
7	Absolutist/ Situationist	Fairness (workload)	Clinical Experimentation
8	Situationist	User perspective; Goal-directed	Project Management/ Clinical Experimentation

mentioned most as being primarily responsible for each of the moral issues (this column shows the aggregated results of the second distribution round only). Afterwards, the participants were asked whether the final distribution of responsibilities was 'fair'.

5.4.2   Analysis of Empirical Results

When analysing the empirical results, we have to keep in mind that several things run together. First, the ethical parallel research itself probably had some effect on the way the research project was carried out and how the different responsibilities were distributed. The technical researchers are probably more attentive to moral issues due to the presence of an ethicist at their project meetings. Hence, this might already have triggered some learning processes. Second, the workshop was structured along the lines of the wide reflective equilibrium approach so that the different elements in the workshop were not only used to *assess* the individuals' moral opinions but also to *encourage reflection*. When we try to analyse the resulting distribution of responsibilities in terms of the Rawlsian procedural framework and try to see whether this approach did indeed reconcile the tension between the different conceptions of responsibility, it is somewhat difficult to separate the effect of the workshop itself from the effect of the procedural approach. However, notwithstanding these multiple effects, we can still derive some interesting points from the ethical parallel research and the workshop.

180 *Neelke Doorn*

First, the workshop prompted discussion on the distribution of responsibilities in the project. In their evaluation of the workshop, most participants indicated that they had become more aware of certain moral issues (e.g., the need to involve end users). There was a general agreement that most moral issues span several activities within the project and that it is therefore difficult to single out one activity where it should primarily be addressed. The primary responsibility was in those cases ascribed to the project management for coordinating this joint effort, to the experimentation phase where all activities were supposed to come together, or to the clinical partner. Some participants explicitly mentioned that this workshop made them realise that some moral issues were currently not addressed adequately. The idea that the work should shift from research towards laboratory or clinical experiments with a (prototype) application was shared by all. Soon after the workshop, a brainstorm meeting was scheduled in which the requirements for clinical experimentation were discussed in more detail. Hence, one effect of the workshop was certainly to pay more attention to the end users and to involve them in the research.

Second, although the participants endorsed rather different conceptions of responsibility with different foci (consequences, fairness, tasks, duties, professionalism), they tended to be sensitive to one another's arguments. Although it proved difficult to attain consensus on all points, the opinions of the different participants tended to converge between both 'distributing exercises' (remember that the participants were asked to distribute the responsibilities twice, with a discussion in between). Whereas the first distribution of responsibilities showed a significant scatter of tasks over different project activities and partners, the second distribution showed more responsibility for the project management and the clinical partners. Because all discussions and responsibility ascriptions were done anonymously, this can be considered a genuine convergence and not the result of group pressure. The participants were also asked about the fairness of the resulting distribution of responsibilities. Interestingly, although the participants perceived the end result in rather different ways, they all seem to interpret the end result more or less as a consensus on how the responsibilities are to be distributed. Some interpreted the outcome of the workshop as the insight that the 'ethics' of the project is, in the end, a joint effort, whereas others interpreted it as primarily a responsibility of the clinical partners or the project management to coordinate the joint efforts. However, all participants agreed that, in the end, all project members should have a commitment to the project as a whole (including the moral aspects).

Third, when asked whether the workshop would affect the work in the project, most participants indicated that it would indeed have implications for their work, though for some only minor ones. All participants expected a shift in focus from research towards either laboratory or clinical experiments with a (prototype) application. One participant expected that the enduring impact of the workshop would be to make more explicit what the project in fact aims for. Before the workshop took place, the goal of the project was still rather ill defined. Additionally, the opinions on what is part of the project became clearer and also more inclusive. Some researchers initially considered most moral issues as being beyond the scope of the present project. However, during the discussion and in the second 'distributing exercise', most issues were included in the scope of the project, with a central role for the project management.

5.4.3 Discussion

When we assess the project in terms of the two procedural norms: first and second order reflective learning, and openness and inclusiveness, we can identify the following points. First, both levels of learning seem to have occurred. The various participants' remark that they became more aware of ethical issues is a clear sign of first-order learning. However, the discussions indicate that the workshop prompted second-order learning processes as well. Some senior participants worried about the fairness of the load for the PhD and postdoctoral researchers, which indicates openness to other people's interests. Moreover, the emphasis that the work requires a *joint* effort, spanning all the project activities, also points to (second-order) reflective learning processes. Lastly, the fact that the problem definition itself became object of discussion is also an indication of reflective learning.

In terms of inclusiveness, the project clearly aims to be inclusive. It was deliberately chosen to include a clinical partner in the project as well, herewith attempting to make the project more than just a technological project. However, the cooperation between the technical partners and the clinical partner proved difficult in practice. During the workshop it was also mentioned that the user involvement was in fact rather weak. In that sense, the project was less inclusive than aimed for at the start. However, soon after the workshop, more tangible attempts were made to include end users. Because the researchers sincerely aimed at openness and inclusiveness and because they did not raise formal obstacles for including more people, we can conclude that this criterion is, at least partly, fulfilled.

What does the foregoing teach us about the necessity of the two procedural norms? Are these norms indeed required? Regarding inclusiveness, the answer is obviously yes. If the criterion of inclusiveness is released, the method loses its justificatory force. In practice, it will be difficult to involve all relevant people in the decision-making directly. However, in a case such as the current project, the interests of those people that are affected by the technology should at least be represented. If we look at the end users, for example, it is important that their interests are looked after. Even though they do not have to be involved in the actual distribution of responsibility, the ultimate distribution of responsibility should include the task to look after their interests. So, though indirectly, they should be included or represented in the decision-making process.

The second norm is learning. During the workshop, it was investigated to what extent the moral background theories (Column 2 in Table 5.2) were

182 Neelke Doorn

predictive for the actual distributions of responsibility (Column 4 in Table 5.2). The empirical findings of the case suggest that there is no correlation between these two 'layers of morality'. People with similar moral background theories might come to different responsibility distributions and people with different moral background theories might come to similar responsibility distributions. This suggests that reflective learning (here, a willingness to change one's moral background theory) is not required to come to a similar distribution of responsibilities. However, without reflective learning, people will probably not recognise the legitimacy of other people's arguments in the first place. So, reflective learning is probably still required to agree on the possibility and legitimacy of disagreement. People do not have to change their own conception of what responsibility amounts to, but they do have to acknowledge that their conception is one among many. In the empirical case, reflective learning processes were present, especially in the discussion of the fairness of responsibility ascriptions. It is questionable whether the outcome would have converged as it did now without these reflective learning processes. This suggests that both norms are indeed beneficial for getting a justified overlapping consensus and that the norm of inclusiveness is also required.

5.4.4 Further Investigations

Three points deserve further investigation. First, because the workshop was structured along the lines of the wide reflective equilibrium approach, it is difficult to assess whether it is the workshop itself or the 'procedural approach' that encourages reflection and alleviate the tension between the different responsibility conceptions. If the workshop was structured in a different way, not focusing on the different layers of morality, would the result have been the same? This question cannot be answered on the basis of this single case alone. Related to this point is the question whether the method should be applied in its full justificatory function or mainly as a constructive approach. Both questions need further research.

Second, the present case does neither confirm nor refute that (higher-order) reflective learning processes are indeed indispensable for recognising the legitimacy of other people's conceptions. Reflective learning proved, strictly speaking, not a necessary condition: it may be theoretically possible to think of a situation where people commit to reasonable pluralism without any instance of reflective learning. However, in practice it is highly unlikely that people will recognise the legitimacy of other people's responsibility conceptions in the absence of reflective learning processes. Hence, although reflective learning is not logically necessary, in practice it probably *is* required.

Third, due to the divergent interpretations of the final distribution of responsibilities, this final distribution cannot straightforwardly be interpreted in terms of an overlapping consensus or in terms of individual wide reflective equilibriums. In that sense it is maybe somewhat artificial to talk about 'procedural justice' in this context. The workshop did not explicitly derive or discuss procedural justice or cooperation norms. However, the fairness of responsibility distributions was explicitly discussed, including the question whether the final responsibility distribution could be considered fair. Together this seems a first step to deriving procedural justice norms.

More studies are needed for further developing the present approach to discuss responsibility. Remaining questions are the role of reflective learning processes and the different aims of the approach. Our hypothesis is that the more challenging the moral disagreements are, the more important these reflective learning processes become and the more important it becomes to systematically touch upon the different layers of morality. Alternatively, a discussion might easily arrive at an impasse in which opposing opinions are merely expressed rather than being listened to.

5.5 CONCLUSIONS

In this chapter, we developed a procedure for distributing responsibilities based on Rawls' political liberalism. The procedural model was applied to a technological project that was carried out between 2007 and 2011. This project was studied as part of an ethical parallel study. An interactive workshop was organised to discuss the responsibilities for moral issues in the project. During the workshop, it appeared that the team members endorse a large variety of responsibility conceptions and rationales for distributing them.

The case shows that, in a pluralist setting, a procedural approach can be useful for prompting discussion on the legitimacy of the different conceptions and the question what a fair distribution of responsibilities amounts to. Although a full overlapping consensus regarding the distribution of responsibilities is probably too demanding, the case shows that the tension between the different conceptions can be alleviated by structuring the discussion along the lines of the different layers of Rawls' wide reflective equilibrium approach, because this encourages participants to think in terms of 'fair' workload and the legitimacy of other people's arguments. Although some differences in opinion remained, the effect of the workshop was that the work became more focused and that certain moral issues that were until then not recognised, became part of the work. The two procedural norms (reflective learning and inclusiveness) were both (partly) fulfilled.

More generally, it may be concluded that the procedural approach that was developed in this chapter can be instrumental in overcoming the problem of many hands with respect to responsibility-as-obligation. As we have seen in Chapter 2, this is the situation in which a collective can be properly ascribed a responsibility-as-obligation whereas it is unclear how this responsibility distributes over the individual members of the collective, so that none of them may be responsible-as-obligation. This was also the situation that occurred in the case we described in detail in this chapter. The procedure presented in this chapter may help to distribute responsibility among the individual members of the collective and might so help to avoid the problem of many hands. The emphasis on the fairness of the procedure thereby is not only important from

184 *Neelke Doorn*

a moral point of view but also because a distribution that is the result of a fair procedure is more likely to be accepted and to be lived by.

NOTES

1. In this chapter, pluralism is understood as the acknowledgment of diverse and competing values and visions of the good life. The freedom to pursue one's own objections and shape one's life is assumed to be the cornerstone of democracy (Dryzek and Niemeyer 2006). Accordingly, conflicting private values stemming from these diverse and competing visions of the good life cannot simply be reduced to one overarching public value.
2. We do not want to suggest that Rawls' theory is the only procedural theory. Deliberative democracy, such as defended by, among others, Cohen (1989, 1997) and Elster (1986, 1998), is another example of a highly developed procedural theory. The concept of deliberation can also be linked to the work of the German philosopher Jürgen Habermas (1990).
3. The term "justice as fairness" is used by John Rawls to refer to his distinctive theory of justice in which he developed two principles for organising modern welfare state. The first principle, known as the equal liberty principle, states that each person is to have an equal right to the most extensive basic liberty compatible with similar liberty for others. The second principle describes two conditions that are to be satisfied in case of social and economic inequalities: (a) The inequalities are to be attached to positions and offices open to all under conditions of fair equality of opportunity (the fair equality of opportunity principle); and (b), The inequalities are to be to the greatest benefit of the least advantaged members of society (the difference principle) (Rawls 1993: 5–6; Rawls 2001: 42).
4. We admit that this definition of 'relevance' is only a first order approximation and that what is relevant or reasonable may always be a point of debate. That is the reason we add the criterion of openness, which warrants the possibility of reformulating the central issue of the network, such that new aspects not considered relevant or reasonable before may be introduced and will become part of the considerations.
5. Ambient Intelligence reflects a vision of the future of ICT in which intelligence is embedded in virtually everything around us, such as clothes, furniture, etc. The technology consists of Wireless Sensor Networks (WSN), the combination of body sensors, ambient sensors, and wireless networks.
6. For a more elaborate description of the project, including the results of the ethical investigations, the reader is referred to (Doorn 2010c; Doorn 2012). The project officially ran from December 2007 through November 2010, but it continued until mid-2011.
7. Although the term "social acceptance" suggests a strategic or prudential rather than moral intention, in the interviews the technical researchers interpreted the term "acceptance" as referring to both *acceptance* and *acceptability*. In the remainder we use the term to refer to this broad interpretation of social acceptance.
8. We realise that this description of moral issue is not as well-defined as some philosophers would like it to be. However, because the interviews and the workshop were explicitly aimed at tracing the opinions of the engineers themselves, we did not give any constraints on what counts as a moral issue nor did we introduce issues that were not mentioned by the engineers themselves. For a more well-wrought description of when a value can be considered a *moral* value, see Nagel (1979, Chapter Nine: The fragmentation of value).

9. These ideologies indicate the background considerations underlying moral deliberation, classified along the two dimensions universalism and idealism. The first dimension refers to the extent to which individuals reject universal moral rules in favor of relativism. The second dimension refers to the degree to which individuals are idealistic or pragmatic in their attitude toward the consequences of actions. On the basis of Likert scale responses to 20 statements, respondents were classified into one of the four ideological categories without the need for interpretation by the interviewer. These categories are situationism, absolutism, subjectivism and exceptionism. Situationists share with subjectivists a low score on the universalism dimension (and similarly, absolutists and exceptionists share a high score); comparably, subjectivists and exceptionists have a low score on the idealism dimension, whereas situationists and absolutists share a high score on this dimension.
10. In order to avoid a discussion on a too personal level ("*you* should have done that!") we used the more neutral terms project "activities" or "phases" as the organisational entities to which to ascribe responsibility.

REFERENCES

Argyris, C., R. Putnam, and D. McLain Smith 1985. *Action science*. San Francisco; London: Jossey Bass Publishers.

Argyris, C., and D.A. Schön. 1978. *Organizational learning: A theory of action perspective*. Reading: Addison-Wesley.

Brown, H.S., P. Vergragt, K. Green, and L. Berchicci. 2003. "Learning for sustainability transition through bounded socio-technical experiments in personal mobility." *Technology Analysis & Strategic Management* 15(3): 291–315.

Cohen, J. 1989. "Deliberation and democratic legitimacy." In *The good polity: Normative analysis of the state*, edited by A. Hamlin and P.H. Pettit, 17–34. Oxord: Blackwell.

Cohen, J. 1997. "Procedure and substance in deliberative democracy." In *Deliberative democracy*, edited by J. Bohman and W. Rehg, 405–437. Cambridge: MIT Press.

Daniels, N. 1979 "Wide reflective equilibrium and theory acceptance in ethics." *Journal of Philosophy* 76(5): 256–282.

Doorn, N. 2010a. "Applying Rawlsian approaches to resolve ethical issues: Inventory and setting of a research agenda." *Journal of Business Ethics* 91(1): 127–143.

Doorn, N. 2010b. "A Rawlsian approach to distribute responsibilities in networks." *Science and Engineering Ethics* 16(2): 221–249.

Doorn, N. 2010c. "A procedural approach to distributing Responsibilities in R&D networks." *Poiesis & Praxis. International Journal of Technology Assessment and Ethics of Science* 7(3): 169–188.

Doorn, N. 2012. "Exploring responsibility rationales in R&D Networks." *Science, Technology & Human Values* 37(3): 180–209.

Dryzek, J.S., and S. Niemeyer. 2006. "Reconciling pluralism and consensus as political ideals." *American Journal of Political Science* 50(3): 634–649.

Elster, J. 1986. "The market and the forum." In *Deliberative democracy*, edited by J. Elster and A.Hylland, 103–132. Cambridge: Cambridge University Press.

Elster, J. (1998) "Deliberation and constitution making", in *Deliberative democracy*, edited by J. Elster, 97–122. New York: Cambridge University Press.

Fischer, F. 1980. *Politics, values, and public policy*. Boulder: Westview Press, Inc.

Fischer, F. (1995) *Evaluating public policy*. Chicago: Nelson-Hall.

Forsyth, D.R. 1980. "A taxonomy of ethical ideologies." *Journal of Personality and Social Psychology* 39(1): 175–184.

186 Neelke Doorn

Forsyth, D.R., J.L. Bye, and K.N. Kelley. 1988. "Idealism, relativism, and the ethics of caring." *Journal of Psychology* 122(3): 243–248.

Goodin, R.E. (1995) *Utilitarianism as a public philosophy.* Cambridge: Cambridge University Press.

Grin, J., and H. van der Graaf. 1996a. "Technology assessment as learning." *Science, Technology & Human Values* 21(1): 72–99.

Grin, J. and H. van der Graaf. (1996b) "Implementation as communicative action: An interpretative understanding of interactions between policy actors and target groups." *Policy Sciences* 29(4): 291–319.

Habermas, J. 1990. *Moral consciousness and communicative action.* Cambridge: MIT Press.

Hoogma, R., Weber, M. and Elzen, B. 2005. "Integrated long-term strategies to induce regume shifts to sustainability." In *Towards environmental innovation systems,* edited by M. Weber and J. Hemmelskamp, 209–236. Heidelberg: Springer.

Ladd, J. 1991. "Bhopal: An essay on moral responsibility and civic virtue." *Journal of Social Philosophy* 32(1): 73–91.

Law, J. and Callon, M. 1988. "Engineering and sociology in a military aircraft project: A network analysis of technological change." *Social Problems* 35(3): 284–297.

Mouffe, C. 2000. *The democratic paradox.* London: Verso.

Nagel, T. 1979. *Mortal questions.* Cambridge: Cambridge University Press.

Nihlén Fahlquist, J. 2006. "Responsibility ascriptions and vision zero." *Accident Analysis and Prevention* 38(6): 1113–1118.

Oakley, J., and D. Cocking. 2001. "Virtue ethics and professional roles." Cambridge: Cambridge University Press.

Rawls, J. 1993. *Political liberalism.* New York: Columbia University Press.

Rawls, J. 1995. "Political liberalism: Reply to Habermas." *The Journal of Philosophy* 92(3): 132–180.

Rawls, J. 1999 [1971]. *A theory of justice.* Cambridge (Ma.): The Belknap Press of Harvard University Press.

Rawls, J. 2001. *Justice as fairness: A restatement.* Cambridge (Ma.): The Belknap Press of Harvard University Press.

Sabatier, P.A., and H.C. Jenkins-Smith. 1993. *Policy change and learning: An advocacy coalition approach.* Boulder: Westview Press, Inc.

Schön, D.A. 1983. *The reflective practitioner. How professionals think in action.* New York: Basic Books.

Schot, J.W., and A. Rip. 1997. "The past and future of constructive Technology Assessment." *Technological Forecasting and Social Change* 54(2/3): 251–268.

Sclove, R.E. 1995. *Democracy and technology.* New York: The Guilford Press.

Senge, P.M. 1990. "The leader's New Work: Building learning organizations." *Sloan Management Review* 32(1): 7–23.

Van de Poel, I.R., and S.D. Zwart. 2010. "Reflective Equilibrium in R&D networks." *Science, Technology & Human Values* 35(2): 174–199.

Van de Poel, I.R., and N. Doorn. 2013. "Ethical parallel research: A network approach for moral evaluation (NAME)". In *Early engagement and new technologies: Opening up the laboratory,* edited by N. Doorn, D. Schuurbiers, I.R. van de Poel, and M.E. Gorman, 111–136. Dordrecht: Springer.

Van Hooft, S. 2006. *Understanding virtue ethics.* Chesham: Acumen Publishing.

Williams, G. 2008. "Responsibility as a virtue." *Ethical Theory and Moral Practice* 11(4): 455–470.

Wynne, B. 1995. "Technological assessment as reflexive social learning: Observations from the risk field." In *Managing technology in society. The approach of constructive technology assessment,* edited by A. Rip, T. Misa and J. Schot, 19–36. London: Pinter.

Young, I.M. 2000. *Inclusion and democracy.* Oxford University Press.

6 Responsibility as a Virtue and the Problem of Many Hands

Jessica Nihlén Fahlquist

6.1 INTRODUCTION

It is reasonable to think that the problem of many hands (PMH) becomes more prevalent the larger the projects and activities in business and technology become. Some of the more recent examples are the bank crisis in 2008–2009 and the Deepwater Horizon disaster in 2010. In both cases, there were huge societal, economic, and environmental costs, respectively, but it was difficult to pinpoint individuals to hold responsible. This was due to the complexity of the cases and the complicated web of causalities and interdependencies that led to crisis and disaster. However, in both cases, there are also clear signs of irresponsible behaviour by individuals. Although PMH, like these ones, cannot be solved merely by responsible individual behaviour, agents who *take* responsibility would potentially reduce the risk of PMH. This is the notion I will defend in this chapter. As we will see, this requires not just virtuous individuals but also an institutional context that is conducive to responsibility-as-virtue.

In Chapter 2, the problem of many hands was discussed as the situation in which it is not reasonable to hold any individual responsible for some collective harm while it would be reasonable to hold the collective responsible for that harm. The examples of the problem of many hands in Chapter 2 focused on responsibility-as-blameworthiness and on responsibility-as-obligation. This chapter focuses on responsibility-as-virtue. In order to avoid the problem of many hands, a broad outlook is needed, that takes all the different meanings of responsibility into account. Whereas part of the problem could be dealt with by distributing responsibility-as-obligation, this is facilitated by a willingness to take on responsibility and by people with certain characteristics. Thus, to 'be responsible' can refer to 'seeing to it that φ', i.e., to fulfil one's obligations, or to a certain kind of person with a specific set of character traits, attitudes and emotions. Both are essential and, as argued in Chapter 1, people who are 'responsible' in the virtue ethical sense are more likely to take on and fulfil responsibilities-as-obligations. However, the two meanings are not identical and we need to have a closer

188 *Jessica Nihlén Fahlquist*

look at the notion of being a responsible person to grasp how it adds to what has been said so far.

When used in the virtue ethical sense, a person is responsible if she has certain character traits, attitudes, and emotions, and behaves in a certain way over time. One major difference between responsibility-as-blameworthiness and responsibility-as-accountability on the one hand, and responsibility-as-virtue on the other hand is that whereas the former two are backward-looking the latter one is primarily forward-looking. A difference between responsibility-as-obligation and responsibility-as-virtue is that whereas the former is more definable in a specific task or set of tasks, the latter is more open-ended and voluntarily assumed. Neither responsibility-as-blameworthiness nor responsibility-as-obligation pay attention to the agent herself or her character, but are attached to actions.

The purpose of this chapter is to show how responsibility-as-virtue might help in avoiding the PMH. The suggestion is that responsibility-as-virtue should be seen as consisting primarily of care, moral imagination, and practical wisdom. This conception puts emotions to the fore of responsibility. Unless one cares or empathises with potential victims of the unintended as well as the intended consequences of one's actions, one does not act responsibly in the virtue sense. In order to be a responsible person in this sense it is necessary that one *feels* responsible and in order to feel responsible one needs to *care*.

This chapter proceeds as follows. In section 6.2, a tentative sketch of responsibility-as-virtue is presented. Subsequently, virtue ethics is discussed in section 6.3 as the main theoretical background of responsibility-as-virtue and in section 6.4 it is argued that responsibility-as-virtue consists of three main elements: care, moral imagination, and practical wisdom. After analysing, in section 6.5, how the institutional context can promote responsibility-as-virtue, the question of how the PMH may be avoided through responsibility-as-virtue is discussed in section 6.6. Section 6.7 provides a discussion of how this could work out more practically in dealing with technological risks, and attention is paid to the question of whether responsibility-as-virtue might be too demanding. The chapter ends with a conclusion (section 6.8).

6.2 RESPONSIBILITY-AS-VIRTUE: A FIRST SKETCH

When the *Deepwater Horizon* oil spill occurred in April 2010 (see Introduction) this was not the first time BP's activities caused harm in terms of lives lost, health and environmental problems. They had previously neglected adequate upgrading of safety systems at their Texas City Refinery, causing fatalities on several occasions. The most well-known accident previous to the *Deepwater Horizon* oil spill occurred in March 2005, when one of their largest refineries in Texas City exploded. Management had not paid

Responsibility as a Virtue 189

due attention to the engineering problems, and maintenance and safety had not been upgraded according to best practice for reasons of cost (Hopkins 2011). BP had ignored safety and environmental regulations and had not implemented the necessary improvements, their safety culture and safety practices were flawed, and there were poor management decisions (cf. Steffy 2011, Baker et al. 2007, Bakolas et al. 2011).

Arguably, BP's management did not take safety seriously enough and acted in ways that are blameworthy. It is clear that most people feel, for good reasons, a need to blame someone in cases like this one if BP's management is judged to have done things wrong, for example, because they had information on how to improve safety but chose not to do it. In such a case, conditions of responsibility-as-blameworthiness are fulfilled and blaming is appropriate. However, at some point someone neglected to take a forward-looking responsibility and this is what led to the unwanted situation. That some people did not take their forward-looking responsibility can mean that (1) they violated their obligations to do x, y, and z (responsibility-as-moral-obligation), or (2) that they did not act in a responsible manner (responsibility-as-virtue). Whereas obligations are relatively specific, being a responsible person or acting responsibly can mean something beyond doing what the obligations prescribe. It is, in this way, a thicker concept and more related to virtues than obligations. In the following, we will have a closer look at responsibility conceived in this way.

It is reasonable to have greater expectations, in terms of responsibility, of someone who takes part in an activity that creates risks to other people's health and the environment than from an individual who does not. Changing status quo by creating opportunities and risks entails more responsibility. Arguably, we expect that certain professionals whose activities affect people's lives and health are responsible to a greater extent than people who do not have that power to change people's lives in a good or bad way. This means that they are praised when things go well and blamed when things go wrong. When we talk about responsibility in this way we are referring to backward-looking responsibility because we are pointing at what was done and the consequence of what was done.

However, intuitively, responsibility for risk-generating activities also means taking responsibility during the very process in which risks are generated. In the case of BP, it would be reasonable to expect employees to step up and do something to stop the neglect of safety and environmental concerns. Although some employees appear to have done that, this did not change the outcome. It is reasonable to think that people working with research and development of risky technologies are *responsible* people and that if they see something which could potentially be dangerous they do something about it, i.e., that they make a serious effort, deliberate about potential risks and uncertainties, and do not act recklessly or are not too risk-prone and not too "adventurous". It is reasonable to hope that people working

190 *Jessica Nihlén Fahlquist*

with risk-generating activities are empathetic and have the ability to think about potential victims of materialised risks. However, it is not common to conceive of engineers as empathetic. It is important to note that the image of an engineer does not necessarily have anything to do with the personality of people who are engineers. Engineers are probably as empathetic as non-engineers. However, engineers are commonly thought to make decisions in a rational and quantifiable way, meaning that emotions have little to do with engineering and should perhaps be left out completely. Roeser argues that instead of unemotional calculators, engineers should cultivate their moral sensitivity by learning to use their emotions. This should be done because engineering design is not morally neutral, but involves values (Roeser 2012). This ability arguably requires a certain emotional maturity and empathetic attitude, i.e., being a certain kind of person.

Responsible people, in this sense, both seek to avoid risks to people's health, lives, and the environment, and do everything in their power to reduce the negative impact of their activities. Thus, partaking in risk-generating activities entails forward-looking responsibility and a sense of responsibility.

The aim in the remainder of this chapter is to explicate what is involved in the notion of responsibility-as-virtue and to sketch what responsible people are like. To do that, we need to have a brief look at virtue ethics. The reason for that is that virtue ethics is the ethical theory concerned with character traits, emotions, attitudes, and people's behaviour over time, as opposed to utilitarianism and deontological ethics, which are more concerned with the moral quality of isolated actions.

6.3 VIRTUE ETHICS

Virtue ethics is usually seen as the third ethical theory, the other two being deontological ethics and consequentialism. Deontological ethics is based on the notion of duties and, very simplified, calls an action right if it is in accordance with universal duties and wrong if it violates a duty. Consequentialism, again very simplified, calls an action right if it brings about good outcomes, e.g. happiness, and wrong if it produces the opposite, i.e., disutility or unhappiness. Whereas these two focus on actions, virtue ethics is more concerned with the person and her character.

The word virtue means 'excellence', 'capacity', or 'ability', and being virtuous is being able to or having the power to achieve something. Virtue ethics is concerned with traits of character that are admirable. However, the lack those character traits would not necessarily lead to blaming or accusations of acting immorally. A moral agent is motivated to the extent that she wants to be a morally good person and because she recognises certain values, e.g. honesty. Virtue ethicists attempt to find answers to questions of what an agent should do by considering the agent's character and the morally relevant features of the situation (van Hooft 2006).

Responsibility as a Virtue 191

Possessing the virtues, in virtue ethics, is the basis of being good as a human being. According to Swanton (2007: 209), "a virtue is a disposition to respond to or acknowledge items in its field or fields in an excellent or good enough way". Excellence includes not only actions, but also emotions and motivations. Swanton defends a pluralist account of virtues, which entails that virtues make the possessor excellent in responding to the 'demands of the world', including demands of the self. Oakley and Cocking (2001) argue that the best way to understand a virtue ethics criterion of right action is in terms of 'regulative ideals'. An agent who has a regulative ideal has internalised a specific conception of correctness or excellence in a way that they are able to adjust their behaviour and motivation in accordance with that standard.

If a virtue is a disposition to respond in a certain way to the demands of the world we are concerned with people's behaviour over time. Against this background, what is required of a person to be called "responsible"? What would responsibility-as-virtue entail? In everyday situations, we talk about responsible and irresponsible people, leaders, parents, teachers, politicians, and so forth all the time. Responsibility as a virtue, i.e., as a way of responding to the demands of the world, has been explored by some philosophers. According to van Hooft (2006), who briefly discusses the notion, responsibility-as-virtue is about a "willingness to take responsibility" and "being responsible", i.e., being a responsible person. It is not the same as a willingness to accept blame for things an agent has done wrong, although that may be one part. Emotions like personal involvement, commitment, and "not leaving it to others", a feeling that it is "up to me", and a "willingness to make sacrifices in order to get involved" are also involved in the virtue of responsibility.

Williams (2008) argues that responsibility-as-virtue represents a "readiness to respond to a plurality of normative demands". The key to understand responsibility in this sense is the notion of plurality, i.e., in a typical case where responsibility is called for, there are more than one important demand and the responsible agent needs to use her judgment to balance these demands in order to form an appropriate response. Most of us are employees, parents, friends, colleagues, and someone's child at the same time and being responsible requires juggling the different concerns implied by these different roles in a sensible way and respond in appropriate ways (Williams 2008). As the complexity of society increases, this approach to morality becomes even more relevant.

Discussing one of the greatest industrial disasters in history, the Bhopal accident in 1984, Ladd (1991) conceives of responsibility as connected to 'civic virtue': "A virtuous citizen, and that should include everybody, should have a concern for the common good and for the long-range welfare of other people in the society, even where this concern demands individual sacrifices of one sort or another or simply giving less priority to one's own private interests and to one's advancement on the escalator to worldly success" (Ladd 1991: 90).

192 *Jessica Nihlén Fahlquist*

There are some theories of responsibility which include similar notions of without referring directly to virtue ethics. First, Iris Marion Young (2006) talks about responsibility due to social connections. Second, Fredriksen (2005) discusses responsibility due to social involvement.

The common characteristics of responsibility-as-virtue in these theories are the following: Responsibility (1) is forward-looking, (2) focused on the person and her relations to other people and the world as opposed to individual actions, (3) requires that the person sees herself as part of a greater context within which she acts, and (4) requires the agent to act in a certain way over time. A virtuous-responsible person feels responsible for more than she directly causes. This does not mean that she fears blame or would be blamed in case something happened and it does not necessarily mean that she needs to feel responsible for others to the extent of self-effacement.

I have now very briefly discussed what virtue ethics is and we have a sketch of what responsibility-as-virtue could involve. I will now argue that the most important ingredients in responsibility-as-virtue are care, moral imagination, and practical wisdom.

6.4   CARE, MORAL IMAGINATION, AND PRACTICAL WISDOM

My proposal to what it means that an agent acts responsibly in the sense of responsibility-as-virtue is that (1) the agent cares about other people and the way the activities in which she partakes potentially affect other people (and the environment), (2) the agent has the emotional ability to morally imagine what those effects could be like and what risks might be involved in those activities, and (3) the agent has the cognitive ability to transform these concerns into practice and actions. When someone partakes in an activity that might risk other people's health and wellbeing (although they may not be aware that it does) it is reasonable to ask that this person has the intellectual-emotional capacity to imagine potential victims, the risks that may be generated and that the person cares about her fellow human beings. In addition to that, the agent should be able to transform those emotions and attitudes into actions to go beyond good intentions. If we take BP[1] as an illustrative example, what character traits would we have wanted the managers and employees to possess? What would, in this case, be a responsible response to the demands of the world? It would have been reasonable to expect that someone who is involved in a company whose activities can damage the world, including people's health and wellbeing, the environment and the economy *cares* about how their actions might affect the world. Furthermore, they ideally have the ability to *imagine* the risks and to transform these concerns into actions, i.e. they possess *practical wisdom*. Let us now discuss these intellectual-emotional character traits in turn.

6.4.1 Care

Care, which is the central notion in the normative theory called the ethics of care, can be described as a virtue, a relation, or a practice (cf. Slote 2007, Slote 2001, Noddings 2002, Held 2006). Arguably, care involves all these aspects. It includes emotions and attitudes associated with a virtue, but it is also important to take into account whether it has the intended effects and it should involve or lead to some kind of actions. This means that it involves an attitude or concern for other human beings, an acknowledgment that it matters how that concern is received, and a method to transform the concern into actions. The ethics of care emphasises the central role of relationships and, initially, it arose as a critique against the allegedly "male" rule- and principle-based ethical theories. Carol Gilligan's book *In a Different Voice: Psychological Theory and Women's Development* came out in 1982 and was the first book to argue that women have a different way of thinking about moral matters and that this female morality should be acknowledged. She argued that women emphasise care and particular connections to others instead of universal principles like autonomy, rights, and justice. In the beginning, the ethics of care focused on the practice of caring for family, i.e., work which has been carried out by women throughout history. However, the most recent theories are applied to wider contexts and show how care can be seen as the central notion for ethics generally. The ethics of care is now not merely seen as a feminine kind of ethics, but a theory that covers both men and women and that can be applied to most areas. Slote (2007) argues that care, understood as empathy, works for the whole of ethics, and that one can have a caring attitude "towards (groups of) people one is never going to be personally acquainted with, inasmuch as one is genuinely, altruistically concerned or worried about what happens to them" (Slote 2007: 11, see also Held 2006). This is important for our purpose to find the place of care in the context of responsibility as a virtue. If care was only relevant in relation to our close ones, it would not be appropriate to see it as essential to responsibility because clearly we talk about and should talk about responsibility in relation to distant others or others who are unknown to us. The crucial thing is that we can imagine those others and care what happens to them even if we never get to know them personally. This does not mean that our caring emotions and efforts are equally strong for distant others as they are for our family and close ones. There is a difference in strength between humanitarian concern for others and caring for our loved ones. This difference is natural and morally permitted (Slote 2007).

The distinction between different spheres of caring has also been made by other ethicists of care. Noddings (2002) distinguishes between caring-for and caring-about. The former is the kind of care that takes place in ideal homes and the latter is the kind of care that we engage in with distant others, i.e., other people whom we do not know yet. Caring-about is dependent on caring-for, because we learn to care-about through our experience of being cared-for, and caring-about may be seen as the link between caring and justice: "caring-about (or, perhaps a sense of justice) must be seen as instrumental in establishing the conditions under which caring-for can flourish. Although the preferred form of caring is cared-for, caring-about can help in establishing, maintaining, and enhancing it. Those who care about others in the justice sense must keep in mind that the objective is to ensure that caring actually occurs. Caring-about is empty if it does not culminate in caring relations" (Noddings 2002: 23–24).

To be a responsible person is to feel responsible and to feel responsible is to care about others' wellbeing and how one's actions affect fellow human beings. Little argues that caring is not only important, but a necessary condition for seeing the moral landscape (Little 1995). The emotional component is what distinguishes acting from duty or a sense of duty on the one hand and acting responsibly on the other. Roeser (2012) argues that engineers who work with risky technologies should use their emotions in order to judge the moral acceptability of risks. If we want members of innovation networks to be responsible and argue that one essential part of this is that they care about potential victims, naturally they need to use their emotions. It is simply not possible to care without using emotions. Care and empathy are to a great extent emotional. As Roeser (2011) shows, this does not mean that they are irrational or non-rational. Instead, moral emotions are cognitive and affective at the same time.

To act responsibly requires that one genuinely cares about the ways in which one's actions affect other people's wellbeing. If I am a responsible-virtuous person, it matters to me how others are affected by the activities in which I take part. I can act from a sense of duty by using wisdom, applying principles, and rules. However, if I act responsibly in the sense presented here, I have to take many different normative demands into consideration and in order to know how to respond I need to use my emotions and put myself in the affected persons' shoes. Emotions are crucial to care and hence, crucial to responsibility-as-virtue.

6.4.2 Moral Imagination

As mentioned above, we can care not only for people we know well, but for people we will never know. What makes this possible is our ability to empathise with other people's wellbeing and misery, happiness and sorrow. The emotional ability to care about potential victims also requires moral imagination: the ability "to imagine how your actions influence others, being able to empathically understand others, and being able to envisage alternative courses of action if necessary" (Coeckelberg 2006: 253). As argued by Coeckelberg, "[t]he enhancement of moral imagination can help engineers to discern the moral relevance of design problems, to create new design options, and to envisage the possible outcomes of their designs" (Coeckelbergh 2006: 237).

Moral imagination has a significant role in the exploration of possibilities and projection of future scenarios (Coeckelberg and Mesman 2007), which also includes the consideration of the concerns of the wider society (Davis 1989). This is especially important in engineering and innovation contexts, because those involve a lot of uncertainties. The problem with new technology is, of course, that we cannot always have a reliable estimate concerning risks, because some older technologies may be similar in some respects, but different in others. There is a lack of information or knowledge about the consequences of what one is deciding and doing. Coeckelberg and Mesman (2007) discuss another context in which risks and uncertainties are a salient feature of the professional environment, i.e., the neonatal ward at a hospital. They argue that imagination is needed in order to fill the gap left by lacking information, in their example whether the baby would survive, die or survive with a severe handicap. What these different contexts have in common is that professionals working within engineering and health care have to confront uncertainties and risks to people's health and wellbeing. People who are able to imagine risks will be somewhat more cautious in their activities. According to Werhane (2002), moral imagination can help someone to disengage from a situation and think creatively within the constraints of what is morally possible.

Werhane (2002) argues that moral imagination is not only beneficial for individuals, but that it is also applicable to organisations and systems. She illustrates the need for moral imagination with Eskom, a South African power company, which was an all-white managed company. Eskom was a successful company during the apartheid system providing only services to the white communities. Even before apartheid ended, Eskom started to question and re-evaluate its own practices and came to the conclusion that they should provide electricity to the whole nation and train non-whites for management positions. Said and done, Eskom found ways to provide electricity to the poor, non-white South African people and is today a very successful company.

Eskom appears to have become morally imaginative and it appears reasonable to think they also cared about people enough to be willing to make a change. They acted responsibly. In addition to this, they were also able to transform this concern into actions that changed the company and potentially contributed to moral progress in society as a whole. This brings us to the last component in responsibility as a virtue.

6.4.3 Practical Wisdom

If an agent cares and has the ability to imagine how the activities in which she partakes could affect people and the environment does that mean that she is a responsible person or a responsible member of an organisation or network? Care and moral imagination are the emotional-attitudinal requirements of responsibility-as-virtue. This needs to be combined with a way to transform them into practice. If care is to be effective and useful, it should

196 Jessica Nihlén Fahlquist

be focused. Noddings (2002) points out that the relational aspect of care requires that the agent acknowledges how the recipient of care experiences the caring efforts. There is always the risk of care being too superficial or merely rhetorical, for example stating that "I care *so* much for people in poor countries!" without actually doing anything about it. It could also be too intrusive and paternalistic, for example "I care so much about my teenage children that I never allow them to go outside the house without me" (Noddings 2002). To be responsible, one needs to care in a relatively focused and effective way. This is why practical wisdom is also needed to complete the picture of what responsibility-as-virtue consists of.

Practical wisdom is needed in order for care and moral imagination to transform into actions. Care is essential, but a responsible agent also needs judgement in order to prioritise her caring efforts. An agent cares about other people, e.g. her family, friends, co-workers, people in general and the environment, and judgment/practical wisdom guides her care. Judgment provides the person with a compass and shows her how to balance different concerns. Aristotle discussed phronesis as one of the intellectual virtues. Phronesis can be described as "administrative ability" (Pakaluk 2005).

Practical wisdom is less an ability to apply principles correctly than an ability to see situations correctly (Crisp 2000: xxiv–xxvi). The person who possesses practical wisdom knows how to behave in particular circumstances and this can never be reduced to knowledge of general truths. Phronesis involves deliberation about values and is oriented towards actions and based on judgment and experience (Flyvbjerg 2001).

Although virtue ethics is to a great extent focused on agents and the character of agents, actions are important as well. It makes no sense to talk about a virtuous-responsible agent if this character trait never reveals itself or materialises in actions and behaviour. Phronesis in the context of responsible behaviour is what makes a person able to respond to the plurality of normative demands (compare Williams 2008) of the particular context within which she is situated. This skill is what makes it possible for the agent to prioritise and decide what is relevant and what is less relevant.

6.5 'RESPONSIBLE' ORGANISATIONS AND NETWORKS

How can a situation be achieved in which people are more responsible in the virtue ethical sense described above? If responsibility-as-virtue consists of care, moral imagination, and practical wisdom, what does that mean in the context of organisations and networks? The challenge when applying the concept to such institutional contexts is that it does not immediately make sense to apply virtues to a group of people. It appears that care is primarily

Responsibility as a Virtue   197

a personal quality. Individuals are more or less caring and empathetic, but it seems awkward to talk about caring organisations or caring networks (other than in PR campaigns). Care and empathy should probably be seen as individual qualities, i.e., as a combination of certain character traits, attitudes, and emotions. However, the other two components of responsibility-as-virtue, i.e., moral imagination and practical wisdom, could more easily be applied to the collective context. Moral imagination could probably be practiced and improved if time and energy is devoted to collectively detecting risks and to discerning the ethically relevant aspects of an activity. Practical wisdom is the ability to deliberate about values and transform the concerns raised through care and moral imagination into actions and behaviour over time. This is also something that can be facilitated and made more systematic by institutional means, e.g. by rewarding responsible employees.

Upbringing, education and peer influence as well as genes are likely to create people's personality. For such reasons, we may not be able to affect people's personality. What, nevertheless, what can be done is to create a situation in which it is possible and encouraged to behave responsibly, i.e., an institutional environment conducive to responsible behaviour. Obstacles can be removed, systems of incentives and rewards for good behaviour can be created and it can be made easier to do good in the context of large innovation projects to counteract the image of the engineer or manager as a cog in a cog wheel.

I will give two illustrations of how the institutional context can be shaped to encourage or discourage responsibility-as-virtue. The first example is to show how choices can be affected. Thaler and Sunstein (2008) have described how all choices are affected by the way alternatives are presented and argue that even a libertarian needs to be paternalistic in this sense: there are no choices completely unaffected by the number and presentation of alternatives. The person who contextualises a choice in this way is called a 'choice architect'. One of their examples is a cafeteria where the manager needs to decide how to present the food products sold: fruit, candy, food, and so forth. One decision would be to put candy first to make people buy a lot of candy. Another option, arguably a more responsible option, is to put the fruit in the more visible place and the candy in a less visible place. This way, the managers have not removed any of the options, but they still potentially contribute to healthier choices.

A second illustration is the case of John Tozer in which a professional code silences dissident voices.[2] In 1989 the Australian engineer John Tozer criticised the decision of the Coffs Harbour authorities to pump sewage into the sea. According to him the engineers employed by the local authority had given a misleading impression of the effects on the environment and they had failed to properly investigate the alternatives. The engineers in question were subsequently successful in removing Tozer from the Association of Consulting Engineers Australia (ACEA). Tozer was accused of having contravened the professional code by openly criticising the work of other

198 Jessica Nihlén Fahlquist

(associated) engineers. One should expect a responsible engineer to disclose abuses or potential risks, and organisations stimulate that it becomes a norm or habituation that employees discuss and think about potential risks to people and the environment.

These two examples illustrate how a social or institutional context conducive of (ir)responsible behaviour can be created. Virtue ethicists argue that habituation and moral exemplars can make people more virtuous. If it becomes the norm for engineers, managers, and the like to discuss and always think about potential risks and ethical aspects of the activities they are involved in, and if they get used to this norm, it will become a habit. If leaders talk and act in a responsible manner, i.e., if they care, use their moral imagination and transform these emotions and attitudes into action, this is likely to have a positive influence. And if people are habituated and 'program' themselves into acting responsibly they are more likely to do it even when there is a cost. Even in a network, there are some kind of leaders or initiators and if these people make sure good and responsible behaviour is rewarded instead of punished this too is likely to have some effect. If 'choice architects' make it easier to choose the responsible behaviour than the irresponsible behaviour that will influence people's behaviour.

To stimulate responsibility-as-virtue in collective settings, the first thing to do is to incorporate ethics in organisations in a more profound way than what is common today. It has been suggested that attention should be focused less on codes of conduct and regulation and that instead one should acknowledge the important role of virtues, character, and attitudes (Clegg and Rhodes 2006). An organisation does not become ethical by establishing rules which aim at preventing wrongdoing by its employees. For an organisation to become an ethical organisation, it should consist of people with a high moral standard, who aspire for excellence, who do good things and who care both about doing a good job as well as about other people. This obviously means that the most excellent people are to be recruited. However, against the background of the power and risk-generating nature of innovation, excellent *and* responsible people should be recruited. Responsible network members do not see themselves merely as their professional role (engineer, manager, government representative, politician, etc.) and do not compartmentalise, but attempt to see the whole instead of merely the respective parts. People who lack caring attitudes and emotions should not work in risk-generating activities. From an ethical point-of-view it may be as simple as that. Unless one cares and has the emotional ability to be concerned with how the activities in which one partakes create risks to people's health, lives, and the environment one should not be entrusted with such power.

In order to achieve a situation in which members of innovation networks are ethically aware and emotionally-morally sensitive, we need not only to focus on recruiting the right people, but also on training them to develop these skills and character traits. Character traits are of course partly a matter of genes and upbringing, but also of habituation. The latter should be

Responsibility as a Virtue   199

encouraged through the organisational cultures, something which most likely was not the case at BP. Managers are obviously important as well and can serve as moral exemplars. Even if networks do not have hierarchies and management is less salient, organisations are involved to some degree and there are always some people who take the role as a leader.

In addition to recruiting virtuous-responsible people, some work can be done to develop the ethical and emotional sensitivity in employees, e.g. by ethics courses and discussions of scenarios and cases. The general aim of both recruiting the right people and continue to develop their attitudes is to establish an organisational culture conducive of ethical behaviour, which includes doing good and a caring attitude in addition to the avoidance of wrongdoing. Kaptein (2011) has shown that the ethical culture of an organisation strongly influences the ethical behaviour of employees. For example, management can reduce unethical behaviour by creating an organisation in which managers and supervisors act as ethical role models. Unless managers themselves are responsible and caring, it is difficult to see how they would be able and willing to create an organisational culture characterised by virtuous-responsible behaviour.

6.6   AVOIDING THE PROBLEM OF MANY HANDS

We have now seen that responsibility-as-virtue consists of three main character traits: care, moral imagination, and practical wisdom, and we have seen how institutional contexts may be shaped as to be conducive to responsibility-as-virtue. Let us now turn to a main claim of this chapter: that responsibility-as-virtue can contribute to solving or avoiding the PMH.

Although all normative meanings of responsibility discussed in Chapter 1 (blameworthiness, accountability, liability, moral obligation, and virtue) are important for the PMH, there is one aspect in with responsibility-as-virtue is different from especially the backward-looking meanings of responsibility. In cases of backward-looking responsibility (blameworthiness, accountability, liability), an agent is usually *held* responsible, and for this attribution of responsibility to be fair, certain conditions have to apply. If these conditions are not met, it will—at least in normal circumstances—not be considered fair to hold an agent backward-looking responsible. In contrast, responsibility-as-virtue does not refer to holding responsible but to *taking* responsibility. Although there are limits to which responsibilities agents can (rationally) take, agents can take responsibility for issues for which they cannot reasonably be held responsible by others.

When we look at forward-looking responsibility, it could be argued that responsibility-as-obligation is also voluntarily assumed by an agent rather than attributed by others. Still, there are important differences between both meanings of forward-looking responsibility. In Chapter 1, three routes for acquiring responsibility-as-obligation were discussed: the consequentialist,

200 *Jessica Nihlén Fahlquist*

the deontological, and the virtue route. One of the things that sets the virtue route apart from the other two is that virtuous agents will assume responsibilities-as-obligations, even when it is not strictly required. In other words, virtuous agents now and then act *morally supererogatory*, i.e., beyond what is strictly morally required or can be demanded by others. In the deontological route, agents can also assume responsibilities-as-moral obligations beyond what is required from them, by making a promise or commitment; however, in that case the additional responsibilities need not be morally desirable, they should just be morally acceptable (i.e., they can be morally neutral). Typically responsibility-as-virtue encourages an agent to take on responsibilities-as-obligations that are morally desirable but not strictly required.

There is also another aspect that sets responsibility-as-virtue apart from responsibility-as-obligation. Obligations are usually relatively specific, they refer to specific state-of-affairs to be attained or avoided. To take on such responsibilities-as-obligations, one first need to be aware what is morally at stake in a situation. This often requires moral imagination and care, two of the main elements of responsibility-as-virtue as we have seen. Responsibility-as-virtue thus is conducive to an awareness of moral issues, which is a precondition for identifying the relevant moral responsibilities-as-obligations that are to be assumed (or attributed).

In Chapter 2, the PMH was defined as the situation in which the collective is responsible (in a certain sense) for some φ, whereas none of the individuals making up the collective is responsible (in the same sense) for that φ. How does encouraging responsibility-as-virtue avoid the problem of many hands? There are two ways in which responsibility-as-virtue might do so. First, as argued above, virtuous agents will assume more responsibilities-as-obligations and will better see what kinds of responsibilities-as-obligations are desirable to assume. So in an organisation or network that is conducive to responsibility-as-virtue, more agents will assume more responsibilities-as-obligations. This will reduce the occurrence of the PMH with respect to responsibility-as-obligation.

If more individuals assume a responsibility-as-obligation, this will also increase the 'amount' of responsibility-as-accountability in the organisation or network. That this is the case can easily be seen from one of the conclusion in Chapter 1:

> *Proposition 1: If agent i had a forward-looking responsibility-as-obligation for φ and φ did not occur and 'not φ' is not caused by exceptional circumstances then agent i is accountable for 'not φ'.*

From this it follows, that if more agents assume more forward-looking responsibility-as-obligation for φ, where φ is some morally desirable outcome or the avoidance of some morally undesirable outcome, there will also be more accountability might φ not occur. This makes the PMH with respect

Responsibility as a Virtue 201

to responsibility-as-accountability less likely to occur. As accountability, in our conceptualisation presented in Chapter 1, is a precondition for blameworthiness, this will also increase the 'amount' of individual blameworthiness in the organisation or network. Not every case of accountability will lead to blameworthiness, because agents may have a proper excuse which frees them from blameworthiness. Nevertheless, the PMH with respect to responsibility-as-blameworthiness will become less likely in an organisation or network that is conducive to responsibility-as-virtue.

There is an additional way in which responsibility-as-virtue can contribute to avoiding the PMH with respect to responsibility-as-accountability and to responsibility-as-blameworthiness. Chapter 2, focused on when it is fair to hold an agent accountable or blameworthy, and it was concluded that sometimes gaps may occur because no agent can be fairly held accountable or blameworthy, on the basis of a number of conditions. However, accountability and blameworthiness can also sometimes be voluntarily assumed, or taken, by an agent even in circumstances in which it would be improper or unfair for others to hold that agent accountable or blameworthy. For example, if we want to hold someone fairly accountable or even blameworthy for a collective decision, like in the case of the discursive dilemma of Employee Safety that was discussed in Chapter 2, we would need to know how each of the agents contributed to the collective decision. However, as Michael Davis (2012: 22) notes: "I can take responsibility for what happened even if I have no idea how I contributed to the ultimate decision [as, for example, President Truman did when he said, "The buck stops here"]". As Davis suggests, we can take responsibility for things for which others cannot hold us responsible. This can be the responsibility to do better in the future, which is primarily a forward-looking responsibility, but it will usually also include an element of accountability, because it requires an analysis of what went wrong in the past to know how to avoid harm in the future. Analysing what went wrong in the past seems to imply, at least de facto, assuming responsibility-as-accountability.

6.7 AN EXAMPLE: DEALING WITH TECHNOLOGICAL RISKS

In this section, it will be shown how responsibility-as-virtue can help solve dealing with technological risks in better detecting, better preventing, and better dealing when they materialise.

6.7.1 Detecting Risks

Roeser (2012) argues that it is highly important that engineers, who partake in risky activities, use their intuitions and emotional abilities to detect risks. Engineers should use their worries in the design of their research and

202 Jessica Nihlén Fahlquist

technologies, e.g., by building barriers to prevent certain hazards from occurring or by applying a precautionary principle, meaning that technologies of which the consequences are hard to predict should first be investigated in a safe setting. The precautionary principle should also be applied to new technologies with potential hazards when there is scientific controversy or uncertainty about these hazards. One technology to which the precautionary principle has been applied is nanotechnology, because experts had great concerns about its potential risks. These worries can "point to a source of danger to our well-being" (Roeser 2012: 109).

Engineering students should therefore learn to use their imaginative and emotional skills at engineering universities. This means that ethics modules for engineers should not merely be focused on reasoning skills and argumentation, but also on developing sympathy and similar emotions in order to raise awareness of values in design. I agree with this view and would add that the emotions involved in care are a necessary condition for responsibility-as-virtue. This implies that unless someone has this emotional capacity they are unable to exercise this kind of responsibility. Unless someone is a responsible person that person should not be entrusted with the power involved in generating risks to health and the environment. Whereas people's upbringing cannot be influenced, what can be done is to include these elements in educating people who will be involved in this kind of activities, as suggested by Roeser (2012).

6.7.2   When Risks Are Detected

In an ethical parallel research about the development of a new sewage treatment technology performed by van de Poel and Zwart (2010), it was observed that the researchers and users did not consider themselves responsible for potential so-called secondary emissions of sewage treatment plants, e.g. hormone-related substances, heavy metals, and pathogenic bacteria. The different actors believed that secondary emissions were not likely to be a major risk factor, but whereas the researchers allocated the responsibility for investigating and preventing secondary emissions to the users the latter generally thought it was the researchers' responsibility to investigate and prevent such emissions. After this observation by the ethicists was fed back to the technological researchers, some of the latter began to take the potential risk of secondary emissions more seriously and they, consequently, applied for funding to find out more about the risks of secondary emissions (De Kreuk et al. 2010). This shows that there is a lot of conventional and habitual thinking involved in innovation and once the actors involved are encouraged to reflect and discuss risks and responsibility, they can assume responsibility for risks which they initially did not consider their responsibility. Thus, habitual thinking can be changed. If efforts are made to make members of innovation networks more prone to detect risks their agenda of risks to manage is expanded.

A second example is from a trailer design project where it was shown that the engineers developing trailers plainly did not see it as their responsibility to do anything beyond what the customer requested. Traffic safety, for example, was not considered part of that responsibility. Even if there were measures they could take to improve safety, they did not do that and they did not even suggest it to the customer (van der Burg and van Gorp 2005). The point of bringing up this example is not to blame the engineers. It shows how we habitually see engineers as solving technical problems in an amoral, i.e. not immoral but not moral either, way. This could and should be changed. A responsible engineer takes responsibility for important values, e.g. for doing their utmost to ensure the safety of those people who will be inside or outside of the vehicle. If engineers get used to using their emotional ability and to develop their moral sensitivity they will care about potential victims of the risks that their activities generate and use their imagination and practical wisdom to avoid unnecessary risks.

The next step is that everyone takes responsibility for managing those risks. This does not mean that everyone is equally responsible, but that everyone is adequately concerned to make sure tasks are distributed. When everyone involved cares and is able to imagine together what potential risks there are and take responsibility for creating an accurate and inclusive agenda of risks, responsibilities in terms of tasks can be distributed. Chapter 5 discussed how responsibilities can be distributed in a fair way.

In situations where risks are assessed trough a cost-benefit analysis, a decision is made to accept the risk if the benefits outweigh the costs and vice versa. Psychologists have shown that lay people do not merely calculate risks based on costs and benefits, but include more qualitative concerns such as whether the risk is taken voluntarily, whether the benefits and costs are distributed fairly, whether the consequences might be disastrous, and so forth (Slovic et al. 1979). Ethicists have shown that many, if not all, of these concerns are normatively justified (cf. Roeser 2012). These other concerns should be taken into account by people who work in risky innovation projects. As discussed in section 6.4.3, care is crucial to responsibility-as-virtue.

Another aspect of the detection of risks is that these risks should be taken seriously, and that persons who partake in risky activities are open to criticism. For example, LeMessurier (see Chapter 2) took the objections of a student and his professor seriously, instead of ignoring them because the construction met the safety requirements. LeMessurier decided to check everything and recalculate it. This demonstrates his dedication to safety of the general public. The case shows that care can direct the responsible actions engineers need to take in professional practice. For many engineers, LeMessurier's actions with regard to the CitiCorp building exemplify the highest virtues of the engineering field. Nevertheless, many will wonder why LeMessurier deserves so much praise, because it was his professional duty to report mistakes to the authorities. However, as Pritchard points out (2001), the way in which LeMessurier acted was morally exemplary can

204   *Jessica Nihlén Fahlquist*

make colleagues more virtuous—for the following two reasons. First, courage was needed to report the error, even though not reporting it would have been highly reprehensible. The report could have damaged his reputation considerably. Second, LeMessurier not only reported the problem, but he also proposed a solution to it, which is characteristic of a responsible engineer in Pritchard's opinion.

6.7.3   When Risks Materialise

When risks materialise, a responsible member of an innovation network does not immediately respond by pointing at someone else, by buck-passing or finding a scapegoat, but makes sure actions are taken to give an accurate account of what happened, even if it is not clear whether she was at fault (cf. Davis 2012). She acts in this way because she cares about victims, she has the cognitive-emotional ability to imagine what to do and how victims could be affected and she acts on those concerns.

The potential to solve the problem lies in the different attitudes and behaviour following the occurrence of an undesired event. I will illustrate this with the case of IKEA and child labour in 1998. The Socialist Party (SP) in the Netherlands started to boycott IKEA, because its suppliers were involved in child labour in the third world, particularly in India, and demanded that IKEA guarantee that children would never be involved with the production of IKEA products. In India, child labour is not illegal, but in the Netherlands, where IKEA is located, it is illegal and considered highly unethical. Now, when confronted with this, the management of IKEA has roughly the following options concerning how to react:

1. "We did nothing wrong. We did not know anything about the involvement of our suppliers in child labour".
2. "The suppliers follow the law in the country where they are based. One cannot demand anything more than law-abidance. Neither we nor our suppliers did anything wrong".
3. "The children have not been treated with care and we will do everything we can to make sure that our suppliers take action to change the situation by contributing to the improvement of the working conditions of the children, such as working times, medical care, training, etc. If they refuse, we will end our contract with the suppliers in question".

The focus in 1 and 2 is on blameworthiness and it is argued that because the condition of knowledge or the condition of wrongdoing was not met, it entails that IKEA is not responsible. In contrast, 3 is the response of a management team who cares about people and takes responsibility in a virtue-sense. To guarantee that children in the third world would never be involved in child labour can actually harm the children in question, if their families have no other means to survival: many of these children could end up as criminals. This response shows moral imagination: imagining how your actions influence the future of those children, which plays a significant role in the exploration of the possibilities. For example, to stop child labour instantaneously could be devastating for the children involved. It is common to hear all three kinds of reactions from companies which have been confronted by accusations of this kind. If managers abandoned 1 and 2 and instead focused on developing attitude 3, that would bring the organisation closer to a situation where the problem of many hands is less likely to occur. Innovative excellence should be combined with ethical excellence and responsible attitudes and behaviour.

6.7.4   Is This Demanding too Much?

Someone may object to the suggestions in this chapter. It could be argued that this is demanding too much from people. We could conceive of a notion of *balanced responsibility*, inspired by care ethicist Michael Slote's idea of *balanced care*. Slote argues that we should strive for a balance among three kinds of caring: self-concern, intimate caring, and humane or humanitarian caring:

> Concern with intimates as a class and excluding the agent must be balanced against concern for (the rest of) humanity. This much is required. But then it is merely permissible that self-concern be in balance with each of these other concerns. That is, someone whose actions express or reflect some sort of balance among self-concern, intimate caring, and humane caring acts rightly or permissibly, but s/he may also act permissibly and will indeed act supererogatory if her actions reflect a *lesser* degree of self-concern than just mentioned.
>
> (Slote 2001: 78)

If this qualification is applied to collective settings, it means that members of a collective are allowed to have several affiliations and obligations. What is characteristic of a responsible person, i.e., someone who cares, have moral imagination and practical wisdom, is that these cognitive-affective abilities facilitates their capability to respond to a plurality of normative demands and to know how to prioritise them.

6.8   CONCLUSION

In this chapter, I have argued that responsibility-as-virtue consists of care, moral imagination, and practical wisdom. To be responsible in this sense involves having a certain attitudinal-emotional concern and the ability to

206 Jessica Nihlén Fahlquist

transform those concerns into actions and responsible good behaviour over time. Part of the explanation why some people are responsible in this sense whereas others are not obviously has to do with genes and upbringing, i.e., things we can do little about when dealing with grown-ups. Nevertheless, as we have seen there are various things we can do to stimulate responsibility-as-virtue in collective settings. We can shape institutional settings so as to make them more conducive to responsibility-as-virtue. We can hire people, for example in organisations, who are not just excellent professionals but who also exhibit responsibility-as-virtue and, finally we can train people to acquire the competences and attitudes that are required for responsibility-as-virtue.

As we have seen, responsibility-as-virtue could potentially help to overcome or at least diminish the problem of many hands. There are several reasons why responsibility-as-virtue might help to reduce the PMH. The main underlying reason, however, seems to be that responsibility-as-virtue in contrast to the other senses of responsibility is not about holding others responsible or attributing responsibility to others but about taking responsibility oneself. Even in situations in which it may be inappropriate or too strict to hold another responsible one might take responsibility oneself.

Responsibility-as-virtue requires a certain attitude. Part of this attitude is that people who work in collective settings in which risks are generated see themselves as a part of a greater context. Everyone should feel responsible for the consequences of the activities of the collective. This does not mean that each and every one is equally blameworthy if something negative happens. I am not suggesting that everyone should be blamed when things go wrong as a consequence of a collective project. However, it may be a positive thing that people feel ashamed or morally tainted by what happens as a consequence of the collective activities even if they did nothing to directly cause it. This may be a proof of the fact that one cares about the victims, can imagine what it feels like to be in their shoes and that one will do what one can to reduce the negative effects of what happened.

NOTES

1. In this context, I refer to BP during the years between 2005 and 2010 to include the Texas refinery explosion and the Deepwater Horizon disaster, but without saying anything about what BP is like now or in the future.
2. Based on Beder (1993).

REFERENCES

Baker, J. A. III., F. Bowman, G. Erwin, S. Gorton, D. Hendershot, N.G. Leveson, S. Priest, I. Rosenthal, P.V. Tebo, D.A. Wiegmann, and L.D. Wilson. 2007. *The report of the BP U.S. refineries independent safety review panel.* (http://www.propublica.org/documents/item/the-bp-us-refineries-independent-safety-review-panel-report)

Bakolas, E., and J.H. Saleh. 2011. "Augmenting defense-in-depth with the concepts of observability and diagnosability from control theory and discrete event systems." *Reliability and System Safety* 96(1): 184–193.

Beder, S. 1993. "Pipelines and paradigms: The development of sewerage engineering." *Australian Civil Engineering Transactions* CE35(1): 79–85.

Clegg, S.R., and C. Rhodes. 2006. Introduction: Questioning the ethics of management practice. In *Management ethics: Contemporary contexts*, edited by S.R. Clegg and C. Rhodes, 1–9. London: Routledge.

Coeckelberg, M. 2006. "Regulation or responsibility? Autonomy, moral imagination, and engineering." *Science, Technology, & Human Values* 31(3): 237–260.

Coeckelberg, M., and J. Mesman. 2007. "With hope and imagination: Imaginative moral decision-making in neonatal intensive care units." *Ethical Theory and Moral Practice* 10(1): 3–21.

Crisp, R. (ed. and translator). 2000. *Aristotle: Nicomachean ethics*. Cambridge: Cambridge University Press.

Davis, M. 1989. "Explaining wrongdoing." *Journal of Social Philosophy* 20(1–2): 74–90.

Davis, M. 2012. "Ain't no one here but us social forces: Constructing the professional responsibility of engineers." *Science and Engineering Ethics* 18(1):13–34.

De Kreuk, M., I.R. van de Poel, S.D. Zwart, and M.C.M. van Loosdrecht. 2010. "Ethics in innovation: cooperation and tension." In *Philosophy and engineering. An emerging agenda*, edited by I.R. van de Poel and D.E. Goldberg, 215–226. Dordrecht: Springer.

Doorn, N. and Nihlén Fahlquist, J. (2010) "Responsibility in engineering: Toward a new role for engineering ethicists." *Bulletin of Science, Technology & Society* 30(3): 222–230.

Flyvbjerg, B. 2001. *Making social science matter. Why social inquiry fails and how it can succeed again*. Cambridge: Cambridge University Press.

Fredriksen, S. 2005. "Luck, risk and blame." *Journal of Medicine and Philosophy* 30(5): 535–553.

Held, V. 2006. *The ethics of care. Personal, political and global*. Cambridge: Cambridge University Press.

Hopkins, A. 2011. "Risk-management and rule-compliance: Decision-making in hazardous industries." *Safety Science* 49(2): 110–120.

Kaptein, M. 2011. "Understanding unethical behavior by unraveling ethical culture." *Human Relations* 64(6): 843–869.

Ladd, J. 1991. "Bhopal: An essay on moral responsibility and civic virtue." *Journal of Social Philosophy* 22(1): 73–91.

Little, M.O. 1995. "Seeing and caring: The role of affect in feminist moral epistemology." *Hypatia* 10(3): 117–137.

Noddings, N. 2002. *Starting at home. Caring and social policy*. Berkeley: University of California Press.

Oakley, J., and D. Cocking. (2001). *Virtue ethics and professional roles*. Cambridge: Cambridge University Press.

Pakaluk, M. 2005. *Aristotle's Nicomachean ethics: An introduction*. Cambridge: Cambridge University Press.

Pritchard, M.S. 2001. "Responsible engineering. The importance of character and imagination." *Science and Engineering Ethics* 7(3): 391–402.

Roeser, S. 2012. "Emotional engineers: Toward morally responsible engineering." *Journal of Science and Engineering Ethics* 18(1): 103–115.

Roeser, S. 2011. *Moral emotions and intuitions*. Basingstoke: Palgrave Macmillan.

Slote, M. 2001. *Morals from motives*. Oxford: Oxford University Press.

Slote, M. 2007. *The ethics of care and empathy*. New York: Routledge.

208 *Jessica Nihlén Fahlquist*

Slovic, P., B. Fischhoff, and S. Lichtenstein. 1979. "Rating the risks." *Environment* 21(3): 14–20, 36–39.

Smiley, M. 1992. *Moral responsibility and the boundaries of community. Power and accountability from a pragmatic point of view.* University of Chicago Press.

Steffy, L. 2011. "BP's long history of neglect will prove difficult to outrun." *Herald Tribune* (8 February). (http://www.heraldtribune.com/article/20110208/columnist/102081017)

Swanton, C. 2007. "Virtue ethics, role ethics and business ethics." In *Working virtue: Virtue Ethics and Contemporary Moral Problems*, edited by R.L. Walker and P.J. Ivanhoe, 207–225. Oxford: Clarendon Press.

Thaler, R.H., and C.R. Sunstein. 2008. *Nudge: improving decisions about health, wealth, and happiness.* New Haven: Yale University Press.

Van de Poel, I.R., and S.D. Zwart. 2010. "Reflective equilibrium in R&D networks." *Science, Technology & Human Values* 35(2): 174–199.

van der Burg, S., and A. van Gorp. 2005. "Understanding moral responsibility in the design of trailers." *Science and Engineering Ethics* 11(2): 235–256.

Van Hooft, S. 2006. *Understanding virtue ethics.* Chesham: Acumen.

Werhane P.H. 2002. "Moral imagination and systems thinking." *Journal of Business Ethics* 38(1–2): 33–42.

Williams, G. 2008. "Responsibility as a virtue." *Ethical Theory and Moral Practice* 11(4): 455–470.

Young, I.M. 2006. "Responsibility and global justice: A social connection model." *Social Philosophy and Policy* 23(1): 102–130.

Conclusions
From Understanding to Avoiding the Problem of Many Hands

Ibo van de Poel and Sjoerd D. Zwart

In this book we have tried to philosophically clarify and analyse the problem of many hands (PMH). Loosely, this problem may be described as the problem of attributing or allocating individual responsibility in collective settings. As we have seen in the introduction, the problem has a backward-looking variety and a forward-looking one. In the backward-looking case, something has gone wrong, often as a consequence of collective action or inaction, and we wonder which individual, if any, is responsible for what went wrong. In the forward-looking case, the problem of many hands is more a problem of distributing responsibility regarding a collective action. Something has to be accomplished, which cannot be accomplished by the individuals in isolation, and we wonder how to distribute individual responsibilities so that the desirable aim is indeed actually accomplished.

Both varieties of the PMH are pretty common in our society: the financial crisis, global warming, poverty in the third world, the Fukushima disaster, just to name some examples. The PMH, however, occurs also on a somewhat smaller scale, think of the bankruptcy of a company, misspending of public funds, or the failure of the PROMEST plant, which we discussed in Chapter 4. Or even more mundane: the loss of the local football team, or miscommunication about an outing. We use to think that the impact of an accident varies with the moral blameworthiness of individuals who produced it. There must be somebody to blame for the financial crisis. In the more mundane cases, we typically tend to see the PMH as a practical rather than as a moral problem: We should just better communicate or better play together in the local football team.

We have tried to show that despite the wide variety in the ways the PMH surfaces in society, from disasters on a world scale to inconveniences in a local community, it displays a common structure. We have tried to capture this common structure in Chapter 2 by characterising the PMH as the situation in which a collective is responsible for some φ, whereas none of the individuals in that collective is responsible for that φ. To make this common structure of the PMH even more explicit, and to be able to detect it more precisely in concrete settings, we have also developed a formalisation of the

210   *Ibo van de Poel and Sjoerd D. Zwart*

PMH in Chapter 3. In this concluding chapter, we come back to the characterisation we have offered and we will point out why we think it is a good way to capture the common structure of the PMH.

Another main aim of this book has been to elaborate possible ways of avoiding or at least diminishing the likelihood of the occurrence of a PMH. This was a main focus in Chapters 4–6, which focused respectively on institutional design solutions, procedural solutions and on the role of virtues in helping to avoid the PMH. These chapters contained not only philosophical analyses, but also empirical ones. We indeed believe that empirical research is indispensable in developing possible solutions to the PMH. Although we will do suggestions in this concluding chapter on how to deal with the PMH, it must be stressed that many of these suggestions are still rather preliminary and require further empirical study and corroboration, or, of course, refutation, and the formulation of new working hypotheses on the basis of the more conceptual and theoretical elaboration of the PMH.

In this concluding chapter, we aim to do two things. First, we will look again at our characterisation of the PMH and we will argue why we believe it is an appropriate characterisation of the main features of the PMH. Second, we will discuss possible ways to avoid or alleviate the PMH. We will do so by formulating five hypotheses about what (institutional) characteristics of collectives may decrease the chances of occurrence of the PMH.

THE CHARACTERISATION OF THE PMH

In Chapter 2 we characterised the PMH as follows:

> *(PMH): The problem of many hands (PMH) occurs if a collective is morally responsible for φ, whereas none of the individuals making up the collective is morally responsible for φ.*

We illustrated various examples of the PMH, especially in Chapters 2, 3, and 4. One thing that these examples showed is that there is not necessarily a complete disconnection between individual and collective responsibilities even if the PMH occurs. For example, the collective might be blame-responsible for φ, whereas individuals are blame-responsible for $\varphi 1$, $\varphi 2$, $\varphi 3$, which together cause φ.

The reader might ask herself why such cases constitute a problem that we call the problem of many hands. After all in these cases, the collection of agents is responsible, so why calling this a problem? Moreover, one might wonder why we take the responsibility of the collective for φ to be a necessary condition in the definition of a PMH. We will discuss both issues below and point out why we think that our characterisation of the PMH is adequate.

Why Is the Moral Responsibility of the Collective a Condition for the Occurrence of the PMH?

The main reason why we have introduced this condition is to limit the set of consequences for which the PMH can occur. We want to rule out cases in which it is unreasonable to hold anybody responsible. This includes examples such as avalanches, earthquakes, or volcano eruptions. Now, it may be objected that such cases can also avoided by requiring a form of collective *causal* responsibility, rather than collective moral responsibility, an option that we briefly considered and rejected in Chapter 2. The main reason to reject this option is that whether it is reasonable to hold at least someone responsible does not solely depend on causality, although that also plays a role, but also on other reasons, in particular on the normative reasons why we attribute responsibility in the first place.[1]

Introducing the requirement of collective moral responsibility as a condition to speak of a PMH raises the question of how to delineate the possible responsible collection of actors. As we discussed in Chapter 4, there is a danger that we might define the collection deliberately in such a way that the collection of agents is not collectively moral responsible, and avoid the PMH by a methodological choice rather than by substantial arguments derived from actual practice. To avoid that pitfall, in Chapter 4 we argued for delineating the collection of relevant actors along causal lines, i.e., along the lines of proximate and distal causes.

The advantage of this approach is that it does not take the way a collection of actors is currently organised as decisive for the question whether a PMH has occurred. That would make it too easy to avoid a PMH because it would mean that as long as a collection of agents is unorganised, maybe even deliberately so, it does not form a collective that can bear responsibility. Our approach instead delineates the collection of agents that could potentially undertake action because it is causally related to the φ in which we are interested. As we pointed out in Chapter 2 for so-called occasion collections, the crucial question is not whether they are currently well-organised or involved in a joint action but rather whether it would be reasonable to expect them to organise themselves in other to contribute to good or to avoid harm.

In our approach, then, the delineation of the responsible collection of agents follows a causal criterion; the normative considerations only come in once we have delineated the possible responsible collection and apply the conditions for collective responsibility, which vary with the different types of moral responsibility. They include in all cases, however, the capacity condition, which is related to the question whether it is reasonable to expect the collection of agents to organise itself better. This approach is not very different from how we usually attribute individual responsibility. Also there, we first look at the causal involvement of the agents (through actions or omissions) and we then ask whether these individuals are also morally responsible (by applying normative considerations).

212 *Ibo van de Poel and Sjoerd D. Zwart*

It should also be noted that our current characterisation of the PMH is not substantially different from what we proposed in a 2012 article (van de Poel et al. 2012; see also the introduction). There rather than requiring that the collective was responsible we required that the gap in the individual responsibility distribution was morally problematic. We also pointed out that the judgment on what we consider morally problematic depends on the meaning of responsibility considered and the aims we have in attributing that meaning of responsibility. We consider our current requirement of collective responsibility a further clarification of when a gap in a responsibility is morally problematic. It spells out in detail when a gap in a responsibility distribution is problematic by referring to the conditions for collective responsibility (that we discussed in Chapter 2). Recall these conditions are somewhat different for different kinds of collective responsibility, so doing justice to the different aims of attributing responsibility for the different meanings of responsibility.

Why Is It Problematic if None of the Individuals Is Responsible for φ?

As we have seen in several of the examples of the PMH we discussed in this book, often individual and collective responsibility are not completely disconnected even if the PMH occurs. There might be no individual that is responsible for the φ for which the collective is responsible, but individuals may still be responsible for state-of affairs $\varphi1$, $\varphi2$, $\varphi3$, that together cause or are otherwise (closely) related to φ. Why would such cases nevertheless be problematic and count as an instance of the PMH? The answer to that question is based on the reasons why we attribute responsibility and these reasons vary among the different kinds of responsibility. For each case we encountered strong reasons as to why it is problematic when no individual is responsible. We will expound them for the cases of blameworthiness, accountability, and responsibility-as-obligation.

Let us start with *blameworthiness*. The main aim of attributing moral blame is retribution. Why is this aim not achieved if only the collective is responsible? Why is it problematic only to blame the collective and not one of its agents? A first thing to note here is that moral blame is a response to an intentional action. And in Chapter 2 we have argued that collectives do not have intentions, at least not in the usual sense of the term; for that reasons we preferred to talk about collective aims rather than collective intentions.

If collectives have no intentions no moral blame is possible and, consequently, retribution is also impossible. But does retribution really require moral blame? After all, we can punish collectives in various ways. The government can fine or even forbid certain groups and we can punish collectives involved in a joint action by forbidding, or otherwise discouraging, the joint action. The point, however, is that these types of punishment do not have a *moral* component, i.e., they do not express, or at least not necessarily so, a blaming reactive attitude towards the collective. In words attributed to Baron Thurlow: "Did you ever expect a corporation to have a conscience, when it has no soul to be damned, and no body to be kicked?" (cited in Coffee 1981).

Note that this does not rule out that collections can be legally punished or that they can be blameworthy in a legal sense; however, moral blameworthiness and therefore moral retribution seems quite problematic if not impossible for collectives.

The above does not rule out that we can still technically attribute what we have called responsibility-as-blameworthiness to organised collectives, namely if that collective meets all conditions for collective responsibility-as-blameworthiness formulated in Chapter 2. None of these conditions refers to collective intentions. However, in our framework the meaning of that attribution is not that we morally blame the collective for an intentional action, but rather that it should be the target of retribution and if the collection cannot be such a target it is reasonable to take some individual agent of the collection as target and therefore as blame-responsible. If this is not actually the case in practice, we have a PMH.

It can still be asked whether it is also necessary that an individual is blame-responsible for the total harm done, for the φ in which we are interested. In the case of the Bhopal disaster, it seems as if we can blame various individuals for their mistakes, and for their contributions, but none of them for the overall disaster, and the resulting fatalities (cf. Kutz 2000). In terms of retribution, this seems an unsatisfactory outcome; it seems appropriate that someone should be blameworthy for the overall effect and not only for smaller mishaps, like insufficient communication, especially because the disaster was probably preventable if the collective had been better organised.

Let us now look at the case of *accountability*. We have said in Chapter 1 that accountability is related to maintaining or restoring the moral community in two senses, namely (1) in establishing or confirming the agency of the accountable agent and (2) in (re)confirming certain moral rules. Especially the first cannot be attained if only a collective is accountable. The reason is that a collective is not an agent in the usual sense of the term because it lacks collective intentions as we have argued. Moreover collectives cannot give an account because they cannot speak. Of course, individuals can speak on behalf of a collective. They do so, however, as individuals with a specific role, for example, in their capacity as leader of the collective or their capacity as spokesperson of the collective. But if they give an account in such a capacity it means that in addition to accountability of the collective at least one individual is also accountable, and the PMH does not occur. However, when only the collective is accountable (in a technical sense again, i.e., as meeting the conditions for responsibility-as-accountability at the collective level), no account can be given, i.e. the PMH occurs and this is problematic because the aim of accountability cannot be achieved.

214 *Ibo van de Poel and Sjoerd D. Zwart*

We finally turn to the case of *responsibility-as-obligation*. Here the aim is efficacy, i.e., the effective attainment of something good or the effective avoidance of harm. Now suppose that we have three individuals who are responsible-as-obligation for $\varphi 1$, $\varphi 2$, $\varphi 3$, respectively, and further suppose that $\varphi 1$, $\varphi 2$, $\varphi 3$ together cause φ. However, none of these individuals is responsible-as-obligation for φ. Why does this case constitute a PMH?

It could be argued that in such cases the aim φ is effectively achieved if the agents properly discharge their individual responsibility-as-obligation. There is certainly some truth in this argument. The point, however, is that responsibility-as-obligation implies certain supervisory duties to see to it that φ. It should be noted that in the described hypothetical case, none of the three individuals has the supervisor duty to see to it that φ. According to our framework, the collective has this supervisory duty if it meets all the conditions for obligation-responsibility. However, *as a collective*, it cannot exercise this duty; after all collectives can only act through individuals agents that are part of the collective. But if none of the agents has the supervisory duty to see to φ, the collective can also not discharge its responsibility-as-obligation to see to it that φ. In other words, the attribution of responsibility-as-obligation to the collective means that the collective should somehow distribute that responsibility to the agents within the collective. If that does not happen, the PMH occurs.

We would like to stress that this is not just a scholarly argument for why the PMH for responsibility-as-obligation (PMH_O) occurs if no individual has a responsibility to see to it that φ. In Chapter 2, we followed Goodin (1995) in introducing responsibility-as-obligation to see to it that φ in addition to duties to do α. The reason to make a distinction between responsibilities and duties is that responsibility has a discretionary component that allows for improvisation. In many real-life situations this is important because we often do not exactly know beforehand how to achieve φ (or whether our current plan to achieve φ will be successful). The supervisory duty that comes with responsibility-as-obligation helps to deal with such uncertain situations, because we can adjust plans and can improvise. However, in the case that we only have three individuals doing their part ($\varphi 1$, $\varphi 2$, $\varphi 3$), and no one exercising the supervising duty, we cannot deal with unexpected situations and we cannot improvise because no one is overseeing the situation, and, as a consequence, no one is responsible for adjusting the plan. For example, it may turn out that for some reason individual 1 cannot make $\varphi 1$ happen. However, maybe this individual can still assure $\varphi 1'$, and perhaps $\varphi 1'$ together with $\varphi 2'$ and $\varphi 3'$, will still assure φ. Such a change of plan, however, requires someone, at least one individual, carrying out the supervisory duty relation to obligation-responsibility to see to it that φ. For this reason, we speak of a PMH if the collective is obligation-responsible for φ, whereas none of the individuals is obligation-responsible for φ.

Conclusions 215

AVOIDING THE PROBLEM OF MANY HANDS

The PMH constitutes an undesirable situation; so a natural question is how to avoid the PMH. The second part of the book mainly focused on that question, with a somewhat different emphasis in the various chapters. In this concluding chapter, we want to combine a number of insights and suggestions developed in the Chapter 3 through 6, by formulating five hypothesis about the occurrence of the PMH that contain hints on how to avoid the PMH. We call these hypotheses because although we have arguments to believe that they hold, in all cases further empirical research is needed to confirm (or reject) them.

The first hypothesis is:

(1) The PMH is less likely to occur in better organised collectives.

This directly follows from Chapter 3, section 3.4 and from proposition (org) in Chapter 4, section 4.5.2. Better organised here refers to the dimensions of power, coordination, and control discussed in the Chapters 3 and 4. It should be stressed, as we also did in Chapter 4, that better organised should not simply be understood in terms of power; in that case, the hypothesis would say that the PMH is less likely to occur in hierarchical organisations. However, that is often not the case. As Bovens (1998) already pointed out the problem of organising responsibility along strictly hierarchical lines is that those higher up in the organisations may have the power but often lack the relevant information (our coordination dimension) to be responsible; those on the work floor might have the required information but will lack the power in a strictly hierarchical organisation. Somewhat similarly, it was pointed out in Chapter 4, that a strict hierarchy will often result in little room for manoeuvre, i.e., little room for discretion and improvisation lower in the organisation, resulting in less monitoring and feedback options, so weakening the control dimension. What is important then is that collectives are well-organised in the three dimensions in a way that reinforces the taking and discharging of responsibility in the collective. Well-organised collectives are thus not restricted to hierarchical organisations or to what we have, in Chapter 2, called 'organised groups'.

(2) The PMH is less likely to occur in collectives that have effective and fair procedures to distribute responsibility internally.

This follows from proposition (appoint) in Chapter 4, section 4.5.2 and from Chapter 5. It should be noted that an active distribution of responsibility is especially relevant for responsibility-as-obligation, because this responsibility can be voluntarily taken, as we have seen in Chapter 1; this is less the case for responsibility-as-accountability and for blameworthiness.

216   *Ibo van de Poel and Sjoerd D. Zwart*

However, if responsibility-as-obligation is better distributed and the PMH_O is avoided, also the PMH for responsibility-as-accountability (PMH_A) and for responsibility-as-blameworthiness (PMH_B) are less likely to occur.

It is important to have not just an effective but also a fair procedure for distributing responsibility. Fairness is in itself desirable for moral reasons, but it is also instrumentally important because if individuals perceive the distribution of responsibility as fair it is more likely that they will live by the responsibility distributed to them. For this reason, responsibility distribution through a fair procedure is more likely to be effective than delegation and attribution of responsibility along strictly hierarchical lines. As we have seen in Chapter 5, fairness can be conceived in a procedural way and it can do justice to different legitimate conceptions of responsibility, i.e. it can deal with pluralism in responsibility conceptions.

(3) The PMH is less likely to occur in institutional settings that encourage individual responsibility-as-virtue, including the taking of initiative, the exercise of judgement (practical wisdom), care, moral imagination, and the willingness to reflect and learn.

This follows directly from Chapter 6, which also explains how collective settings can nurture virtues in individuals. As explained in Chapter 6, virtue-responsible individuals will actively assume responsibility which makes the PMH, in all its varieties, less likely to occur. It should be stressed that this may be especially important in combination with a procedure for distributing responsibility as referred to in hypothesis (2). Virtue-responsible individuals will take initiative and exercise judgment so that it seems more likely that the following of a procedure will result in a complete distribution of responsibility, i.e., a distribution in which for all relevant responsibilities-as-obligations at least one individual is responsible. It also seems that virtue-responsible individuals will have a disposition to live by the responsibilities they have assumed.

We also think that responsibility-as-virtue may be conducive to what we called second order reflective learning in Chapter 5. Such reflective learning requires one to look beyond one's concerns and considerations, and it also seems to require the exercising of care and moral imagination, which according to Chapter 6 is part of responsibility-as-virtue.

(4) The PMH is less likely to occur in collectives that balance internal cohesiveness with inclusiveness and openness.

The importance of internal coherence follows from proposition (cohesive) in Chapter 4, section 4.5.2. Also in Chapter 5, we saw that a certain degree of agreement and internal cohesiveness are necessarily in a network for first order reflective learning to occur, and in order to attain certain outcomes. However, in Chapter 5, we also saw that such a desideratum may be at tension with the network norm of inclusiveness and openness. More inclusive or more open social networks (or collectives) may be characterised by more disagreement and conflicting interests and values. Although some disagreement might be conducive to especially second-order reflective learning, too much may lead to stalemates or to unanticipated consequences, for which no one is willing to take responsibility, as in the PROMEST case discussed in Chapter 4.

(5) The PMH is less likely to occur in institutional settings that provide for *independent* supervision and redundancy.

This follows from proposition (control) in Chapter 4, section 4.5.2. Although the term 'control' might suggest that what happens in the network is controlled from a centre of control, our notion of 'control' also includes decentralised supervisions and fall-back options. In particular, it allows the detection of issues not developing as expected (and desirable) and for the ability to improvise to get thing back on track. Control so conceived is closely related to the self-supervisory duty that comes with responsibility-as-obligation.

Although we have argued that self-supervisory duties come with obligation-responsibility, preferably agents other than the ones having the obligation-responsibility should (also) have a supervisory role. This would increase the chances of supervision being properly carried out especially when the interests of the agents with the obligation-responsibility conflict with their obligation-responsibility. The supervision should therefore be independent.

Similarly, but for different reasons, redundancy should also be independent. A paramount principle in safety engineering is the provision of redundant (safety) systems that are not plagued by the same (root) causes of defect as the original system. For example, in nuclear reactors redundant cooling systems preferably rely on other modes of energy supply than the normal cooling system; otherwise a hick-up in the energy supply would lead to the non-functioning of both the normal and the back-up system. Similarly, independent redundancy should be built in social networks to help fulfilling certain responsibilities-as-obligations.

Thompson (forthcoming) pleads, using an analysis of three cases of the PMH (*Deep Water Horizon*, 9/11, financial crisis), for the establishment of independent bodies with oversight responsibility. Although this may seem to multiply the number of hands involved, he argues: "But the multiplication is not the same. The difference is that the hands would be specifically charged with oversight and nothing else, and they would be independent in the sense that neither their mission nor their interest would conflict with their responsibility for oversight" (Thompson forthcoming: 14). Thompson's idea of oversight responsibility then is similar to our idea of independent supervision.

218 *Ibo van de Poel and Sjoerd D. Zwart*

According to Thompson, the oversight bodies might also be charged with what he calls design responsibility. This is the responsibility to (re)design the institutional setting in such a way that the PMH is less likely to occur. This design responsibility does not only relate to the pursuit of redundancy but also relates to our other four hypotheses. What is particularly attractive about Thompson's proposal is that it attributes the responsibility for the institutional design of the collective setting in a clear way to an agent that can oversee what is happening. In addition, this agent can take initiatives for adjusting the institutional design in time if this turns out to be necessary. Thompson claims, as we do, that this decreases the probability of the occurrence of a PMH.

NOTE

1. It should further be noted that opting for collective causal responsibility of collectives only shifts the normativity question from the *normative responsibility* of the collective toward the *reasonable* causal responsibility contribution, which is also a normative issue.

REFERENCES

Bovens, M. 1998. *The quest for responsibility. Accountability and citizenship in complex organisations*. Cambridge: Cambridge University Press.

Coffee, J.C., Jr. 1981. "No soul to damn: No body to kick": An unscandalized inquiry into the problem of corporate punishment". *Michigan Law Review* 79(3): 386–459.

Goodin, R.E. 1995. *Utilitarianism as a public philosophy*. Cambridge: Cambridge University Press.

Kutz, C. 2000. *Complicity: Ethics and law for a collective age*. Cambridge: Cambridge University Press.

Thompson, D. forthcoming. Designing responsibility: The problem of many hands in complex organizations. In *The design turn in applied ethics*, edited by J. van den Hoven, S. Miller and Th. Pogge. New York and Cambridge: Cambridge University Press.

van de Poel, I., J. Nihlén Fahlquist, N. Doorn, S. Zwart, and L. Royakkers. 2012. "The problem of many hands: Climate change as an example." *Science and Engineering Ethics* 18(1): 49–68.

About the Authors

Ibo van de Poel is Anthoni van Leeuwenhoek Professor in Ethics and Technology, and head of the section Ethics and Philosophy of Technology of the department Values, Technology and Innovation, school of Technology, Policy, and Management at Delft University of Technology. In 1998, he obtained his PhD in science and technology studies (STS) with a dissertation on the dynamics of technological development. Since his PhD, he has done research and published in the following areas: engineering ethics, the moral acceptability of technological risks, values and engineering design, moral responsibility in research networks, the problem of many hands, ethics of new emerging technologies like nanotechnology, technology as a form of social experimentation, and the dynamics of technological development. He has written eight (edited) books (five in English, three in Dutch), over 30 international peer reviewed articles, and over 30 international book contributions. He is a co-editor of the Springer book series in the *Philosophy of Engineering and Technology* and was co-editor of *Techne*, the journal of the Society for Philosophy of Technology. He is member of the editorial board of the journals *Science and Engineering Ethics* and *Accountability in Research*, and of the book series *Philosophy, Technology and Society* (Rowman & Littlefield). In 2011, he has received a VICI grant for his research proposal *New Technologies as Social Experiments: Conditions for Morally Responsible Experimentation* from the Netherlands Organisation for Scientific Research (NWO).

Lambèr Royakkers (1967) is Associate Professor in Ethics and Technology at the Department School of Innovation Sciences of the Eindhoven University of Technology. Lambèr Royakkers has studied mathematics, philosophy, and law. In 1996, he obtained his PhD on the logic of legal norms. During the last few years, he has done research and published in the following areas: military ethics, robo-ethics, deontic logic, and the moral responsibility in research networks. In 2009, he started as project leader the NWO-MVI research program 'Moral fitness of military personnel in a networked operational environment' (2009–2014). Central in this research are the questions about the role of technology in military

220 *About the Authors*

operations in the 21st century. His research has an interdisciplinary character and is on the interface between ethics, law, and technology in a military context. He is also involved in a European project, as chairman of the ethics advisory board of the FP7-project SUBCOP (SUicide Bomber COunteraction and Prevention, 2013–2016). He is co-author of the book *Ethics, Engineering and Technology* (Wiley-Blackwell, 2011, with professor Ibo van de Poel). In 2015, his book on Social Robots will be published (Routledge).

Sjoerd D. Zwart is Assistant Professor in the Philosophy of Technology and Engineering Sciences at the Delft (1997) and Eindhoven (2002) Universities of Technology, The Netherlands. He has studied mathematics, has a master's degree in the formal philosophy of science, and wrote a PhD-thesis on verisimilitude distance measures on Lindenbaum algebras that bear a considerable similarity to classical Belief Revision (*Refined Verisimilitude.* Dordrecht, Kluwer, 2001). Subsequently, his research efforts shifted towards subjects within the philosophy of technology and engineering viz., methods and techniques in engineering design (modeling, scaling, measurement, functional and means-ends reasoning, and causality), and norms and values in engineering and its ethics (just design and norms in modeling). In 2009 he edited "Modeling in Engineering Sciences", part IV of A.W.M. Meijers, H. Radder, W. Houkes, P.A. Kroes, S.D. Zwart, I.R. van de Poel and S.O. Hansson (Eds.), *Philosophy of technology and engineering sciences,* published by Elsevier, North-Holland. Most recently he has taken up studies into practices and tacit knowledge in the engineering sciences and technology. Witnesses of these activities are: co-editorships with M. Peterson and contribution to a *SHPS* special issue on "Values and Norms in Modeling" (2014) and co-editorship with L. Soler and contribution to a *Philosophia Scientiæ* special issue on Collins's account of Tacit Knowledge (2013). Finally, he is co-editor with Soler, Léna, Vincent Israel-Jost, and Michael Lynch of a book called *Science after the Practice Turn in Philosophy, History, and the Social Studies of Science,* published in 2014 by Routledge in New York.

Tiago de Lima obtained his PhD in Artificial Intelligence at the Université de Toulouse in 2007. He was as a postdoc at the Eindhoven University of Technology from 2007–2009. During that period, he worked on the project Moral Responsibility in R&D Networks funded by the Netherlands Organisation for Scientific Research (NWO). In 2009, Tiago became associate professor at the Université d'Artois, France, on the framework of CNRS-higher education chairs program and also became member of the Centre de Recherche en Informatique de Lens (CRIL). He has published several papers on logics for dynamics of knowledge, agency and responsibility, tableaux methods, and reasoning about actions and change in multi-agent environments.

About the Authors 221

Neelke Doorn holds a master degree in civil engineering (MSc, cum laude) and philosophy (MA, cum laude) and a PhD degree in philosophy of engineering and technology. She wrote her PhD thesis on moral responsibility in R&D networks. Dr. Doorn is currently employed as assistant professor at the faculty of Technology, Policy and Management of the Technical University Delft, department of Values, Technology and Innovation. Her research focusses on moral and distributive issues in engineering and technology development. In 2013, she was awarded a prestigious Venigrant for outstanding researchers from the Netherlands Organization for Scientific Research (NWO). In 2014, Dr. Doorn was shortlisted for the engineer of the year award from the Dutch professional engineering organization (KIVI-NIRIA) for her work on the interface of ethics and engineering. Dr. Doorn is Editor-in-Chief of *Techné: Research in Philosophy and Technology* (Journal of the Society for Philosophy and Technology).

Jessica Nihlén Fahlquist is a senior lecturer at the Centre for Research Ethics & Bioethics at Uppsala University. She is also a postdoctoral researcher at the Philosophy section at Delft University of Technology. She received her PhD in Philosophy in 2008 from the Royal Institute of Technology, Stockholm. Generally, her research focuses on issues related to risk and ethics with a particular interest in notions of moral responsibility. In her research, she has explored the distinction between backward-looking and forward-looking responsibility and how to distribute responsibility between individuals and the government for public health problems and environmental problems. Additionally, she is interested in topics related to children and risk, particularly how to balance the protection of children and respect for their developing autonomy. Jessica Nihlén Fahlquist has published articles in the areas of public health ethics, ethics of technology, and environmental ethics.

Index

accountability: conditions for 24–5, 37–9, 41, 112–14; formalisation 112–14; implication 24; and maintaining moral community 19, 213; relation with blameworthiness 25, 42, 116; routes to 37–9

action: collective 58, 62–4; joint 58–9, 69–74, 96–9, 135, 142–4

agent: ability 104–8; corporate 135

Agricultural Board: Christian in Brabant (NCB) 135; National (*Landbouwschap*) 138, 152; northern southern 147; regional NCB and LLTB 37

Agricultural-Economic Institute (*Landbouw-Economisch Instituut*, LEI) 137

ambient intelligence 177

Aristotle 22, 24, 196

authority structure 118

background theories 170–4, 178–81

backward-looking responsibility: formalisation 112–15; problem of many hands for 5, 209; relation with forward-looking responsibility 36–41, 116–17; *see also* accountability; blameworthiness; liability

blameworthiness: conditions for 21–3, 41, 114–15; excuse conditions for 25; formalisation 114–15; implication 21, 42; relation with accountability 25, 42, 116; and retribution 19–20, 42, 212

Boudon, Raymond 160

care 193–4; balanced 205

causal efficacy 32, 36; of a group 53, 59–61, 76, 145

cause: causal chain 148; as condition for responsibility 22, 32, 35, 41; distal 133; proximate 133; as unusual 80

Central Manure Exchange (*Mestcentrale*) 136, 138

Chronic Obstructive Pulmonary Disease (COPD) 177

CitiCorp (building): responsibility for 69–74, 133, 155; structural deficiency 70

climate change: causality 76, 79–80; international agreement 75, 82–4; knowledge of 76–7, 80; mitigation 74, 77; responsibility for 74–89

Coalition Epistemic Dynamic Logic (CEDL) 94–109

coercion 22–3, 25, 62–3

cohesiveness 163, 216–17

collateral damage 148

collection of agents: cohesiveness 163; delineation along causal lines 132–5, 211; involved in a joint action 58–9; occasional collection 59–61

collective: action 58, 62–4; agreement 82; aim 56–9, 62, 64, 70, 75–6, 212; freedom 62–3; intention 8, 55–6, 212–13; involved in joint action 58–9; knowledge 62, 103–4; occasional collections of individuals 59–61; organised group 56–8; types of 55–61

collective responsibility 55–66; capacity condition for 55–61; for climate

224 *Index*

change 75–7; conditions for 61–4; discrepancy between individual and collective responsibility 6, 89; irreducibility of 65; reducibility thesis 65; strong reducibility thesis 66
conditions for responsibility: capacity 21, 35, 41, 75, 79; causality 22, 32, 35, 41, 76; freedom 22–3, 41, 77, 79; knowledge 22, 41, 76, 79; normative 35, 41, 63; wrong doing 23, 77
consensus: justified 169, 175; overlapping 170, 172
considered moral judgments 170
contributory factor 133

decision procedure 56–7, 62, 66–8, 143
Deepwater Horizon disaster 1–3, 187
delegation 44–5, 110, 118–24, 157, 160, 216
discursive dilemma 66–9; of Employee Safety 67–9
distribution of responsibility 31–2, 84–5, 167–8, 174–84, 215–16; complete 216; fair 162, 167–8, 174–84, 215–16; principles for 31–2, 84–5, 167; procedural approach for 167–8, 174–8, 215–16
duty (duties): moral 81; supervisory 28–9, 153, 214, 217; in a tragedy of the commons 81–4; transgression of 23, 39
dynamic logic: epistemic 94; propositional 94

Employee Safety 67–9
Ethical Position Questionnaire 178
European Community: Common Agricultural Policy (CAP) 142

fairness *see* distribution of responsibility, fair
farmers: as a group 141, 146, 151; individually 146; livestock 148
fertilizer granules 136
forward-looking responsibility: conditions for 35; consequentialist route 31–2; delegation of 44–5, 109; deontological route 32–4; formalisation 109–12; implication 27, 29, 42; as

obligation 14, 27–9, 109–12; problem of many hands for 5, 209; relation with backward-looking responsibility 36–41, 116–17; and supervisory duties 28–9; as virtue 14, 29–30, 188–90, 192–6; virtue route 34–5; *see also* causal efficacy
freedom: as the ability to avoid an outcome 23, 63; as the absence of coercion 23, 62, 81; as the availability of alternative actions 23; as the availability of reasonable alternatives 23, 81; as condition for responsibility 22; of a group 62–3
free will 23

General Inspection Service (*Algemene Inspectie Dienst,* AID) 141
global warming *see* climate change
Group Decision Room (GDR) 177

hierarchical line 63, 215

ignorance 22, 25, 38, 98, 114; non-culpable (excusable) 18, 22, 36, 46, 80–1, 86
IKEA 204
inclusiveness 174–5, 216–17
institutional design 9, 210, 218
intention: overlapping participatory 58–9; *see also* collective, intention

Jesse James train robbery 59
joint action *see* action, joint
justice: as fairness 171, 184; procedural 168; to victims 19, 42, 54

knowledge: as condition for responsibility 22, 41, 76, 79; distributed 103; group 103–4, 162
Kyoto Protocol 74, 78, 79, 82

LeMessurier 70–4, 133, 155–6, 203–4
lessons: control 163; degree organization 159; task distribution 161
liability: conditions for 25–7; as doing justice to victims 19; implication 26; legal 25; moral 15, 25; and remediation 19, 26; strict 19, 25

Index   225

liberalism 168
luck 69

manure: buying duty 140; surplus 137
methodological individualism 58
Ministry of Agriculture 139, 147, 153
moral agency 21, 25, 46
moral community 19
moral imagination 194–5

National Manure Bank 140
9/11 hijacked planes 60
no-forgetting 98
no harm principle 19
norms: procedural 172

openness 174–5, 216–17
organisation: intermediary 158, 161;
    see also collective, organised
    group
organisational activities: delegation
    119; information 119
organisational dimensions 94, 119–22
    134–5, 156–64, 215; control
    134–5, 158–9, 163–4, 215;
    coordination 94, 119–21,
    134–5, 157–8, 215; power
    94, 119–22, 134–5, 156–7,
    160–1, 215

perfect recall 98, 103–4
practical wisdom 195–6
problem of many hands: avoiding
    the 122–4, 159–64, 199–201,
    215–18; backward-looking 5,
    209; characterisation 4, 51–4,
    210–14; in a computerized
    society 50; epistemological
    dimension 52; formalisation
    117–22; forward-looking 5,
    209; moral dimension 52; as a
    problem of control 52
problem owner 162
procedural justice 169
procedure see decision procedure;
    voting, procedure
profession 34
project management: role 181
PROMEST: B.V. 136; collection 149;
    consortium 137; plant 137
promise 32–5
pro tanto justification 172
punishment see blameworthiness, and
    retribution

Rawls, John 168–72
reasonable stake 174
reducibility thesis 66; strong
    reducibility thesis 66
redundancy 161, 217
reflective equilibrium 170–1
reflective learning 173
responsibility: as accountability
    14, 24–5, 112–14; aim of
    attributing 18–20, 54; as
    answerability 24; assuming
    18, 34–5, 199–200; as
    authority 14; backward
    looking 17–18, 20–7, 112–15;
    as blameworthiness 14,
    21–3, 114–15; as capacity 14,
    55–61; as cause 14; collective
    6–7, 55–66; consequentialist
    perspective 18, 20; delegation
    44–5; design 218; distribution
    of 31–2, 84–5, 167–8, 174–84,
    215–16; excuses 24; as the
    fittingness of reactive attitudes
    17–18; forward looking
    16–17, 27–39, 109–12;
    indirect 121; as liability 14,
    25–7; meanings of 5, 13–15,
    42; merit based perspective
    18, 20; as obligation 14,
    27–9, 109–12; oversight 217;
    pluralist conception 168; and
    promises 32–4; as a relational
    concept 16–18; relations
    between different kinds of
    36–41, 116–17; rights based
    perspective 18, 20; as task 14;
    as virtue 14, 29–30, 188–90,
    192–6; see also delegation
retribution see blameworthiness, and
    retribution
Rio Declaration 75–6
risk 201–5
Robertson, Leslie 36

social network 143
social ties 131–4
stakeholders 132
Strawson, P. 17
Stuurgroep Mestproblematiek Noord-
    Brabant 134
supervisory duty see duty (duties),
    supervisory
systems: functional 160; interdependence
    160; organized 160

226 *Index*

Thompson, Dennis 4, 50
Tozer, John 197
tragedy of the commons: responsibility in a 81–4
Twin Towers 36–7

uniform strategy 107
United Nations 74

vertical differentiation 118
virtue: civic virtue 191; due care to others 19–20, 42, 54; responsibility as virtue 14, 29–30, 188–90, 192–6
voting: paradox 66–7; procedure 57–9, 66–8; strategically 68